# WOMEN AGAINST FUNDAMENTALISM

This book is dedicated to Cassandra Balchin and Helen Lowe, wonderful WAF women and hugely energetic and persistent activists.

# WOMEN AGAINST FUNDAMENTALISM

## Stories of Dissent and Solidarity

Edited by Sukhwant Dhaliwal
and Nira Yuval-Davis

London Lawrence & Wishart 2014

Lawrence and Wishart Limited
99a Wallis Road
London, E9 5LN


ISBN 9781 909831 025

British Library Cataloguing in Publication Data.
A catalogue record for this book is available from the British Library

# Contents

# Acknowledgements

We would like to express our deepest gratitude to all the WAF women who have contributed chapters to this book, for taking the time to tell their stories and then translating these into a form that they are willing to share in public. As much as we all espouse the personal as political, we are not used to speaking about our personal lives, and most of us have been invested in helping others with their personal difficulties; so for some, though not all, it's been a difficult step to write a chapter about themselves. Thanks also for offering us rich feedback on the Introduction.

We would also like to thank Chitra Nagarajan and Ashika Thanki for their comments on an earlier draft of the Introduction and for all their enthusiasm. Also special thanks to Sue O'Sullivan, who has provided additional editorial support on our own personal chapters, as we felt it vital that more than one person should read each input.

Big thanks to Sally of Lawrence and Wishart for all her support and help and belief in the importance of the project.

And, of course – to our wonderful partners, Paolo and Alain, for their consistent and constant support and patience.

Last – but not least – thanks for all the local and global anti-racist anti-fundamentalist feminists, in and outside WAF, who've been carrying on the important political work that we, all the participants in this book project, have been involved in. We draw comfort from your courage, hard work and solidarity, and see in this book a small contribution to our global transversal project.

'Our tradition: Struggle not Submission!'
(WAF's slogan)

*Sukhwant and Nira*

# 1. Introduction

*Sukhwant Dhaliwal and Nira Yuval-Davis*

This book celebrates – while also acknowledging the huge challenges it faces – a particular kind of feminism, one that has been concerned with challenging both fundamentalism and racism. It consists of the autobiographical political narratives of feminist activists of different ethnic and religious backgrounds who have been members of Women Against Fundamentalism (WAF), a feminist anti-racist and anti-fundamentalist organisation that was established in London in 1989, at the heart of the Salman Rushdie affair.

Political narratives have been described as 'stories people tell about how the world works', the ways in which they explain the engines of political change, and as reflections on the role people see themselves and their group playing in their ongoing struggles.[1] And the contributors to this book offer just such narratives – they talk about the trajectories of their lives, and how they see themselves and the groups to which they belong in relation to the wider political struggles in which they have been involved. WAF women have shared solidarity and trust, based on common political values, but, as can be seen from the chapters of this book, their perspectives – as well as their personal/political histories – have also differed.[2] This variety of voices is significant not only for these women as individuals but also for WAF as a political organisation. In this introduction we highlight what we as editors perceive to be the most important issues for WAF's activism throughout its history. However, the book has been constructed in such a way that reading all the chapters will itself provide a more pluralistic and contested flavour of WAF's politics.

This introduction outlines the rationale for the book, introduces WAF and its political context, explains the book's theoretical and methodological framework, and explores some of the themes that have emerged from the activists' stories.

## THE RATIONALE FOR THE BOOK

The impetus for this book is threefold. Firstly, it aims to explore how, both within Britain and across a closely related global context, a particular arena of feminist activism – that of anti-fundamentalist anti-racist feminism – confronts and analyses contradictory pressures. On the one hand it is faced with a growing majoritarian politics of belonging that is exclusionary and often anti-Muslim, and draws on either civilisational or Christian fundamentalist discourses.[3] On the other hand it is confronted by an undercutting of secular and other emancipatory movements by fundamentalist absolutist and authoritarian political projects in all religions. What's more, these latter projects are also connected to a growing identity politics among some minorities (especially but not only Muslims) that often utilise human rights and anti-imperialist discourses. And all of this is taking place within a local and global crisis of neoliberal political economy and a securitarian 'war on terrorism'.

Secondly, the book stems from a motivation to understand the specific pathways that have led particular women to choose these complex arenas of feminist political activism, and how these choices relate to other aspects of their lives – their social locations, their identity constructions and their political and moral value systems.

The third impetus for this book was a sense of the urgent need for documenting and understanding the lives of WAF women before it's too late to do so. This was prompted partly by the death of two central members of WAF, Helen Lowe and Cassandra Balchin, to whom this book is dedicated; and partly by a political crisis within the organisation that has meant that its formal days of activism are over.

## FOUNDING WAF

As mentioned above, Women Against Fundamentalism was formed in 1989 in London, during the height of the controversy surrounding the publication of the novel *The Satanic Verses* by Salman Rushdie, but with the express objective of challenging the rise of fundamentalism in all religions. Its members included women from a wide range of ethnic, national and religious backgrounds, who were primarily united by their position as feminists and as dissenters within their communities. Fundamentalism as defined by WAF refers to modern political movements that use religion to gain or consolidate power, whether working within or in opposition to the state. We strictly differentiate fundamentalism from religious observance, which we see as a matter of individual choice.[4]

WAF established itself as a women-only organisation because it recognised that the control of women's bodies and minds lies at the heart of the fundamentalist agenda. Fundamentalists perpetuate women's role as upholders of community morals and traditions; and women who refuse this role risk being demonised, outcast from their community, subjected to physical violence or even killed. So WAFers' resistance was shaped by their experience as women and as dissenters. They persistently asserted women's right to contest and doubt manifestations of religion, culture, tradition and norms, and to challenge self-styled leaderships that claim to represent them. This was most clearly reflected in WAF's adoption of the powerful slogans initially coined by members of Southall Black Sisters – 'our tradition, struggle not submission'; 'religious leaders do not speak for us'; and 'fear is your weapon, courage is ours!'

This did not mean that WAF was opposed to religion per se, but rather that its members emphasised the crucial role of secular spaces in ensuring equality for people of all religions and none. In its later years WAF discussed and rejected the proposal to change its name from the singular 'fundamentalism' to the plural 'fundamentalisms', because it wanted to emphasise the continuities rather than differences across authoritarian mobilisations within all religions.[5]

WAF's work carried several objectives: highlighting the resurgence of fundamentalism in *all* religions and lobbying for a secular state; demanding women's rights over their own bodies and control over their own lives; opposing institutionalised Christian privilege; and resisting ethnic minority parity demands for religious accommodation, such as demands to extend rather than abolish the blasphemy law (and later legislation on incitement to religious hatred) and to extend rather than abolish state funded religious schools.

Over the years WAF organised seminars and public meetings, and produced a journal, an education pack and a website. It set up two working groups – on religion and the law, and on religion and education. Although it was based in London (though for a couple of years it had a branch in the north of England), it worked with various feminist groups around the UK, as well as with transnational feminist organisations that shared its perspectives, including Catholics for Free Choice, Women Living Under Muslim Laws and the Association of Women in Development (AWID).[6]

## THE RUSHDIE AFFAIR AND MULTICULTURALISM

Multiculturalism can be a descriptive term that simply expresses an ideal situation in which people of different origins live harmoniously alongside each other. As a state policy, multiculturalism was born out of the political rejection of assimilation, but it went on to become the dominant frame through which relations between the state and ethnic minorities within Britain were managed. The right has always objected to multiculturalism on the grounds that it threatens so-called 'British values' and the 'British character' of the UK. But the women involved with WAF were critical of multiculturalism for different reasons, two in particular. As anti-racists they saw multiculturalism as a mechanism for sidestepping the substantive challenges that were being made to structural racism; while as feminists they were critical of the ways in which multiculturalist practice undermined their concerns about internal community power relations, and about violence against Black and minority women. In fact many women came into WAF through involvement in the search by Southall Black Sisters for political allies to counter both cultural relativism and Black identity politics. WAF's critique of multiculturalist practice drew attention to a layer of unaccountable 'community leaders', and to the projection of minorities as unified and internally homogeneous. It lobbied for public funds to be administered by accountable, democratically elected representatives and not by religious leaders.[7]

In Britain, the resurgence of religion as a political identity began in earnest in the 1970s, among Sikhs mustering support for a separate Sikh state (Khalistan) in India.[8] However, it was the Rushdie affair that heightened the tension that exists between the 'freedom to' assert religious beliefs and make demands for religious recognition, and the need to safeguard people's 'freedom from' religion – the right to critique and live free from the influence of religion, religious leaders and religious organisations. The importance of the Rushdie affair is also that it was one of the earliest examples of new media and communications facilitating the compression of time and space to enable the conjuring up of an imaginary and unified religious community – in this case the emergence of a transnational Muslim 'umma' ('community'); new media allowed the binding together of ethnic, national, cultural and linguistic identities and histories that otherwise might not have had any necessary connection with each other.[9]

Rushdie's *The Satanic Verses* was published by Viking/Penguin in

September 1988. By October 1988 Indian politician Syed Shahbuddin had succeeded in obtaining a ban on the book in India, on the grounds that it was offensive both as 'literary colonialism' and as 'religious pornography'. So, very early on in the debate, a narrative emerged that brought together anti-imperialist sentiment and arguments about the need to protect the sexual purity of Islam.[10] This sentiment then swiftly became part of the transnational activities of the right-wing Jamaat-e-Islami party.[11] However, their fairly mundane lobbying activities intensified rapidly in January 1989, when a number of Bradford Muslims decided to publicly burn the book. This act was then copied in other northern towns, and an ad hoc Islamic defence group was established that organised a march through central London. Following on from this the Jamaat-e-Islami initiated a number of public demonstrations among their supporters around the globe.[12] And so as not to be outdone by JI mobilisations, Ayatollah Khomeini, then leader of Iran, issued a fatwa (Islamic legal pronouncement) condemning to death Rushdie and his publishers. He also declared that defenders of the fatwa would be revered as 'martyrs'.[13] In effect, this was an incitement to murder.

As Julia Bard later described, the Ayatollah's fatwa 'broke the left and liberal consensus on anti-racism' as people in these circles debated whether they should defend the free speech of the protestors as 'express(ions) of their culture' or be seen to be siding with racists by depicting these actions as 'barbaric'.[14] Meanwhile, some members of the Labour Party Black Sections, as well as other anti-racist activists, either overtly or implicitly, framed this new wave of religious fundamentalist mobilisations in 'Black' or 'anti-racist' political terms.[15]

An increasing level of intolerance among some Muslim activists was matched by scathing press coverage that likened Muslims to Nazis, using the now familiar 'backward irrational Muslim' narrative as a way of dismissing multiculturalism, and pointing to the contrast between such backwardness and enlightened progressive (white Christian) British nationalism. One of the more curious examples of this was Fay Weldon's 1989 pamphlet *Sacred Cows*, which drew on concerns about alleged cultural relativism as a justification for asserting the superiority of 'British culture' and Christianity, as Clara Connolly pointed out in her subsequent review.[16] Weldon also entangled together political concerns about 'race', class and gender to depict anti-Rushdie activists as an ignorant, uncultured, working-class mass, and argued that a conservative sexual morality would be the best way to avert a growing Islamist narrative about 'the decadent West'. Clara was also critical of the 'rescue narrative' that underpinned the pamphlet, and countered Weldon's call to 'save' minority women from sexist minority men/cultures with a series of examples of minority women's own autonomous activism.

However, a growing fundamentalist narrative about Rushdie as an 'infidel' and 'blasphemer' whose writing defiled the purity of Islam did ring alarm bells for a number of feminists (as can be seen from the contributions to this book of Pragna Patel, Gita Sahgal, Shakila Maan and Hannana Siddiqui, as well as Clara and Julia). Accordingly, on 8 March 1989 SBS co-organised an International Women's Day event with the Southall Labour Party Women's Section, entitled 'The Resurgence of Religion: What Price do Women Pay?', an event that was attended by around two hundred women. SBS focused their intervention on fundamentalism, and the need to defend secular traditions. At the end of the meeting they surprised the local Labour Party by issuing a statement in defence of Salman Rushdie and the right to free speech, and of the right to dissent and doubt, and to not have their lives determined by so called 'community leaders'; and they also called for the abolition of the blasphemy law – an archaic piece of legislation which at that time censored any criticism of Christianity in Britain, and has only recently been modified.

Encouraged by the response to their Southall meeting, SBS joined forces with other feminists who had attended the event – including members of Voices for Rushdie, Brent Asian Women's Refuge and the Iranian Women's Organisation in Britain – to establish a network of women opposed to fundamentalism in all religions. And at their first meeting, on 6 May 1989, they officially established WAF, in order to highlight the impact on women of fundamentalist mobilisations. The statement from that meeting was later published as a letter to *The Independent* (see Appendix pXXX). WAF women then decided to take a public stand against a large anti-Rushdie march scheduled to go through central London on 27 May 1989, and coined the slogan 'Rushdie's right to write, is our right to dissent!'[17] This stand is now considered a foundational moment in WAF's history. Images of the event provide strong visual representations of WAF's political location – of women from diverse backgrounds shouting slogans both at ethnic minority fundamentalists demanding censorship and at white fascists hurling racist abuse. This demonstration was captured on film by Gita Sahgal in

*Struggle or Submission*, a documentary about the impact of religious pressures on women's ability to determine the direction of their own lives.[18]

When several years later, in 1994, Bangladeshi writer Taslima Nasreen was also subjected to a fatwa and forced into exile, in response to her novel *Lajja* (Shame), WAF again expressed its solidarity; they made the connections between Nasreen's situation and the mobilisation against Rushdie, in that both involved the transnational activities of the Jamaat-e-Islami.[19] Gita's chapter in this volume discusses her research on JI activists who fled Bangladesh after their involvement in the 1971 genocide, and how she discovered them sitting comfortably alongside local authority politicians in the east London borough of Tower Hamlets; while Georgie Wemyss's chapter reflects on her own experience of JI mobilisations (and their front organisations) within Tower Hamlets.

WAF did not focus solely on the violence committed by Muslim fundamentalists however. For example WAF members joined forces with other South Asian activists in Britain to speak out against atrocities committed against Muslims by the Hindu Right at Ayodhya in northern India in 1991, and again in Gujarat in west India in 2002 (see chapters by Pragna and also Rashmi Varma in this volume); while Nira contributed to an international women's delegation to Gujarat whose findings were published as a report by the International Initiative for Justice.[20]

## 'WOMEN WHO WALK ON WATER'

All the accounts we have come across (many but not all of which are contained within this book) describe the first phase of WAF as highly energetic, dynamic, creative and colourful. For example Clara and Pragna recall the picnic in Parliament Square, and Julia played in a klezmer band at a WAF fundraiser. The lyrics of one of WAF's earliest songs proclaimed that 'we are women who walk on water'; and these women did indeed create waves and walk through a sea of voices to confidently assert brave and novel positions. As noted by many contributors to this book, being involved in WAF deeply affected their lives, their thinking, and their way of doing politics. Even during periods of inactivity, WAF continued as a source of inspiration, a resource for political analysis and a method for political engagement. In this section we provide a brief summary of the key moments and context for the first phase of WAF, which ran roughly from 1989 to 1996.

This first phase has to be understood in the context of a decade of Thatcherite governance at the centre, and several years of Ken Livingstone's GLC in London. On the religious-secular front, this gave rise to a number of contradictory pressures and opportunities. As a frontrunner of neoliberal economic policy, Margaret Thatcher was hyper-individualistic and frequently confronted the traditionalism of the Church of England, but she was also a strong defender of the Christian character of British nationalism. Furthermore, while secularism may by this time have become a lived reality for many British people, the British state has never been secular in the sense of a full separation of religion and the state. Indeed, the Church of England continues to enjoy its status as the established church, with the Queen as the titular head, the prime minister appointing the Archbishop of Canterbury and 26 Bishops sitting in the House of Lords; and right up until 2008 Christianity was legally protected by blasphemy legislation (and some would argue that this continues today in lieu of the Incitement to Racial and Religious Hatred Act 2006).[21]

But in spite of its role at the heart of the establishment, during the social fallout resulting from neoliberal economics the Church of England positioned itself as a critic of the state, and tasked itself with providing a safety net and voice for the increasing numbers of disadvantaged and unemployed people, particularly within Britain's inner cities – as did the Catholic Church.[22] Christian groups were also an important source of support for anti-racist activism, as places of worship doubled-up as places of sanctuary for those at risk of deportation; while some Christian organisations provided access to a slightly better academic education for working-class children who were being failed by impoverished state comprehensives.

Meanwhile Ken Livingstone's GLC was funding right-wing ethnic minority religious projects under the guise of a multicultural commitment to strengthening minority identities.[23] But at the same time it was enabling and supporting the growth of a radical secular civil society through state funding for autonomous secular women's, LGBT, anti-racist and creative arts projects, which in turn strengthened the foundation for progressive opposition to conservative sections within communities across London.[24]

During this period WAF organised a number of seminars that attempted to grapple with the various dimensions of advocating secularism in the context of imperialism, nationalism, racism and state neutrality.[25] WAF members wanted to reclaim the term as a meaningful principle and practice for ensuring democratic accountability and plurality. During these seminars WAF met with supporters and also (theoretical) opponents. Tariq Modood, for instance, accused WAF of articulating a majoritarian anti-religion (and indeed anti-Muslim) position – as 'partly located in the prejudices of most Britons'.[26] Modood was one of the earliest advocates of what we now refer to as 'multifaithism', and he argued that equality for cultural and religious minorities was to be gained not by severing the ties between religion and the state – which he claimed would 'further marginalise minorities' – but by opening these out to create 'full citizenship' for all groups. This would be achieved by providing religious leaders and members of other faiths with the same representation (for example in the House of Lords) and state funding as the Anglican church, especially where it could be shown that such faiths were 'the primary identity' of a group, or that a group was 'not fully able to identify with and participate in a polity to the extent that it privileges a rival faith'.[27] This was met with a strong counter argument by Clara Connolly, who emphasised that Modood's multifaithism would inevitably be reflected in legal restrictions on the freedoms of women, and of sexual minorities such as gays and lesbians, and could lead to reversals of women's hard-fought-for civil rights on divorce and reproduction.[28] Modood also argued that religious groups ought to be able to influence public policy on the same premise – the personal is political – that feminists had drawn on to push against strong distinctions between public and private spheres. This analogy was met with a firm rebuttal: feminist projects such as WAF were precisely opposing the way that such public/private distinctions were used by religious groups to curtail women's movement and impose differential and subordinate roles on women and girls.

WAF was supported in these arguments by Homi Bhabha, who countered claims that secularism is an alien concept for minority communities. Moreover, Bhabha defended the normative importance of secularism as enabling and protecting the changeability of religions over time, and the multiple forms of religious practices that develop with the movement of populations within and across countries (including among ethnic minorities).[29] And Rohini PH emphasised the importance of secularism for averting the worst effects of communalism, in its attempts to seal the boundaries of group identification – attempts that historically had specific and detrimental impacts on women.[30] WAF women believed that many of the demands being made for religious accommodation in Britain – such as for the extension of blasphemy legislation and faith-based schooling – were being made more credible because of the privileged position of Christianity in Britain, and they therefore took the view that disestablishment was both important and necessary. (However, WAF also actively distanced itself from autocratic forms of secularism, such as in Kemalist Turkey, that sought to erase difference in conjunction with a monocultural nationalist project.)

What WAF's campaign for secularism meant in real terms could perhaps be seen most clearly in its call for the withdrawal of all state funding for faith schools, and its opposition to the Education Act 1988, which imposed Christian worship within state schools.[31] At the same time WAF also supported attempts to stop the establishment of new faith-based schools, including through the Save Our Schools (SOS) campaign, which pointed to the importance of secular public institutions for safeguarding the rights of women and girls, particularly those within minority communities. SOS was set up by Southall Black Sisters and other secular left and socialist organisations in Southall in order to resist attempts by Sikh parents and governors to establish autonomous but state funded Sikh schools under Thatcher's new rules for taking local secondary schools out of the control of the local state. Parents and residents also complained that the Sikh groups were using this Tory attempt at privatisation to establish more conservative schools that would enable greater policing of young people – particularly young women; such schools would allow them to closely monitor, regulate and restrict the life choices of their students.[32]

WAF also drew to a considerable extent from discussions and models of secularism around the world; and this led to a deeper understanding of the context-specificity of policies and strategies, and also of the increasingly sophisticated games that fundamentalists play in order to impose their agenda. For instance, WAF expressed solidarity with Indian feminists who were highlighting the way that religious 'personal laws' for family and property matters were meted out as differential rights for Muslims, Hindus and Christians in India, and pointing out how this contradicted the secular universalist ethos of the post-colonial Indian constitution. They were of course equally critical of attempts by Hindu fundamentalist political parties to hijack the feminist campaign for a single secular gender-just civil law through their advocacy of their own idea for a single system – one that sought to privilege Hindu provisions on marriage and property and to impose these on others while dressing them up as nationalist demands.[33]

Back in Britain, at a WAF public meeting on 'Resisting Religious Fundamentalism World-Wide', on 8 March 1990, Rabia Janjua spoke from the floor about her own personal experiences at the hands of the complex intertwinings of immigration law, religious persecution and gender. Rabia had been forced to marry her rapist in Pakistan, who had then fled to England to escape prosecution under Zina laws (for adultery/unlawful sex) – which both of them faced. He made arrangements for Rabia to join him in England but never enabled her to resolve her immigration status. When he became violent and abusive she left him, but then risked deportation back to Pakistan, where she would face a prison sentence of up to ten years and public flogging. Her situation was a stark reminder of the way in which racist immigration laws in Britain could compound the impact on women of fundamentalist interventions on 'personal laws' in other parts of the world. Rabia was subsequently supported by WAF and SBS, who campaigned for her right to stay in Britain, and this campaign was one of the earliest to highlight the need for the British government to recognise the gendered dimensions of religious persecution as grounds for asylum.[34]

Many of the founder members of WAF originated from countries where religion had a stranglehold on public affairs, including from places where this had resulted in a concerted assault on women's reproductive rights – such as in Ireland and Iran.[35] Campaigning against restrictions on abortion rights was therefore an important part of WAF's political work: as Ann Rossiter has pointed out, in Britain it is 'religious fundamentalism which forms the basis of most, if not all, the recurring challenges to the 1967 Abortion Act'.[36]

As can be seen from Clara's chapter in this volume, a number of Irish women who joined WAF were also involved in the Irish Women's Abortion Support Group, which provided urgent support for women travelling from Ireland to England to undergo abortions. The personal biographies and bodies of these women were marked by forces that drew on a potent synthesis of anti-imperialism and religious nationalism, as well as by transnational activism. In Ireland, the Catholic Church traditionally drew its strength both from its special relationship with the state and from its projection of itself as heroically standing up to British imperial forces and assimilationist pressures. In

1983 a constitutional amendment had secured equal rights for the foetus, and in 1986 pressure from the British-based Society for the Protection of the Unborn Child (SPUC) had led to the suspension of non-directive pregnancy counselling and criminalised the provision of information on abortions. SPUC then extended their reach by campaigning for restrictions on abortion information offered by Irish student unions, censorship of women's magazines and restrictions on contraception. In May 1990, therefore, Dublin Well Woman Clinic and Open Line Counselling decided to pursue the matter in the European Court of Human Rights, citing the restrictive measures as violations of Article 10 of the European Convention of Human Rights, the right of access to information.[37] In London WAF members showed their support for this legal action in their second ever demonstration, a noisy picket outside the Irish embassy; and in October 1990 Rita Bertenshaw, the Director of the Dublin Well Woman Clinic was invited to address WAF's first ever public seminar, and participate in a discussion on religious fundamentalism and reproductive rights alongside activists on abortion rights in the USA and Latin America.[38] At the time of the third anniversary of the fatwa against Salman Rushdie, in February 1992, WAF were once more demonstrating outside the Irish embassy in London, against a decision by the Irish courts to prevent a 14-year-old rape victim from travelling to England for an abortion.[39] The chapters within this book by Clara, Shakila, Sue O' Sullivan and Ritu Mahendru are a testimony to the ways in which working on or writing about sexuality, sexual health and sexual violence necessitates a fight against fundamentalism.

For WAF the demonstrations outside the Irish embassy were also important for the part they played in showing that the organisation was not focused solely on Muslim fundamentalism, but was concerned about fundamentalism in all religions. Several other connections were made during these campaigns. The battle over reproductive rights in Ireland had revealed the growing influence of transnational Christian fundamentalist campaigns – bringing together as it did a range of US Christian denominations in the Moral Right and British groups like SPUC in order to bolster the legal and normative power of the Catholic Church.

The Dublin Well Woman Clinic's appeal to Strasbourg was also reflective of the increasing recourse by both feminists and fundamentalists to supranational rights institutions and an international language of human rights. By the mid-1990s, when WAF activists were participating in UN conferences in Vienna (1993), Cairo (1994) and Beijing (1995), fundamentalists across a number of religions had formed alliances to lobby those spaces for the restriction of access to abortion and contraception (including through the use of the language of women's empowerment).[40] These international dimensions, and the growing relevance of an international language of rights and UN conventions, marked an important step-change for political activity within the domestic context. And this in turn led to many discussions about the possibilities and limitations of 'universalism'. In a *WAF Journal* special issue on reproductive rights, Gayatri Spivak highlighted the limits of universalism by pointing to the disjuncture between Northern feminists lobbying for reproductive rights at the 1994 UN International Conference on Population and Development in Cairo and the subjection of their sisters in the South to population controls.[41] This was countered by WAF's Rayah Feldman, who identified examples where women in the South were also campaigning for the right to abortion and contraception.[42] Nevertheless, issues of context, geography and feminist solidarity did arise; and here Nira made the argument that 'transversalism' could offer a way out of the schism between universality and cultural relativism or contextual particularism (which is discussed further in the second half of this chapter).[43] WAF also began to discuss the language and meaning of feminism, and whether or not this could be articulated through religious discourse.[44] The group had already worked closely with Catholics for Free Choice and Women Living Under Muslim Laws, but, as is clear from Cassandra Balchin's chapter, some WAF members wanted to explore religious frameworks, while others (Sukhwant Dhaliwal, Pragna and Hannana) pointed to the dangers of travelling this road within a British context in which secular alternatives could be compromised.

In spite of the challenge from within deconstructionist postcolonial discourses to the use of the term 'fundamentalism' and a universalist discourse of rights – and criticisms levelled at WAF for fuelling imperialism and racism by campaigning on these issues and in these terms – WAF members proved time and again that they could speak out about religious absolutism and simultaneously challenge, rather than give way to, racism and imperialism. On the heels of the Rushdie affair, WAF women joined forces with Women in Black to oppose the bombing of Iraq in the first Gulf War in 1991 (see Nadje Al-Ali's chapter for a detailed account of this period, and Rashmi Varma's chapter for concurrent campaigning on the other side of the Atlantic). Furthermore, amidst the heat of racist mobilisations in Tower Hamlets, WAF members from east London joined other local women in setting up Women United Against Racism to assert the right of women to simultaneously campaign against the British National Party and against the sexism and harassment of male anti-racist activists, including those associated with fundamentalist organisations (see Georgie Wemyss' chapter in this book).[45]

## POST 9/11 AND THE RE-BIRTH OF WAF

In 1996, WAF closed its office (Sukhwant's chapter talks about putting WAF into storage) and experienced a period of inactivity, due to a cumulative sense of over-commitment among the various WAF members, who were all, as the many chapters of this book demonstrate, already fully engaged in other forms of political activity. However former WAF members continued to interact in campaigns against fundamentalism, violence against women, on racism and against immigration controls through the ongoing activities of other political groupings, such as SBS, Women in Black, WLUML, Interights, refugee and migrant forums.

Then on 11 September 2001 the Al Qaeda suicide attacks on the Twin Towers in New York unleashed a new political world. Tony Blair dutifully lined up behind George Bush's enraged patriotism and war-mongering. Political discussion in the UK became extremely polarised between a racist discourse about Muslims forming dangerous 'fifth columns' and an anti-racist defensiveness against any critique of Islam. If it had been difficult before, it now became almost impossible to have a rational debate about Muslim fundamentalism, the actual existence of terrorist networks within Britain, or the role that ought to be played by both the state and civil society in challenging fundamentalism.

So, after a few years of remission, WAF women started to meet again. At first they met in each other's homes over pots of vegetarian soup, exchanging analyses of the new national and global political realities. WAF opposed Blair's claim to be carrying the mantle of freedom, democracy and Afghan women's rights, but many were also uncomfortable with the Stop the War Coalition's response, which was to build a majoritarian alliance with factions of the right-wing Muslim Brotherhood and Jamaat-e-Islami networks based in Britain. While there were some good people involved in this coalition, producing really important critiques of British and US foreign policy, Stop the War foreclosed any attempts to talk about the resurgence of Muslim fundamentalism. It also Islamicised its demonstrations by allowing prayers from the podium, and eventually also hosted Islamic Right speakers on its platforms.

When Bush and Blair began their assault on Afghanistan, Women Living Under Muslim Laws (WLUML) organised a meeting that was attended by a number of WAF women.[46] This meeting highlighted the problem for women's rights under both imperialism and fundamentalism. Then in September 2002 WAF joined forces with Act Together, Women in Black, Southall Black Sisters, Women Living Under Muslim Laws and the Women's International League for Peace and Freedom to run a women's teach-in on 'Anti-militarism, Fundamentalism, Secularism, Civil Liberties and Anti Terror Legislation after 9/11'.[47] Alongside this re-emergence into the public arena, some women took it in turns to lead informal discussions within WAF in order to debate the dramatic transformation of the political landscape and to share information about fundamentalist mobilisations.

At this time there was little scrutiny of global fundamentalist networks by anti-racist and feminist activists or academics. WAF saw it as important for feminists and the left to disavow the imperialist agenda in Guantanamo, Iraq, and Afghanistan, and also agreed on the necessity of critiquing the co-option of feminist claims by neoliberal and neo-fascist politicians. However they also objected to the way in which these justifiable concerns were then mobilised to marginalise or silence critical discussion of the growing global strength of fundamentalist tendencies (see Nadje's chapter) and to reinforce the 'faith agenda' within Britain (see Pragna's, Hannana's and Sukhwant's chapters). Eventually WAF called a public meeting and began giving out leaflets at Stop the War demonstrations that spelt out its arguments against *both* the War on Terror *and* fundamentalism (see Appendix 2 pXXX). More women started to join WAF, and the organisation began a series of women-only meetings for those on its email list, as well as larger public meetings that were open to all.

Some members of the Stop the War Coalition looked to capitalise on widespread disenchantment with Blair and the Labour Party by attempting to transform the mass demonstrations against the war into an electoral challenge. The Socialist Workers Party and the Muslim Association of Britain joined forces to establish the Respect Party, and once again Tower Hamlets became a focal point for religious-political machinations when George Galloway became the Respect Party candidate for Bethnal Green and Bow in the 2005 general election. WAF women voiced their concern about the dirty games of Respect and the myopia of the Socialist Workers Party during the campaign, but were also critical of the sitting Labour MP's support for the war on Iraq.[48]

## FROM MULTICULTURALISM TO MULTIFAITHISM

New Labour was a paradoxical project, often pushing in contradictory directions, and this was particularly the case in its attempts to simultaneously revive both social democracy and religious communitarianism. It promoted a human rights and anti-racist agenda while simultaneously carrying out policy that actively undermined its own measures.

New Labour established the Human Rights Act 1998, looked to extend the anti-discrimination provisions to incorporate all six European equality strands, and established the Equality Act 2010. In 1998, then Home Secretary Jack Straw initiated an inquiry into the murder of the black teenager Stephen Lawrence and supported Lord Macpherson's findings of 'institutional racism' within the police force; and this led to a new Race Relations (Amendment) Act 2000 that compelled public bodies to promote good race relations and produce racial equality impact assessments, thereby providing another important tool for demanding accountability.[49] It was also New Labour that initiated the first government working group on violence against Black women – the Forced Marriage Working Group (discussed in the chapters by Hannana, Gita, Pragna and Sukhwant) – and it was the New Labour Home Office minister Mike O' Brien who engaged with feminist critiques of multiculturalism to coin the phrase 'mature multiculturalism', and, influenced by SBS, applied a human rights framework to tackling violence against women.

However, this was compromised by its counter push towards religious communitarianism, the tightening of immigration controls and asylum provisions and the pursuit of a neoliberal economic agenda that encouraged the outsourcing of public services and privatisation. Under Tony Blair, the Labour government nurtured a new settlement that involved the state in active moves towards de-secularising its relationship with civil society, particularly as regards ethnic minorities. Thus a new 'Faith and Cohesion' Unit was established within the Department of Communities and Local Government (DCLG), which administered a range of funds to encourage and consolidate a role for religious organisations in the public sphere, including a 'Faith Communities Capacity Building Fund' (FCCBF) and a 'Faiths in Action' programme.[50] Moreover, the DCLG produced 'myth-busting guidance' in order to counter the concerns of local authorities that were cautious about contact with religious organisations, with little pause for reflection on the historical reasons for supporting secular public services. These New Labour commitments then trickled down through state apparatus at national, regional and local levels, including to the Greater London Assembly and government-led quangos. All this enabled religious organisations to have formal lines of influence over policy and practice in a wide range of areas, including domestic violence – an area where they had previously been accused of compromising the safety and rights of women and children.[51] Alongside this government policy, both civil society mobilisations and academics started to project religion as 'cohesive', 'faith communities' as central players in tackling terrorism, and religious groups as important carriers of social capital and providers of welfare support.[52]

Community Cohesion was a concept widely promoted after the Cantle report of 2001, published after an inquiry into the Northern 'race riots' of 2001. It marked a turn away from cultural diversity and tolerance, and towards an earlier form of assimilationism; it sidestepped the direct racist abuse, structural racism and socio-economic disadvantage that had led to the disturbances and instead placed the onus on ethnic minorities to 'integrate'.[53] Various members of the teams inquiring into the causes of the 'race riots' expressed concern about segregation between the white majority and ethnic minority communities: they believed that the distance between communities could grow into a fear of difference and could be exploited by extremist groups.[54] Yet there was little or no reflection on the contribution of government policy to such segregation, including its local authority housing and dispersal strategies, New Labour's commitment to faith schools and a faith agenda that further fragmented and communalised minority communities.

As the 'War on Terror' got underway, this concern about cohesion was bolstered by the Preventing Violent Extremism (PVE) programme of 2007, which funded Muslim community organisations under the guise of 'tackling radicalisation'. PVE gave rise to a number of new actors and systems, and a large-scale transfer of public resources to 'Muslim' specific programmes.[55] Ironically, although government reports on cohesion and extremism had drawn attention to the propensity for religious organisations to encourage both segregation and extremism, the PVE agenda was being filtered through the same government's faith agenda, in order to strengthen religious identification above all else. New Labour's response to the events of 2001 should be seen as reflective of Blair's view that Britain had become a post-class, post-race society. The effect was to exacerbate a situation where religion had become the primary legitimate signifier of difference.[56]

In 2007 WAF and SBS made a joint submission to the government's Commission on Integration and Cohesion's consultation document 'Our Shared Future'.[57] This submission was critical of the Commission's terms of reference, particularly its focus on 'cohesion' and 'integration' rather than on human rights, equality and non-discrimination. They questioned whether there was any such thing as a set of fixed or distinctive 'British values' (and especially whether these were superior to others), but at the same time defended the values that had emerged from the Enlightenment tradition, particularly the universality of human rights; it was these that provided the common basis for fighting discrimination and inequality. And WAF also stood by the Enlightenment emphasis on the right to question, doubt and dissent. (Indeed many of the chapters contained within this volume – Ruth Pearson, Pragna, Clara, Gita, Nira, Hannana, Nadje, Cassandra, Georgie, Rashmi and Sue – reflect a simultaneous desire on the one hand to challenge imperialism and eurocentrism, and on the other to safeguard an international language of rights, principles and values as articulated through the human rights framework and enforced through a number of human rights conventions.)

Women within WAF coined the term 'multifaithism' to describe New Labour's stance on religion: the party had overseen a transition from multiculturalist governance to a multifaithist public policy that privileged religious identity and religious representation over all others. The Labour Party had heavily relied on ethnic, religious, caste and kinship networks to help rebuild popular support during their long years in the opposition wilderness;[58] and now the government – with the assistance of the newly galvanised religious councils modelled on the Jewish Board of Deputies (the Muslim Council of Britain, the Network of Sikh Organisations and the Hindu Forum of Britain) – was well placed to push multifaithism. This was done – of course primarily through working with male representatives, although the initiation of a Muslim Women's Network in 2002 by then Minister for Women Patricia Hewitt was also part of this shift.

The WAF/SBS submission to the Commission on Integration and Cohesion stated that the institutionalisation of religious communitarianism in public policy and practice was 'accelerating the process of the communalisation of what were once Asian or even Black communities'.[59] The submission identified the Muslim Women's Network as part of a trend that took issues affecting Black and minority women and reframed them as issues facing 'Muslim women'. This denied both the importance of secular Asian women's projects and the role that Muslims had already played in democratic processes within Britain – not as 'Muslims' but as people actively engaged with Black, Asian, anti-racist and other struggles.[60]

However WAF members interacted with these new religious discourses and layers of religious leadership in different ways. Indeed Cassandra Balchin became the Chair of the Muslim Women's Network, and her chapter in this book explains her commitment to engaging with these new bodies – whether driven by government or civil society – in the hope that she could influence the emerging 'Muslim' political spaces in a progressive way. Pragna, Hannana and Sukhwant, on the other hand, found the practice of speaking of specific 'Muslim', 'Hindu' or 'Sikh' women's 'needs' or 'issues' as problematic, and their chapters highlight the way that religion-speak shifted the terms of debate in areas such as violence against women.

The WAF/SBS submission remains an important contribution to the Cohesion and Prevent debates, in two main ways. Firstly, it draws attention to the state's relationship with fundamentalist partners; and, secondly, it emphasises the implications for women of the revival of 'community' and religious identity politics (issues which are otherwise absent in the literature on Community Cohesion).

WAF noted that the War on Terror had brought a discriminatory pressure to bear on Muslims to demonstrate their loyalty to Britain, but it also highlighted the contradictory response of the British state, which was in search of Muslim allies to fight extremism but at the same time working with (and often funding) a number of the front organisations of undemocratic, violent authoritarian movements, particularly branches of the Jamaat-e-Islami, the Muslim Brotherhood and the Hindu Right in Britain.[61] (Chapters by Georgie and Gita note the local and transnational implications of such actions.)

The WAF submission also criticised the lack of recognition by the Commission of the problems of 'community', especially for women. The Commission on Cohesion and Integration had wilfully ignored several decades of feminist critique of 'community', and the existence of power relations and inequalities within communities. The problems with who it is that defines and represents 'the community' are discussed by almost every contributor to this book. New Labour's promotion of 'faith communities' specifically encouraged fundamentalist and anti-democratic elements to establish themselves as representatives of large groups of people, which in turn served to legitimise campaigns for religious accommodation of all hues – including separate religious based schools; dress codes in secular state schools; personal laws (especially family laws governing marriage, divorce, child custody and inheritance); and legal protection against religious discrimination.

The WAF/SBS submission also highlighted the adverse implications for censorship and dissent that had arisen from the British state's engagement with fundamentalist forces. In particular it was critical of the invitation to Ramesh Kallidai, Secretary General of the right-wing Hindu Forum, to participate in the board of the Commission for Integration and Cohesion. This was in spite of the Hindu Forum's undemocratic tendencies being in full public view when they had forced the closure of a London art exhibition by the renowned Indian painter M.F. Hussain, on the grounds that Hussain's depiction of naked Hindu female deities offended Hindu sensibilities. The WAF/SBS submission drew parallels between attempts to censor M.F. Hussain and other situations where fundamentalist mobilisations had attempted to censor dissenting artists, including the threats made to the life of Gurpreet Bhatti for her play *Behzti* (Dishonour), which had dared to speak out about rape and power abuse within Sikh gurdwaras.[62] Shakila's chapter in this volume recounts that period from the perspective of an artist who has been forced to deal with the fundamentalist and conservative stranglehold on definitions of 'community', 'religion' and 'ethnicity'. (Similar concerns are raised by the Jewish contributors to this book; in particular, Nira and Julia reflect on the erasure of Eastern European and Yiddish traditions in the cultural politics of Zionism.) It was the experience of dealing with religious opposition to artistic license and intra-community pluralism – right through from the anti-Rushdie protests to the Behzti protests – which had led WAF to oppose the Incitement to Racial and Religious Hatred Act 2006.

In 2007, Southall Black Sisters, WAF's sister organisation, was itself subjected to the hard reality of the Cohesion and Prevent agendas, when Ealing council decided to cut its funding on the grounds that specialist services for black and minority women work against 'equality' and 'cohesion'. Community Cohesion meant that local councils were starting to do away with 'race' equality departments. Moreover, while longstanding progressive secular organisations were facing funding cuts, PVE policy led the same councils to initiate and fund 'Muslim' projects. At the same time that Ealing Council decided to withdraw funding to SBS, it was promoting religious literacy, inter-faith networks and faith-based (largely Muslim) groups to deliver local welfare services.[63] This included the creation of Muslim women-only projects. Ealing chose to ignore SBS's casework with Muslim women, and also to ignore Harriet Harman MP's applause for SBS's work in challenging segregation and extremism.

In fact the threat to SBS's funding can be seen as the culmination of a three-pronged attack by the New Labour government on specialist feminist services: there was a mainstreaming agenda, which pushed for 'difference' to be accommodated within generic service provision; a commissioning agenda, which involved a competitive tendering process that favoured much larger generic providers; and a faith agenda that validated religious organisations whilst simultaneously cutting secular providers. Fortunately, in 2008, SBS won a legal challenge against Ealing Council: the High Court affirmed the organisation's right to exist as a secular specialist provider because of the need for advice and advocacy to be framed within a democratic and secular ethos; and it also recognised the importance of specialist services for enhancing BME women's participation in the public sphere. WAF women supported SBS in their legal challenge and convened a joint public meeting at the House of Commons to highlight these issues. Unsurprisingly, all this led to a renewed sense of urgency about fighting for secular spaces.[64]

## FUNDAMENTALISM, EDUCATION AND THE LAW

Education and the law are two areas that have been subjected to strong and sustained lobbies by fundamentalists, and, accordingly, during its second period of activity WAF set up two sub groups to deal with them. It's impossible to do justice to these in the short space of this introduction, and what follows is therefore a very short summary highlighting a handful of the concerns and debates, beginning with the group on education.

As we have seen, in opposition the Labour Party had courted the ethnic minority vote, including by promising public funding to ethnic minority faith-based schools, on parity grounds. This was acted upon immediately the party took office, through the extension of Voluntary Aided status to minority faith schools (an overall policy commitment from which many Christian organisations also made significant gains). In defence of state funding for faith schools, New Labour utilised a wide variety of arguments: choice and parental power; the high rates of academic success of faith schools; the high levels of demand for them; and the role of faith schools in strengthening moral values.[65] Many of these claims have been subject to challenge.[66]

There were some suspicions that New Labour's interest in faith schools was motivated less by a concern about achievement than by Blair's personal religious belief, the need to give a sop to electoral vote banks and provision of a guise for neoliberal privatisation. WAF's response was to reiterate its position against faith schools, and emphasise the importance of secular schools for teaching critical thinking skills, and for providing young people with coherent personal, sexual and relationships education as well as progressive pastoral support. Moreover, WAF women were concerned that amid all the debates about faith schools little consideration was being given to their impact on gender equality. The government chose to bat away this issue by arguing that an investigation into the impact of faith schools on gender equality would be 'a massively disproportionate use of taxpayers' money' (in spite of the soon to be enacted gender equality duty).[67] As the number of state-funded faith schools continued to grow at an exponential rate, WAF decided to engage with the Accord Coalition, who were campaigning for the regulation of existing faith schools, through challenging their admissions policies and employment practices, and insisting that the national curriculum should be compulsory for all schools.[68] The Accord Coalition hoped that regulation would effectively pull faith schools towards a more mainstream character. WAF sought to add to the Accord discussions by restating the normative implications for gender, sexuality and dissent when religion enters the education system (i.e. they questioned whether simply opening up the admissions criteria is a sufficient goal). And WAF argued that a number of other issues needed to be considered: the use of these spaces for fundamentalist forces to accrue power and influence, and to seal the boundaries of their religion; the lack of plurality on religious holidays; the lack of sex education and PSHE; and the restrictions to women's access to extracurricular activities.[69]

WAF also raised concerns about the incursion of religious discourses within mainstream education subsequent to fundamentalist lobbies of mainstream comprehensive schools.[70] This more sophisticated strategy pushed for the accommodation of religion and religious 'sensibilities' within mainstream education – which effectively meant the encouragement of differential norms for young women, as primarily structured by conservative patriarchal tropes of 'respect' and 'decency'.[71] Importantly, some of the demands around religious accommodation were being made by women utilising a range of rights frameworks (the Race Relations Act 1976; the Human Rights Act 1998; and the new Religion and Belief Regulations 2003 that were part of New Labour's extension of equalities legislation in line with Europe). In 2002, Shabina Begum, a fourteen year old girl from Luton, took her school to court when it refused to adapt the school uniform to accommodate her desire to wear the jilbab (a full length robe). Begum accused the school of breaching her right to exercise her religion, and effectively of also denying her right to an education. The case went all the way to the House of Lords, who decided against Begum and in favour of the school. The judgement quoted from Nira and Gita's book *Refusing Holy Orders* (see note 5) to note the contestatory nature of religious claims; to argue the importance of balancing Begum's needs with the needs of the other girls at the school; and to be wary of the political motivations of specific religious mobilisations, including the desire to make strong distinctions between 'good' and 'bad' Muslim girls.[72]

In 2008, when New Labour proposed to extend the Public Sector Equality Duty to include 'the need to promote equality of opportunity to religion or belief', WAF made a submission to the Discrimination Law Review Team to oppose such proposals. In particular, WAF distinguished between 'religion and belief' and other equalities strands on the basis that the right to express religion is not an absolute right but rather is expected to be tempered in relation to its likely impact on others; in some instances the right to manifest one's religion had been limited in order to safeguard the rights of others. WAF argued that, in the context of resurgent fundamentalist forces and the contestatory nature of religious identities, extending such provisions to include religion would do far more to create inequality than to enable equality. In making this argument WAF found itself ranged against the growing strength of the Christian lobby in Britain, as Christian organisations, particularly Christian schools, campaigned hard for exemptions from the public sector equality duty, so that they would not be obliged to promote equality of gender or sexual orientation.[73]

As to questions about religion and the law, these began to materialise as demands for the recognition of religious councils and religious 'personal laws' as quasi parallel legal systems. This situation was compounded when religious groups began to make use of clauses in the Arbitration Act 1996 to offer cheap alternative dispute resolution forums. On the whole, there was an acceptance within WAF that the push on religious courts and personal laws was politically motivated, and an extension of fundamentalist political projects. Therefore, these were to be recognised as active political bodies with an agenda, rather than seen as passive cultural or religious institutions. Moreover, there was general agreement that such forums discriminated against women and children and were incompatible with human rights; that they were premised on a 'sacred' law, which meant that any legal determinations arising from them could not be challenged; and that many aspects were in direct conflict with UK law with regards to inheritance, property matters, child custody and polygamy. Within WAF there were numerous debates about how to approach this issue, and we began to develop a position paper that did not support a wholesale ban on these bodies (in recognition that people are entitled to seek the views of religious organisations if they so wish), but rather emphasised the importance of secular civil law, and argued the need to ensure that religious courts are not formally legally recognised, particularly in family matters, and that they are not engaged by statutory bodies to resolve issues pertaining to marriage, divorce, child custody and property (there is evidence to suggest that this was becoming the practice[74]). Moreover, there was a keen awareness that the Christian Right, the English Defence League and UKIP were weighing in on debates about Shariah courts, and that WAF's lobbying needed to take place away from these right-wing agendas; and there was also recognition that the problem lay not just with Shariah courts but also with Jewish Beth Dins and other religious dispute resolution mechanisms such as gurdwaras and caste panchayats.

A further discussion among WAF members also revealed concerns that a growing number of women were themselves approaching Shariah councils to intervene in family matters. The debates revolved around two issues. Firstly, there were questions of agency and choice – how far were women choosing this route, and how far were they acting under pressure (whether physical, emotional, normative/societal or because they had entered into religiously sanctioned marriages that were not recognised in civil law and therefore required access to religious divorce). Secondly, there was the question of whether to ban or to regulate – some circles, notably One Law for All, were calling for a ban while some members of WAF (see Cassandra's chapter in this book) wanted to engage with religious councils to attempt to shift their practice to a more feminist position. Other WAF members, however, believed that engagement with religious councils would effectively legitimise the existence of these bodies, and of parallel legal systems, and would thereby undermine the gains of secular civil law.

## COALITION CUTS AND A RESURGENT CHRISTIAN RIGHT

New Labour's engagement with religious organisations was part of their larger discovery of the neoliberal uses of communitarianism, and their development of an 'etho-politics', a new moral vocabulary for public policy that focused on individual behaviour and values as the way to rectify social problems.[75] In this there has been far more continuity than change with the Conservative Party's Big Society agenda. Moreover, to appreciate the ways in which an anti-bureaucracy Conservative Party rhetoric, which questions rather than supports equality legislation, interacts with state-led support for religious organisations, one need only note that immediately on taking office, Andrew Stunnell (a former Baptist lay preacher and at that time Minister for Communities and Local Government) and Eric Pickles (Secretary of State for Communities and Local Government) started to arrange meetings with religious groups such as the Jewish Leadership Council, at which they assured them that the government would cut the red tape on equalities so that religious groups could contribute to the Big Society.[76] In state policy terms, religious groups have gained additional leverage through the Coalition's Localism Act, and their nurturing of Academies (started by Blair).[77]

This continuing religious communitarianism has had a specific impact on people's access to public sector services such as education, youth provision, health and housing.[78] And there have been direct consequences for women's rights from this combination of a neoliberal austerity package, an aversion to equalities and a government that recognises religious groups as pivotal in enabling the decimation of the welfare state. Thus, for example, very soon after the election of the Coalition government, the anti-trafficking feminist group, the Poppy Project, had its funding transferred to the Christian Salvation Army.[79] This should be understood within the wider context of Coalition cuts to women's services and to legal aid, and the comparative rise of faith-based provision.

During this period an emergent network of right-wing Christian organisations has begun to gain public credibility within Britain, partly because of a general boost to critics of New Labour, as people demoralised by their policies were looking for political and electoral alternatives. The Conservative Party has been capitalising on this and revitalising its grassroots (and especially increasing its Black supporters) by tapping into the growing network of evangelical Christian organisations.[80] These new waves of Christian mobilisation raise some interesting issues, as, for example, when the British Pakistani Christian Association (BPCA) invited WAF to join their campaign against blasphemy laws in Pakistan, which have impacted upon Christians, Ahmadis and Shias alike. This was an issue close to our hearts: as well as supporting minority Muslims against persecution (see above), WAF women were also cognisant of the persecution of Buddhists, Hindus and Sikhs by the Taliban in Afghanistan and the Jamaat-e-Islami in Bangladesh. But, although we had campaigned against blasphemy laws in a number of countries, WAF had not as yet supported a Christian mobilisation against religious persecution. The BPCA was very responsive to WAF's suggestions about their campaign, but at the same time they were drawing support in Britain from multifaith platforms and also from the Christian Right. This presented a dilemma: whilst WAF had a lot of space to contribute to the organisation's policy submission, and was able to speak at their rallies with great directness about religious fundamentalism, including Christian fundamentalism, we were also pressurised to work in partnership with key proponents of Christian fundamentalism within Britain. The BPCA were critical of our unwillingness to participate in an alliance with Baroness Caroline Cox and the right-wing Christian Peoples Alliance, even though the Christian Peoples Alliance has been at the forefront of anti-abortion demonstrations against the British Pregnancy Advisory Service (BPAS) and the Marie Stopes organisation, and have been responsible for a new wave of misinformation about reproductive rights. (Indeed WAF had already challenged Caroline Cox during the 1990s, when she had cultivated an alliance with the religious right of all hues to push a multifaith lobby against sex education under the guise of 'parental rights'.) Cox and the CPA are evidence that the ability of fundamentalists to grow their power and sanitise their concerns through working in broad alliances is by no means limited to Muslim organisations.

## CONTEMPORARY FUNDAMENTALIST NETWORKS IN THE UK

This period saw the emergence of new constellations of activists and organisations from many religions but with compatible fundamentalist world views; such groups were actively building alliances with both state institutions and civil society organisations in order to embed themselves within broader discussions about equality, civil liberties and human rights. For instance, a number of Muslim Brotherhood, Jamaat-e-Islami, Salafist organisations and the Hizb-ut-Tahrir began working with each other across different forums and spaces.[81] Moreover, these groups have been projecting themselves as 'moderate'. They have been critical of the anti-Muslim, anti-imperialist nature of the state, but at the same time have worked closely with the police and the state and managed to attract PVE funding, which they have used to strengthen their own position and perpetuate their specific version of Islam.

In February 2010 a flashpoint ignited from the heat of these contradictions. WAF founder member Gita Sahgal, who was at the time Head of the Gender Unit at Amnesty International, made a public critique of Amnesty International's relationship with former Guantanamo detainee Moazzam Begg and his organisation Cageprisoners. To briefly summarise, Gita was critical of Begg's sympathies for the Taliban, and argued that both he and Cageprisoners were located within salafi-jihadi networks within Britain that had been actively promoting Islamic Right tendencies, through publishing and reproducing, in a non-critical way, salafist lectures and books. At the heart of her critique were questions about the legitimacy that right-wing religious organisations could acquire through alliances, and a concern to persuade human rights organisations to work as hard on challenging human rights violations by non-state fundamentalists as those by nation states. Gita called for a clearer distinction to be made between facilitating the telling of the horrendous experiences of former Guantanamo inmates as part of a campaign for the dismantling of Guantanamo Bay and similar spaces used in 'the global war on terror', and the legitimisation of Cageprisoners as human rights defenders and potential partners. She pointed to the propensity of such uncritical alliances to enable the entrenchment of fundamentalist ideas and discourses, and used the word 'sanitisation' to describe this process.

There was some disagreement within WAF on this issue. Some members saw similarities with the Rushdie controversy, and viewed Gita's argument as indicative of all the entanglements and problems of identifying and challenging fundamentalism in the current moment. Others found the argument tenuous, and the focus on Begg and Cageprisoners misplaced, and argued that the way the public campaign had developed was uncomfortable. This was a tense period, during which fissures emerged within WAF that probably caused a stalemate within the organisation, and inhibited its ability to act as a unified political group.

The use of a human rights framework by fundamentalists is by no means confined to Muslim fundamentalism. Hindu Right activists were also lobbying within this frame, while Khalistanis (Sikhs demanding the secession of Punjab from India to establish a separate theocratic state) were positioning themselves as human rights defenders by talking about civil liberties violations and the right to self-determination; and the Christian Right, too, frequently talk about rights, especially the rights of the unborn child.

This complex array of political issues, in combination with the economic crisis and the government's austerity policies, and the need to campaign on green issues, are the context within which women gradually moved away from WAF to focus on different political concerns, though some of us continued to meet as individuals or as members of other organisations, to try to make collective sense of the contemporary political landscape.

## THE THEORETICAL AND METHODOLOGICAL FRAMEWORK OF THE BOOK

Feminism, like all significant social movements and ideologies, is more a cluster than one homogeneous body of principles, perspectives and practices. Early accounts of 'what is feminism' focused on differentiating between liberal, radical and socialist feminisms; later, the homogeneity of women assumed in the feminist slogan 'sisterhood is global' was challenged by particular groupings of women who organised not just as women but also as 'Black', 'lesbian', 'disabled', 'Jewish', etc, to reflect their multiple identities and stipulate simultaneous struggles against multiple axes of oppression.

The kind of feminist activism in which WAF women have been engaged is somewhat different. Although the ethnic, national, religious and racial origins of the women who participate are often important, it is not the ultimate focus of their activism. Rather, their activism is of the kind that can be referred to as 'intersectional politics'.[82] In contrast to early feminists such as Dorothy Smith, who spoke of a 'women's standpoint' in a somewhat similar way to Marx's 'proletarian standpoint', an intersectional approach recognises that people's concrete social locations are constructed along multiple (and both shifting and contingent) axes of difference, such as gender, class, race and ethnicity, stage in the life cycle, sexuality, ability and so on.[83] However, intersecting social divisions should not be analysed as items that are *added* to each other (as is common in identity politics – and in some popular misinterpretations of what intersectionality politics is), but rather as *constituting* each other, and therefore impossible to be experienced separately.[84] There isn't a 'human' who is not gendered, classed, ethnocised, located in a particular stage in the life cycle, etc. Class cannot be experienced or lived outside of 'race', gender, sexuality and the same is true of other categories. Similarly, people's moral and political values are *related to*, but cannot be *reduced to*, their identifications and emotional attachments on the one hand or their social locations on the other. WAF's feminists shared solidarity on the basis of common moral political values, but, as can be seen from the individual chapters in this book, their perspectives also differed in light of their personal/political biographies and locations. The variety of voices within this book is significant in that it illustrates both the diverse political formation of WAF women *and* WAF's specificity as a political organisation.

The autobiographical accounts in this book are based on life history interviews carried out by Nira (except her own, which was carried out by Sukhwant), and then transformed into written narratives by the contributors. There are two exceptions to this format, caused by the greatly mourned loss of two of the WAF members whose contributions were planned for inclusion. Cassandra Balchin died whilst we were putting together this book, and her chapter was therefore edited by us from her interview transcript. Helen Lowe died after the book was conceived but before we had had the opportunity to interview her, and we have therefore included a short biographical piece written by Judy Greenway.

In most narrative studies, interviewers analyse and interpret the narratives from a critical distance. However, with this book, such a 'critical distance' did not exist, since we were all 'WAF women'. As the editors we took the view that each interviewee should decide which issues or aspects of her life she wanted to highlight, and then write this into a short personal-political autobiography. This approach shifted the balance of power from us, as the editors, to the contributors. Such an approach has some disadvantages. One has been that in a couple of cases the contributors decided to withdraw from the book project altogether once they had listened to their own interviews, because they felt too uncomfortable to embark on writing an essay about their own personal lives. Another disadvantage has been that as a result of the need to condense several hours of rich interviews into a fairly coherent five thousand word chapter, the stories have been somewhat flattened, and ambiguities or contradictions that were in the original interviews have been reduced. On the other hand, it has given women control over their own stories: they did not become mere 'case studies' in an illustrative generic study. They were encouraged to decide what should and what should not be included in their narratives. They highlighted different themes according to their own priorities. Another bonus of this process has been that when they listened to the recordings, they often realised that they had left out important issues, which they were then able to include in the final written version.

## THE POLITICAL FORMATION OF WAF ACTIVISTS

As explained above, WAF was formed during the height of the Rushdie affair in 1989, and a common feature of its members has been their critical approach both to the state and to their own communities, including where they have been part of the hegemonic majority. From the beginning its membership included feminists from different origins and cultures, some of whom were mobilised by SBS, who initiated the first meeting of what became WAF on the basis of their previous work on violence against women, anti-racism, state multiculturalist policies and welfare provision. In this way, SBS has always been a collective presence in WAF, while other members have come as individuals. During the heyday of separatist identity politics, at a time when some Black feminists avoided co-operation with white feminists, assuming that 'mixed' activism would always be dominated by white women, SBS activists invited all feminists to Southall to support their activities because they had the confidence to do so. Nira's, Gita's and Pragna's chapters, for example, highlight the significance of all feminists being invited by SBS to the Krishna Sharma demonstration in 1984, when they marched through Southall and picketed the home of Krishna's husband and in-laws to shame them for provoking Krishna's suicide (following the political practice of feminists in India).

Individual members followed a variety of personal pathways that eventually led them to WAF. They came from different religious backgrounds (atheist, of different Christian denominations, Hindu, Jewish, Muslim and Sikh), as well as from different countries of birth (e.g. Czech Republic, India, Israel, Ireland, Kenya, the UK and the USA). The roads to WAF activism among all members were deeply affected by the societies in which they grew up – whether they grew up as members of hegemonic majorities (whether in the West or the South) or as members of racialised minorities. For WAF members who grew up in hegemonic majorities, proto-feminist and/or socialist consciousness (e.g. Clara, Gita, Jane Lane, Natalie, Rashmi, Ritu) often came before proto-anti-racist ones. For others, feminism and/or socialism followed initial experiences which pertained to racism (e.g. Eva Turner, Nira, Pragna, Hannana, Shakila, Ruth and Sue). Green Party leader Natalie Bennett's involvement in WAF highlights the compatibility of WAF's anti-fundamentalist politics not only with anti-racist and socialist feminism, but also with the wider spectrum of contemporary emancipatory politics.

What is specific to WAF politics, however, is not just its combination of feminism and anti-racism, but opposition to religious fundamentalism. Most members of WAF had encountered religious authoritarianism and fundamentalist movements (e.g. Clara the Irish Catholic church; Nira – Jewish fundamentalism in Israel; Pragna – Hindutva; Sukhwant – Khalistanis) long before 9/11 brought a more public awareness of the dangers of religious fundamentalism. A small number of WAF members of UK Christian majoritarian origin had close personal and familial involvement with women and men of Muslim origin (and/or had lived for some years in South Asia, e.g. Georgie, Cass). Other members of Christian origin grew up in Quaker homes and saw their involvement in WAF as compatible with these values (i.e. Jane Lane and Sue O' Sullivan). However, some African Caribbean feminists who originally joined WAF during the Rushdie campaign left shortly afterwards because they resented what they saw as WAF's insufficient regard for the importance of Christian churches as a sanctuary and an organising space against racism (see Jane's chapter for concerns about this).

The political development of WAF women has often been individualistic rather than collective. In part this is connected with a widely shared experience amongst the contributors of discomfort, of feeling 'out of place' or 'out of time' in their activist surroundings, and therefore of searching for (and ultimately finding it in WAF) a political home that fitted more clearly with their perspective (e.g. Clara, Eva, Nadje, Sue and Sukhwant). For some WAF women, books played a particularly strong role during their teenage years, supplying them with inspiration and role models that substituted for more social forms of solidarity in situations in which they felt isolated and confronted by family and/or community (e.g. Nira, Pragna, Rashmi, Sukhwant).

Migration, in their family histories as well as in their own lives, has played a major role in most WAF women's identities. Several women are from families that travelled the routes of colonial labour exchange from countries that were colonised by the British (Pragna, Shakila, Hannana). Many women's lives were made or transformed by the dialectical relationship between particular sections within specific countries and the British state (for example the Congress political elite in the case of Gita, or Jat Sikhs and their role in British colonial rule in the case of Sukhwant). The British colonial dimensions of these narratives are also scrambled by ancestral ties to colonial pasts that drew someone like Georgie out of England to live in India and then Bangladesh, and took Cassandra to Pakistan. And these life histories also recount the lives of new post-colonial/Commonwealth migrants who drifted towards the centre from the periphery (e.g. Clara, Rashmi, Ritu, Sue and Natalie). All these movements across borders share an uncanny connection with an ever present colonial past that refuses to either fix or erase the 'here' and the 'there'. The history of migration and discrimination on the part of the Jewish members of WAF (Julia, Ruth, Eva, Nira and Helen) further complements as well as complicates any binary construction of racialisation which relies on a simplified geo-political dichotomy between 'the West and the Rest'.

Education has played a particularly important role in the lives of most WAF women, often linked to spatial mobility (see for example Eva's chapter – she was the first to get a university education in her family). Migration within the UK was often associated with going to study at university in a different city. This was a common pathway. Given the class origin of many WAF members, education was often possible only because free university education and maintenance grants were still available when they were growing up (e.g. Hannana, Pragna, Sukhwant). The new kinds of people, ideas and organisations that WAF women encountered during their university studies were often a launching pad to new forms of being, as well as activism. This was true also for WAF members who went to study in universities in different cities and in other countries (e.g. Natalie, Nira, Gita, Rashmi, Nadje, Sue and Ritu).

## WAF IS DEAD. LONG LIVE WAF!

The characteristic which we found to be common to all WAF activists is that, whether they are founding members or later joiners, WAF was never their first 'political home' or their only centre of activism. This is because to be a 'WAFer', one's politics had to become not solely feminist, and/or anti-racist and/or anti-fundamentalist: it had to encompass all these different dimensions in order to tread the precarious pathway of 'washing one's dirty linen in public' and simultaneously be anti-racist; to make a distinction between secularism as a separation of religion and the state and secularism as a blanket rejection of any religion or spirituality; to combine all this with a critique of the ethnic 'community', the local, the national and the global. Such a political perspective was achieved in different ways and involved activism in multiple arenas – from racist violence to domestic violence to anti-war to immigration to interventions on multiculturalist and multi-faithist policies to interventions on UN human rights commissions to campaigns on women's reproductive rights. However, what united them was holistic and organic: the specific and the generic were continuously kept together in a dynamic but analytically solid way. WAF was highly valued for many years by virtually all its members as the best context in which they could think and analyse what was happening and learn new ideas and insights – and as a place from which they could take insights back to the other political contexts in which they were operating.

This was both WAF's great strength and its great weakness. Great strength, because in this way WAF members were at the forefront of political analysis, thinking in a complex intersectional way, examining particular social and political issues and policies in a holistic way. Weakness, because it was not easy for new members to join, and even when persevering it often took years before they 'dared' to speak in the name of the organisation (e.g. Eva, Jane, Sue's chapters in this volume).

Moreover, because of the multi-politicking of most WAF members, there was never enough time and energy to accomplish particular WAF campaigns and to nurture the organisation. Eventually – and having been seriously affected by the sudden death of Helen Lowe, a WAF activist who created and sustained the WAF website and email list – the organisation was unable to withstand all the debates and disagreements about new political developments, and eventually it petered out, although, as we have noted, some of the core members continue to meet for occasional political discussions and to attend public symposia, such as the series on Gender and Fundamentalism organised by WAFers Nira and Nadje.[85] The demise of WAF opens up more general questions about the nature and effectiveness of political organisations that resist becoming formally funded and structured bodies or NGOs; about feminist decision-making mechanisms; and about the all too often weakness of intergenerational feminist reproduction.[86]

There were a number of ongoing organisational dilemmas for WAF.

The continuous pull between structuring the organisation, making it function as a formal organisation, and its nature as an activist body with maximum participation, resulted in an uneven relationship between a growing number of e-list members and an ad hoc Organising Group that by default became more of a decision-making and management body than it had intended. This point is connected to the continuous tension between WAF as an activist organisation, supporting and running its own campaigns, and WAF as a space for discussion and reflection. Furthermore, the fact that women involved with this network were already active elsewhere meant that additional activism was restricted, but a simple 'talking shop' was not what everyone wanted. At each stage, newer members in particular had become involved specifically because they felt that anti-fundamentalist activism was needed. In the earlier days, it was this tension between WAF as an academically informed, writing, reflecting space and the practical needs and preferred language of activism that brought about the end of the WAF journal.[87] (This absence of a journal has inevitably meant that in its second phase less of the organisation's work has been recorded.) Finally, WAF's practice of 'speaking in pairs' could be both liberating and constraining for its members. Speaking in pairs was something that emerged in the early days, as a means of countering populist impressions and media coverage that portrayed WAF as anti-Muslim or as only interested in Muslim fundamentalism. By undertaking speaking engagements in pairs of members of different ethnic and religious origin, WAF members made an attempt to deflect such perception, to reflect the diversity of the organisation, and to speak about fundamentalism in all religions. Paradoxically, at times this encased WAF within the same logic that the organisation pushed against – identity politics and all the authenticating and legitimising processes that accompany it.

Needless to say, with the end of WAF's second life we all share a great deal of frustration and the sense of a lost opportunity for social and political impact precisely at a time when the need for it is probably greater than ever.

During the peak of its existence, WAF was used as an example for what is known as 'transversal politics'.[88] This is a kind of politics that feminists and other emancipatory activists developed in many parts of the world, and in transnational and global organisations, in which the solidarity among the activists is not built on common origin or identity but rather on shared political values and they are seen as advocates for rather than representatives of their collectivities. At the same time there is a recognition and respect for the differential intersectional locations of the different participants in the transversal dialogue, and their uneven power relations. The dialogue is sustained by 'shifting' – an empathetic identification with the situated gaze of the other participants in the dialogue – and 'rooting' – a reflective grounding of one's own social as well as ideational location.

The feminists in Bologna who in the 1990s first used the terms 'shifting', 'rooting' and 'transversal politics' in relation to feminist co-operation across borders and boundaries of national and ethnic conflicts borrowed the term from 'the Transversalists' – a group of autonomous leftist liberation activists in Bologna. However, the first person to use the term transversal politics was Felix Guattari, who used it in a very different way.[89] His concern was a dialogue not across borders and boundaries but one that was internal to a political organisation. He felt that only a transversal process of communication, which would encompass both vertical and horizontal layers of the organisation, would ensure that a political organisation would not outlast its purpose, would not continue to exist just because of any organisation's tendency to perpetuate itself.

In the case of WAF it is clear that the reason for its existence, its purpose, is not accomplished. As several chapters in the book indicate (e.g. Gita, Julia, Clara), the changing local and global context of WAF since the days of its establishment, the highly complex, shifting and contested articulations of its politics and priorities, as well as some of its structural weaknesses, have meant that the organisation was not able to sustain the transversal alliance that had kept it working for so many years. This, however, does not invalidate what some of us call the intersectional political perspective of WAF, which argues the need for an encompassing emancipatory political analysis and feminist activism that is at the same time anti-racist and anti-fundamentalist. It is our hope that reading this book will encourage old and new activists to take on this crucial task.

## A NOTE ABOUT HOW THE CHAPTERS ARE ORGANISED

The contributors' chapters are organised according to the time period in which women joined the organisation. So it begins with those that were involved in initiating the earliest meetings, and then moves on to those that joined through those meetings – and so on and so forth.

## NOTES

1. M. Andrews, *Shaping History: Narratives of Political Change*, Cambridge University Press, Cambridge 2007.
2. Some of us called this transversal politics, as discussed towards the end of this introduction.
3. See S. Huntington, 'The Clash of Civilizations', *Foreign Affairs* 72(3), 1993: 22-50); this perspective is also an important feature of contemporary Christian Right interventions in politics.
4. See Women Against Fundamentalism journal archive: www.womenagainstfundamentalism.org.uk; and G. Sahgal and N. Yuval-Davis, *Refusing Holy Orders: Women and Fundamentalism in Britain*, Virago Press, London 1992.
5. For further reading see *WAF Journal*, number 5, 1994, which debates the term 'fundamentalism' and its application across religions and in several different contexts.
6. A few years ago several WAF women, but notably Cassandra Balchin, were involved in an action research project about the impact of fundamentalist movements on the lives and activism of feminists, human rights defenders and development workers in 160 different countries. The publications that emerged from that work can be accessed here: www.awid.org/AWID-s-Publications/Religious-Fundamentalisms.
7. See G. Sahgal, 'Fundamentalism and the Multi-Culturalist Fallacy', in SBS Collective (eds), *Against the Grain*, Southall Black Sisters, Southall 1990; F. Anthias and N. Yuval-Davis, *Racialized Boundaries: Race, Nation, Gender, Colour and Class and the Anti-Racist Struggle*, Routledge, London 1992; Sahgal and Yuval-Davis, op cit.
8. P. Cohen and H.S. Bains, *Multi-Racist Britain*, Macmillan Education, London 1988; V. Das, *Critical Events: An Anthropological Perspective on Contemporary India*, Oxford University Press, Oxford 1996; and S. Dhaliwal, 'Orange Is Not the Only Colour: Young Women and Religious Identity in Southall', in R. Gupta (ed), *From Homebreakers to Jailbreakers: Southall Black Sisters*, Zed Books, London 2003.
9. C. Bhatt, *Liberation and Purity: Race, New Religious Movements and the Ethics of Postmodernity*, Routledge, London 1997, p110.
10. Ibid, p113.
11. The Jamaat-e-Islami is a Saudi-funded fundamentalist group that was formed in 1941 in colonial India, drawing inspiration from Abu a'la Maududi, one of the first thinkers of the Islamic Right, who formulated an ideology of the Islamic state and of modern jihad. Many of its leaders are currently being prosecuted for war crimes in Bangladesh, including

those who have been living in London and/or have been regular preachers at London institutions.

12. Bhatt, op cit.
13. At a recent discussion organised by the Centre for Secular Space, Dr Ghayasuddin Siddiqui provided insights on the connections between Islamist projects, demands for blasphemy laws, persecution of intellectuals and artists, and the eruption of genocidal violence. See: *Bangladesh Genocide: what human rights, anti-racist and peace organisations won't tell you*, speakers: Gita Sahgal, Dr Ghayasuddin Siddiqui and Asif Munier, SOAS, London, 27 November 2012. A full video of the talk is available to view at: www.youtube.com/watch?v=HKEHLvMQm-0, Accessed on 22 September 2013.
14. J. Bard, 'Women Against Fundamentalism and the Jewish Community' in *WAF Journal*, No 4, pp3-5, 1992/1993.
15. See Bernie Grant's statement in *Hullabaloo Over Satanic Verses* (Part 2), a film made by Gita Sahgal for the Channel 4 Series *Bandung File* in 1989. Available at: www.youtube.com/watch?v=cLbx47Nyfio&feature=relmfu; and K. Shukra, *The Changing Pattern of Black Politics in Britain*, Pluto Press, London 1998.
16. C. Connolly, 'Review essay on "Sacred Cows"' in *Feminist Review*, No 35, 1990.
17. The anti-Rushdie march represented the coming together of politically liberal Barelwis, Iranian shias, Wahhabis and Saudi funded networks (particularly Jamaat-e-Islami and the Muslim Brotherhood chapters in Britain). See C. Bhatt, *Liberation and Purity: Race, New Religious Movements and the Ethics of Postmodernity*, Routledge, London 1997.
18. *Struggle Or Submission*, made in 1989 by Gita Sahgal for Channel 4's series *The Bandung File*: www.youtube.com/watch?v=zPZ22wBT46Y.
19. See A. Cummins, 'Taslima Nasreen and the fight against fundamentalism', in *WAF Journal*, No 6, 1995, pp53-57.
20. International Initiative for Justice, *Threatened Existence: A Feminist Analysis of the Genocide in Gujarat*, IIJ 2003.
21. G. Sahgal and N. Yuval-Davis, Introduction, Sahgal and Yuval-Davis, op cit.
22. As articulated in the Church Urban Fund's 1984 report *Faith in the City*, which also represents the first steps that gave rise to the now prominent Christian-led campaigning body, Citizens UK.
23. G. Sahgal, 'Secular Spaces; The Experience of Asian Women Organising' in Sahgal and Yuval-Davis, op cit.
24. Sahgal and Yuval-Davis, op cit.
25. As documented in ibid; and issues 1, 2 and 6 of the *WAF journal*.
26. T. Modood, 'Beware of a Secular Intolerance', in *WAF Journal*, No 6, 1995.
27. Ibid.

28. C. Connolly, 'WAF replies to Tariq Modood' in *WAF Journal*, No 6, 1995.
29. H. Bhabha, 'On Subaltern Secularism', in *WAF Journal*, No 6, 1995.
30. Rohini PH, 'The struggle against communalism: defining our positive alternative', in *WAF Journal*, No 6, 1995.
31. For more detail of WAF's position on religion and education see *WAF Journal*, No 1, p8, November 1990, where there is a copy of the 'WAF Model Resolution on Religious Schools'.
32. Sahgal, 'Secular Spaces' in Sahgal and Yuval-Davis, op cit.
33. See A. Chhachhi, 'Religious fundamentalism and women' in *WAF Journal*, No 1, 1990, pp14-15; and 'Civil codes and personal laws: reversing the option working group on women's rights', in *WAF Journal*, No 8, 1996, pp20-24.
34. 'Rabia Janjua Must Stay: Statement by WAF', dated 29 August 1990, in *WAF Journal*, No 1, November 1990.
35. As well as the chapters in this book, see A. Rossiter, '"Between the devil and the deep blue sea": Irish women, Catholicism and Colonialism'; and M. Poya, *Double Exile; Iranian Women and Islamic Fundamentalism*: both in Sahgal and Yuval-Davis, op cit.
36. A. Rossiter, 'Granting Civil Rights to the Foetus in Ireland – A Victory to Christian Fundamentalists Worldwide', in *WAF Journal*, No 1, November 1990, p9.
37. A. Rossiter, 'Between the devil and the deep blue sea', op cit.
38. Rita Burtenshaw's seminar talk was reproduced in full in *WAF Journal*, number 2, July 1991, pp3-5.
39. A. Rossiter, 'Outraged protestors call for the Irish fatwa against a 14 year old pregnant rape victim to be lifted', *WAF Journal*, No 3, 1992, pp1-3.
40. See *WAF Journal*, Number 7, 1995, which focused on reproductive rights and these international alliances among fundamentalists.
41. G.C. Spivak, 'Public Hearing on Crimes Against Women', *WAF Journal*, No 7, 1995, pp3-5.
42. R. Feldman, 'Reply to Gayatri Chakravorty Spivak', *WAF Journal*, No 7, 1995, pp5-7.
43. N. Yuval-Davis, 'The Cairo Conference, Women and Transversal Politics', *WAF Journal*, No 6, 1995, pp19-21.
44. See the entire WAF Journal devoted to this issue, *WAF Journal* number 8, 1996.
45. See East London WAF Members 'Resistance to fundamentalism in Bangladesh and Britain', *WAF Journal*, No 4, 1992, pp9-11; and 'Women unite against racism: WAF report', *WAF Journal*, No 6, 1995, pp35-36.
46. See A. Imam, J. Morgan & N. Yuval-Davis (eds), *Warning Signs of Fundamentalisms*, WLUML 2004.
47. See WLUML Occasional Paper number 14 (November 2003), which is a written report on this event and can be downloaded from www.wluml.org/node/471.

48. The story of Respect and its alliances is now well documented. See C. Bassi, 'The Anti-Imperialism of Fools: A Cautionary Story of the Revolutionary Socialist Vanguard of England's post 9/11 Anti-War Movement', in *Acme: An International E-Journal for Critical Geographies* 9(2): 113-138, 2009; S. Glynn, 'Bengali Muslims: The New East End Radicals?' in *Ethnic and Racial Studies* 25(6): 969-988, 2002; S. Glynn, *Playing the Ethnic Card – Politics and Ghettoisation in London's East End*, Institute of Geography Online Paper Series, University of Edinburgh 2006; R. Phillips, 'Standing Together: The Muslim Association of Britain and the Anti-War Movement', *Race & Class* 50(2) 2008: 101-13.
49. W. Macpherson, *The Stephen Lawrence Inquiry* (Macpherson Report). HMSO, London 1999.
50. About 45 million pounds have been allocated since 2006 to fund hundreds of religious organisations, and then, in 2009, to establish nine Regional Faith Forums to work with regional statutory bodies and quangos to raise concerns about religion and belief in the region. See E. Spratt and M. James, *Faith, Cohesion and Community Development: Final evaluation report from the Faith Communities Capacity Building Fund*, Community Development Foundation, London 2008; D. Permain and A. Hatamian, *Faiths in Action Interim Report: First Year Evaluation of the Regional Faith Forums and the Faiths in Action Programme*, Community Development Foundation, London 2010.
51. Examples include: the document 'Consulting London: A Framework for the core GLA, LDA, LFEPA, MPA and TFL', published in September 2003, which clearly identifies 'faith groups' as 'stakeholders', and institutionalises their place in consultation mechanisms; the 2006 GLA-organised meeting of religious organisations to discuss their role in tackling domestic violence; and the 'Faith in the Future' project of 2001/02, developed by the Housing Corporation.
52. See for instance: A. Dinham, R. Furbey and V. Lowndes, *Faith in the Public Realm: Controversies, Policies and Practices*, Policy Press, London 2009; A. Dinham, R. Farnell, D. Finneron et al, *Faith as Social Capital: Connecting or Dividing*, Policy Press, London 2006; A. Dinham and V. Lowndes, 'Religion, Resources, and Representation', in *Urban Affairs Review* 43(6) 2008: 817-845; R. Furbey and M. Macey, 'Religion and Urban Regeneration: A Place for Faith?' in *Policy & Politics* 33(1) 2005: 95-116.
53. See L. Back, M. Keith, A. Khan, K. Shukra and J. Solomos, 'The Return of Assimilationism: Race, Multiculturalism and New Labour', in *Sociological Research Online* 7, 2002; J. Burnett, 'Community, Cohesion and the State', in *Race & Class* 45(3): 1, 2004; A. Rattansi, 'Who's British? Prospect and the New Assimilationism', in R. Berkeley (ed), *Cohesion, Community and Citizenship*, The Runnymede Trust 2002, pp96-105; A. Sivanandan, 'Race, Terror and Civil Society', in *Race & Class* 47(3), 2006,

pp1-8; D. McGhee, 'Moving to "Our" Common Ground – a Critical Examination of Community Cohesion Discourse in Twenty-First Century Britain', in *The Sociological Review* 51(3) 2003; 376-404; C. Worley, 'It's Not About Race. It's About the Community': New Labour and Community Cohesion', in *Critical Social Policy* 25(4), 2005: 483-496; A. Kundnani, *The End of Tolerance: Racism in 21st Century Britain*, Pluto Press, London 2007.

54. This was counter to the findings of some of the independent inquiries which expressly talked about the prevalence of racism. For instance, the Oldham Independent Review Panel report, dated 11.12.01, points to: the rise of the far right in the area, including their gaining of seats in local elections; a petrol bomb attack on the then Asian Mayor's house; common usage of the word 'Paki' to refer to Asians in the area; self-imposed curfews amongst ethnic minorities to avoid racist attacks; and complaints by ethnic minorities of people dumping rubbish or throwing bottles, both of which are common forms of racist harassment.
55. Arun Kundnani (2009) and Rahila Gupta (2010) estimated that up to £140 million were disbursed through local authorities to mainly Muslim groups to tackle radicalisation in communities. In the context of an acute shortage of voluntary sector funding, voluntary sector organisations were uncritically signing up to the terms of this new source of funding in order to meet their core costs. See R. Gupta, 'This religious give-away is hard to justify', *Guardian*, 23.1010: www.guardian.co.uk/commentisfree/belief/2010/mar/23/denham-funding-religious-groups; and A. Kundnani, *Spooked! How Not to Prevent Violent Extremism*, Institute of Race Relations, London 2009.
56. Tony Blair (8.12.06), 'The Duty to Integrate: Shared British Values': www.politics.co.uk/news/2006/12/8/blair-warns-of-duty-to-integrate.
57. WAF/SBS Submission to the Commission on Integration and Cohesion, dated January 2007.
58. John Solomos and Les Back coined the term 'machine politics' to describe this phenomenon. See J. Solomos and L. Back, *Race, Politics, and Social Change*, Routledge, London 1995.
59. WAF/SBS submission to the Commission on Cohesion and Integration, London, 2007, p36.
60. Muslim Women's Network, *She Who Dispute; Muslim Women Shape the Debate*, Women's National Commission, London, November 2006.
61. C. Bhatt, 'The Fetish of the Margins: Religious Absolutism, Anti-racism and Post-colonial Silence', *New Formations 59* (Special Issue – Post-colonial Studies After Iraq), 2006; and G. Sahgal, 'Two cheers for multiculturalism', in A. Imam, J. Morgan and N. Yuval-Davis (eds), *The Warning Signs of Fundamentalism*, WLUML, 2004.
62. WAF/SBS Submission to the Commission on Integration and Cohesion, dated January 2007.

63. P. Patel and U. Sen, *Cohesion, Faith and Gender: A report on the impact of the cohesion and faith based approach on black and minority women in Ealing*, Southall Black Sisters and Oxfam, London 2011: www.southallblacksisters.org.uk/reportrequests.html.
64. The public meeting *Faith, Equality and Cohesion* took place on 25 November 2008 at the House of Commons, and included as speakers Karon Monaghan (Matrix Chambers), Pragna Patel (SBS) and Sandhya Sharma (Saheli).
65. The state funding of faith schools remains a scandal. The Coalition government continued the commitment to schools of a religious character and, according to the British Humanist Association (BHA), schools in Britain now take six different forms: local authority owned and managed secular community schools; three types of schools which may be legally registered with a religious character (Voluntary Controlled; Voluntary Aided; and Foundation 'faith' schools, academies or Free Schools); and academies and Free Schools that have no registered religious character but may have a 'faith ethos'. Each of these streams has differing levels of autonomy from state control. The BHA chart is a useful guide and can be found at: http://humanism.org.uk/wp-content/uploads/schools-with-a-religious-character.pdf. Their website also provides annual statistics about schools of a religious character. See: https://humanism.org.uk/campaigns/schools-and-education/faith-schools/.
66. See D. Gillard, *Never Mind the Evidence: Blair's obsession with faith schools*, 2007: www.educationengland.org.uk/articles/26blairfaith.html, accessed 18 October 2013; S. Gibbons and O. Silva, *Faith Primary Schools – Better Schools or Better Pupils?*, Discussion Paper number 4089, March 2009: http://papers.ssrn.com/sol3/Delivery.cfm/dp4089.pdf?abstractid=1369835&mired=2; K.M. Gokulsing, 'Without Prejudice: An Exploration of Religious Diversity, Secularism and Citizenship in England', in *Journal of Education Policy* 21(4) 2006: 459-470.
67. See N. Hanman, 'Unequal Opportunities', *Guardian*, 9.5.06: www.theguardian.com/education/2006/may/09/faithschools.schools, accessed 19 October 2013.
68. See the Accord Coalition website: http://accordcoalition.org.uk/about-us/ Last accessed on 19 October 2013.
69. Julia Bard raised concerns about the links between the growing number of Jewish families sending their children to Jewish schools and the way in which this enabled religious councils and faith schools to determine what it is to be Jewish and to seal the boundaries of the community as a whole. See J. Bard, 'Faith Schools: minorities, boundaries, representation and control' in *FORUM*, vol 49, number 3, 2007, pp277-280. Similar concerns were raised by O. Valins, 'Defending identities or segregating communities? Faith-based schooling and the UK Jewish community', in *Geoforum*, 34, 2002, pp235-247; and J. Romain, 'Faith Schools are Still a Recipe for Social Disaster' in *FORUM*, vol 49, number 3, 2007, pp207-212.

70. See: www.bbc.co.uk/religion/religions/christianity/beliefs/creationism_1.shtml; and www.muslimgovernors.org/; and P. Mukta, 'New Hinduism: Teaching Intolerance, Practising Aggression', in the *Journal of PCIRE*, Autumn issue, 1997.
71. See the research report by two WAF members: S. Dhaliwal and P. Patel, *Multiculturalism in Secondary Schools: Managing Conflicting Demands* (2006): www.workinglives.org/research-themes/discrimination/cre-multiculturalism-in-secondaryschools.cfm, accessed 19 October 2013. More recently the BHA have picked up the concern about sex and relationships education by lobbying government to make this a part of the compulsory national curriculum; for that national curriculum to apply to all schools; and to remove the right of parental withdrawal from these classes. The BHA has also been involved in pushing against pro-life campaigners attempting to influence the school curriculum.
72. R (on the application of Begum (by her litigation friend Rahman)) v Headteacher and governors of Denbigh High School 2006, UKHL 15.
73. D. Gillard, op cit.
74. S. Bano, 'Islamic Family Arbitration, Justice and Human Rights in Britain', in *Law, Social Justice and Global Development Journal*, 2007 (1): http://www2.warwick.ac.uk/fac/soc/law/elj/lgd/2007_1/bano/.
75. See N. Rose, *Powers of Freedom: Reframing Political Thought*, Cambridge University Press, Cambridge 1999; and 'The Politics of Life Itself', in *Theory, Culture & Society* 18(6): 1, 2001.
76. R. Rosen, 'JLC Advises on Big Society' in *The Jewish Chronicle*, 9.1210: http://www.thejc.com/community/community-life/42326/jlc-advises-big-society.
77. According to the British Humanist Association, in 2012 the Coalition government approved 102 Free Schools to open in 2013, of which 33 are faith based. See http://humanism.org.uk/2012/07/14/news-1077/.
78. See S. Dhaliwal, *Religion, Moral Hegemony and Local Cartographies of Power: Feminist Reflections on Religion in Local Politics*, Doctoral thesis, Goldsmiths, University of London, 2012: http://eprints.gold.ac.uk/7802/. In her study of two local areas of London Sukhwant noted the growth of new local systems of election where local areas are being restructured along the lines of believers and non-believers, with the former gaining access to additional educational and welfare resources simply because of the strength of their religious belief.
79. P. Butler and A. Travis, 'Sex Trafficking Charity Loses Out to Salvation Army over £6m Contract', *Guardian*, 11.4.11: www.guardian.co.uk/society/2011/apr/11/eaves-housing-trafficking-salvation-army, accessed 23 September 2013.
80. See A. Brown, 'Tories and the New Evangelical Right', *Guardian*, 10.5.10: www.theguardian.com/commentisfree/andrewbrown/2010/may/10/

evangelical-religion-tory-conservatives; and C. Cook, 'Christian Tories Rewrite Party Doctrine', *Financial Times*, 12.2.10: www.ft.com/cms/s/2/12400596-16ac-11df-aa09-00144feab49a.html#axzz1AJyjO0UY; and J. Doward, 'Secret Christian Donors Bankroll the Tories', *Observer*, 2.5.10:www.guardian.co.uk/world/2010/may/02/secret-christian-donors-bankroll-tories.

81. Tax, M, *Double Bind: The Muslim Right, the Anglo-American Left, and Universal Human Rights*, Centre for Secular Space, London, 2013.
82. See for instance K. Crenshaw, *Demarginalizing the Intersection of Race and Sex*, University of Chicago, Chicago 1989; A. Brah and A. Phoenix, 'Ain't I a Woman? Revisiting Intersectionality', in *Journal of International Women's Studies* 5(3) 2004, pp75-86; N. Yuval-Davis, 'Intersectionality and Feminist Politics', in *European Journal of Women's Studies* (special Issue on Intersectionality) 13(3): 193-209, 2006.
83. D. Smith, *Feminism and Marxism: A place to begin, a way to go*, New Star Books, 1977.
84. For discussion reflecting the 'addition' approach, see for instance Z. Williams, 'Are you too white, rich, able-bodied and straight to be a feminist? *Guardian*, 18.4.13: www.theguardian.com/commentisfree/2013/apr/18/are-you-too-white-rich-straight-to-be-feminist, accessed 14 October 2013; and B. Adewunmi, 'What the Girls Spat on Twitter tells us about Feminism', *Guardian*, 8.10.12: www.theguardian.com/commentisfree/2012/oct/08/girls-twitter-feminism-caitlin-moran, accessed 14 October 2013.
85. N. Yuval-Davis, 'Belonging and the Politics of Belonging', in *Patterns of Prejudice* 40(3) 2006: 197-214. Also see Nira's CMRB UEL website www.uel.ac.uk/cmrb/; and Nadje's CGS SOAS website www.soas.ac.uk/genderstudies/.
86. For an article that critically discusses some of these issues with regards to the feminist movement as a whole see N. Yuval-Davis, 'Human/Women's Rights and Feminist Transversal Politics', in M.M. Ferree and A.M. Tripp (eds), *Global Feminism: Transnational Women's Activism, Organising and Human Rights*, New York University Press, New York 2006.
87. Towards the end of WAF's first phase of existence, some members of WAF criticised the members of the WAF journal editorial team for producing an overly academic journal and wanted to replace it with a more accessible activity oriented one. Alas, the result was the cessation of the journal's production in its previous format and no alternative emerging, either then or during WAF's second phase, although the website aimed to fulfil this need to a certain extent.
88. See for instance: C. Cockburn and L. Hunter, 'Transversal Politics and Translating Practices', in *Soundings* 12, special issue on Transversal Politics, summer 1999; N. Reilly, *Women's Human Rights*, Polity Press, Cambridge 2009; N. Yuval-Davis, 'Women, Ethnicity and Empowerment',

in *Feminism and Psychology* (special issue on Shifting Identities, Shifting Racisms) 4(1) 1994: 179-98.

89. See F. Guattari, *Psychoanalyse et transversalité*, Maspero, Paris 1974.

# 1. Flying by the nets of racism, patriarchy and religion

*Pragna Patel*

My earliest memories of Kenya resemble photo snapshots. Some are blurred whilst others are vivid, but the memory which haunts me most is of an Indian woman (whose name I have never come to know) being dragged onto the streets and publicly abused by a man, presumably her husband. He was holding her with one hand, while his other hand was holding a machete over her head as she lay on the ground pleading for her life. I was three or four years old at the time, and remember standing and peeping from behind the folds of a woman's sari as she and scores of other Indian spectators formed a circle around the couple to watch but not intervene in the woman's shame and humiliation. I was frightened by the spectacle and buried it in the deepest recesses of my mind; it did not surface for many years. I did not realise until years later that what I had witnessed was an act of domestic violence in which the community colluded.

## KENYA

I was born in Kenya in 1960 as was my father before me. He was there due to British colonial policy and its need for indentured labour from India. My paternal grandfather had come from Gujarat in India to Kenya to work on the railways, and from all accounts had led a very modest life. As was common in those days amongst Indian men, my father returned to India for an arranged marriage and was joined by my mother in Kenya shortly afterwards.

My father did not have much of an education and moved from job to job, but his real interest was photography. Around 1964 he decided to move to London, partly out of a desire to improve our lives but also out of fear of being forced out of Kenya as a result of the wave of anti-colonial protests and 'Africanisation' policies that were sweeping through much of Africa in the 1960s. He had no money and so hitch-hiked his way across North Africa and Europe. He eventually arrived at Victoria Station with just a couple of shillings in his pocket. His story was the same as that of many economic migrants – he worked hard, often doing three jobs at a time, to save money to sponsor the rest of us to join him.

## IN THE UK

I arrived with my mother and two younger sisters on a cold December evening in 1965. I was five years old. I remember people staring at us as we got off the plane, but I did not know why. I now realise that my sister and I were wearing sleeveless cotton summer dresses and flip flops. We were not prepared for the British weather.

A sense of insecurity and of being 'stateless' stayed with my parents for many years after leaving Kenya and arriving in the UK. Their entire outlook was shaped by the feeling that they were in the UK temporarily and that they should be prepared to move out at short notice. They were convinced that their early experiences of hardship, racism and poverty were the result of a deliberate policy of the British state towards Asian immigrants, in order to pressurise them to leave the country 'voluntarily'.

My upbringing in a Gujarati Indian working-class family in the UK was dominated by my mother, who did the most to maintain traditional patriarchal family values. She was, in those days, a strong and formidable woman who kept the family together in the face of adversity and poverty. But keeping the family together also meant keeping a tight rein on our behaviour to ensure that we performed according to traditional gender scripts. As the eldest of four girls and one boy – the youngest – I was aware of the immense burden carried by my mother in having had four daughters, and I remember clearly her sheer sense of relief when my brother was finally born: she could finally hold her head up high in the community. My mother had considerable expectations of me as the eldest daughter, but I shattered these when I turned seventeen. My mother's presence was always double-edged. On the one hand it was her will power and strength in times of adversity that kept us fed and clothed, but, on the other, that same strength and determination meant that I constantly clashed with her as I resisted her attempts to put a lid on my dreams of a life outside marriage.

## THE 'GOOD GROUND STEWARDESS'

My early years at school in Willesden were marred by daily low-level occurrences of racism. The now maligned notion of multiculturalism had not yet been invented, and the school's way of dealing with difference was to ignore it altogether. At primary school, I was regularly told that we (Asians) were 'smelly' and that 'we should go back to our own country'. This caused distress and bewilderment, because the abuse came as much from African-Caribbean girls as from white girls. When my father obtained work as a baggage handler at Heathrow Airport we moved to the borders of Southall, and at my secondary school the racism that I encountered in the playground from white working-class pupils was far more menacing and aggressive. However, what confused me most was the attitude of the school. There was no attempt to deal with the racism. In fact the attitude of the school towards its largely working-class Asian students smacked of institutional racism. Asian students were viewed as a pool of potential labour for the Heathrow airport industry. The head teacher's idea of career advice involved telling me that I would make a 'good ground stewardess'!

The school's attitude to racism reached its nadir during the 1979 uprising in Southall. In a rare moment of unity, all sections of the community, supported by the Anti-Nazi League, came out to protest against the racist and provocative actions of the National Front, and the militarised police response which had led to hundreds of arrests of local youth and the death of the anti-racist campaigner Blair Peach. Many of the school's Asian population were directly and indirectly involved in the battle for Southall, but instead of helping us to make sense of the events and to bridge the ever widening gap between the school's Asian and white population, the event was treated as if it had never happened. I was uncomfortable with the silence but, lacking in confidence, I did not think to initiate action or even discussion.

From the age of fifteen, feelings of insecurity, confusion and embarrassment led me to visit the school library on a regular basis to learn more about my Indian background. It was there that I discovered Mahatma Gandhi and how his ideas had changed the course of the British Empire and influenced leading thinkers and freedom fighters around the world. At a time when I was hungry for positive images of Asians, Gandhi became a vital role model. He was to have a profound influence on my political outlook.

## 'I WILL NOT SUBMIT'

Even Mahatma Gandhi, however, could not assist me in my darkest days when, at the age of seventeen, I began to face my most intense battles at home against a forced marriage. During moments of complete desperation and despair, my source of comfort came in the guise of James Joyce's *A Portrait of the Artist as a Young Man*. This book still speaks to me today because of these words, which have become my guiding mantra: 'You talk to me of nationality, language, religion. I shall try to fly by those nets'.[1]

It was a profoundly life-changing book and a source of inspiration for me; it has guided me and set me on a path that has enabled me to make the journey, almost literally, from the personal to the political. *Portrait* not only shaped my resistance to the conservative and traditional values of my family and community, but it has also continued to shape my political outlook in the face of the ever rising tide of racial and religious intolerance.

In 1977 I was taken to a village in India on the pretext of a holiday. It was my first trip to India and I found myself desperately trying to make sense of that vast and complex country of my origin, the birthplace of Mahatma Ghandi, and of the sheer scale of poverty the like of which I had never encountered before. But before I could even begin to take stock, I found myself being forced into a meeting with a young man who was introduced to me by my mother's relatives. I was shocked by the idea of marriage to someone that I had only met for fifteen minutes, but I was alone and trapped in an unfamiliar environment. Events overtook my protests and pleadings, which grew increasingly desperate. Fortunately, I was allowed to return to the UK, but only after I was engaged.

Back in England, I felt confused, frightened and helpless, and tried every tactic in the book to get out of the marriage. Every day was an emotional rollercoaster. Each morning I would wake up determined to resist the idea of marriage, but each day the pressure from my family and relatives multiplied. And then, just when I found myself acceding to the marriage out of sheer exhaustion, I would find myself holding *Portrait* close to my chest, sobbing and repeating to myself again and again the constant refrain by Stephen Daedalus, 'I will not submit'. I found inspiration and comfort in his determination to reject the stifling constraints of his family, language, nationality and religion in order to take flight and find his own voice. Each day, I would wake up with renewed courage, ready to do battle with my family, ready to dissent, struggle and resist.

After a year of civil disobedience, my mother caved in, exhausted by my sheer determination and will to resist. I was free, and I lost no time in getting the grades that I needed to get to college or university – I knew that education was the only way to get away. Looking back, I take great satisfaction in seeing that my defiance opened doors for the rest of my siblings, who were not subject to the same level of constraint.

## FINDING A POLITICAL HOME

In 1979 I fled to Liverpool where I studied English Literature and Sociology. But at college I felt completely isolated: there were only a handful of other non-white students, and I was desperate to be a part of the growing anti-racist Black consciousness that I could see emerging in Southall, especially during the 1979 and 1981 uprisings, and in the Manchester protests against immigration laws that I joined in through student union activities. During the 1981 riots in Southall, I tried to join the Southall Youth Movement (SYM) to volunteer, but I never received a response to my attempts. This was not surprising – as I was to discover later, SYM cultivated a sexist environment and was a 'no go' area for women.

During college summer holidays I met Southall Black Sisters as some of them were selling their Black feminist newsletters on the streets of Southall. In those days it consisted of a campaigning group of feisty and formidable Asian and African Caribbean women. I started going along to their meetings, but by 1981 the group had dwindled considerably, as most left to forge other careers. In 1982 I returned to live and work in Southall, where I cut my political teeth in the anti-racist and Black feminist struggles and activities of that time. I met some male anti-racist activists who had been around since the 1979 uprising, and together we formed the Asian Socialist Collective and the Southall Monitoring Group, which also helped to shape my anti-racist, socialist politics.

It was in 1982, during these local anti-racist and socialist struggles, that I met Raju Bhatt – we worked together at the Southall Monitoring Group. I went on to marry him in 1987, after several years of a live-in relationship. The marriage – which involved a simple civil ceremony with only immediate family members present – was a way for me to appease my mother following our estrangement after I had rejected an arranged marriage and left home to lead an independent life, something which in those days, unmarried Indian women just did not do.. She was of course overjoyed, and for a while my marriage served to reinforce rather than dispel her traditional values. Looking back now, my one regret is that I did not celebrate the moment with friends. I was in a state of denial, and also felt embarrassed about the wedding, because at that time I found myself in rather austere feminist circles, where marriage was regarded as a betrayal of sisterhood and the struggle against patriarchy.

## AGAINST THE POLITICAL GRAIN

From the outset, however, my real mission was to resuscitate what was now a defunct SBS, as all the original members had left. Taking my inspiration from the law centre movement, I re-established SBS and developed it as an advice, advocacy and campaigning centre. I had found my political home: SBS was to be a secular, autonomous feminist organisation, but located within a wider anti-racist and socialist politics.

Between 1982 and 1983 I managed to coax other women to join me at SBS, either as staff or as management committee members – a couple of members of the 'old' SBS and a few 'new' women from the local area. I was joined by Meena and Hannana later in the 1980s, and between the three of us we took SBS into new and exciting directions, a high point of which was the case of Kiranjit Ahluwalia.[2]

SBS was to politically set itself against some aspects of anti-racist and Black feminist orthodoxies, although at the same time remaining firmly within those traditions. We were compelled to adopt different positions because of our daily experiences of working with women who were unable to safely exit abusive situations due to community pressure, and who also experienced state racism or indifference. We had to face some inconvenient truths about multiculturalism and anti-racism, which often lapsed into a narrow and essentialist identity politics, and denied differential relations of power *within* our communities. The struggle against racial inequality was so often reduced to the recognition of cultural difference, of which the only beneficiaries have been fundamentalist and conservative religious leaderships.

We encountered immense hostility from within our movements when we questioned why gender was always subsumed within anti-racist and anti-imperialist politics. Dominant Black feminist thinking at the time asserted that the state was overly keen to intervene in the lives of Asian women, who were being viewed as passive and in need of rescuing from the oppressive yoke of religion and culture. However, our casework revealed that in actual fact the state was not doing nearly enough to rescue minority women from violence and abuse. SBS went against the grain of received wisdom by confronting multiculturalists and anti-racists on the grounds that they were reinforcing rather than challenging the stereotypical victim status of black women.

## WHITE WOMEN LISTEN – THE PROBLEM WITH IDENTITY POLITICS!

Through concrete struggles against violence against women, we were to break the shackles of self-censorship and separatism that prevented dialogue and solidarity between women across the borders of race, religion, ethnicity, nationality and class. We attempted to create a more dynamic framework to address multiple and complex intersections of power stemming from gender, class and race. Out of necessity this also involved a constant search for alliances. We knew that identity and alliance building are closely connected, since the identity that we choose to adopt can limit or increase the potential for alliance building. Moreover, as June Jordan once said, 'identity politics might be enough to get started on but not enough to get anything finished'.

The Krishna Sharma campaign could be seen as a defining moment in the history of SBS, because it was an attempt to cut through the paralysis that had gripped the feminist movement due to guilt-tripping and navel gazing. In 1984 we strode confidently into a conference organised by white socialist feminists and demanded that they show solidarity for our struggle to obtain justice for Krishna Sharma, whose husband and in-laws had subjected her to abuse, and forced her to take her own life. We argued that an alliance across race and class was the most productive way of countering both racism and domestic violence in all communities. We marched through the streets of Southall and protested outside Krishna Sharma's husband's home. Through this public visibility, we wanted to subvert the patriarchal concepts of honour and shame which silence women and operate as powerful barriers to protection. Our tactics were borrowed from the Indian feminist movement, which has a long and rich tradition of very public protests against violence against women. By following in their footsteps, we also demonstrated that feminism is not a 'western' concept. Some of our most enduring slogans were born on that march: 'Black Women's Tradition: Struggle not Submission'; 'What honour keeps us silent? What duty stops us protesting?'. We developed a way of confidently washing our dirty linen in public by using the tools of doubt and dissent – tools that we were to sharpen later in WAF.

## 'WE WILL TAKE UP OUR RIGHTS TO DETERMINE OUR OWN DESTINIES, NOT LIMITED BY RELIGION, CULTURE OR NATIONALITY'[3]

It was against this backdrop that we prepared the ground for the emergence of WAF, and the creation of an alternative feminist vision that could find ways of translating the myriad social and political locations of black and white feminisms into collective action for change. We attempted to overcome the notion that sisterhood is automatic, rather than developed through a politics of solidarity that both recognises difference and also unites around common political values.

WAF was created on the back of a very successful meeting in Southall on 9 March 1989, organised by SBS with the women's section of the Labour Party to mark International Women's Day. The meeting was entitled 'The Resurgence of Religion: What Price do Women Pay?', and was triggered by the Rushdie affair which at that time had burst onto the political and social landscape and helped to shape our politics. By then, the politics of multiculturalism had provided space for the growth of religious fundamentalism, and this in turn provided fertile breeding ground for the rise of communalism within minority communities in the UK.[4] The meeting discussed the alarming rise of religious fundamentalism in countries such as Iran, Pakistan, Ireland and India, but the high point came at the end when, in an act of defiance, SBS issued a statement in support of Rushdie's right to publish *The Satanic Verses*.[5] We opposed the religious assault on his right to free speech, but we also made connections with feminist demands for the right to self-determination and the right to freedom of expression. It was a moment when my personal and political worlds finally collided. *A Portrait of the Artist as Young Man* once again became my touchstone when we penned the line quoted at the beginning of this section.

Our statement provided the blueprint for the foundational principles of WAF. We set about defining fundamentalism as modern religious political movements, and made central to that definition the use of gender and patriarchal systems to control women's sexuality. Our main demands included the disestablishment of the Church of England, cessation of state funding for all religious schools, and the creation of a truly democratic and secular society based on socialist, feminist, anti-racist and anti-discrimination ideals.

## 'FEAR IS YOUR WEAPON: COURAGE IS OURS!'

After much soul searching, WAF decided on its first activity, a public protest in support of Rushdie against the mass mobilisation in London of mainly Muslim men from various mosques, who were calling for his death and for the extension of blasphemy laws. This was not an easy decision. There were intense internal discussions about whether our show of support for Rushdie would feed the racist construction of all Muslims as fundamentalists, and take the focus away from our gendered and anti-racist analysis of religious fundamentalism. I felt strongly that progressive, anti-racist, feminist voices had to be heard, since the voices of support for Rushdie were coming mainly from liberal artists and writers whose analysis was limited to the defence of freedom of expression.

I remember looking for inspiration to the protests organised by Women in Black in Israel. During the first intifada, Palestinian and Israeli women courageously stood together in solidarity against war and demanded peace, in the midst of great hostility and sexualised aggression towards them from all sides. But unlike Women in Black, we decided to wear the most colourful clothes that we could find to assert the joyousness and creativity of life. Colour was important because it symbolised dissent and the possibility of dreaming other kinds of dreams. As I stood in solidarity with other women from WAF, we repeated the words 'We will not submit', knowing that the right to dissent is the only real weapon that we have in our struggle against the power of religious absolutism.

## WASHING EACH OTHER'S DIRTY LINEN IN PUBLIC

For many of us, WAF was a necessary response to the ever rising power of politico-religious and nationalist movements worldwide. But it was by no means easy to navigate between racism and religious fundamentalism. In the early days, a widely respected Black feminist left WAF, following differences about the role of religion; she felt that religion was a site of empowerment and resistance against racism and slavery for many African and Caribbean people, as illustrated by the history of the civil rights movement in the US. She did not feel that this was properly reflected in our analysis, although WAF made clear that we were not anti-religion in circumstances where it aligned itself with secular, feminist and democratic movements. Our alliance with movements such as Catholics for Free Choice attested to this stance. Some feminists of Muslim background also left WAF because they felt that the term fundamentalism was too closely associated with Muslims, and that the climate was not right for our intervention and would encourage a racist backlash. This was also the stance adopted by many anti-racist activists and organisations – including our old political foe, the Institute of Race Relations – as reflected in the old adage 'we know that religious fundamentalism is a problem but now is not the time to talk about it', a constant refrain then as now.

However, for me there were two significant aspects of WAF which made sense. Firstly, in the British context where most of our activism was based, we placed an analysis of the British state at the centre of our understanding of the conditions conducive to the rise of racism and fundamentalism. Secondly, our challenge to the politics of multiculturalism allowed us to collectively wash all our dirty linen in public. We didn't stick to only criticising our own communities, but took a stand on abuses of power committed in the name of religion and culture in other communities. It was this aspect of our critical gaze that made our alliance unique, because it gave us the confidence with which to lift the lid on all our communities, a moral and ethical positioning which was a necessary precondition for our alliance building.

Despite criticism and often intense hostility to our work, we organised campaigns in support of women in a variety of contexts. We challenged laws on the right to information on abortion in Ireland, Sharia laws in Pakistan that were criminalising female sexuality, and the narrowly defined asylum laws of the British state which compound gender persecution.[6]

A particular high point was the WAF journal, which contained excellent essays and articles that were truly international and intersectional in their analysis of the interplay between gender, racism and politico-religious movements in different social and national contexts. The journal issues remain a rich hunting ground for those of us hungry to know about other struggles waged by women. They helped us to think through big questions like the meaning of secularism, and some of the other complexities that arise when creating alternative analysis and strategies for addressing religious fundamentalism.[7]

## BRINGING IT BACK HOME

Membership of WAF fed directly into other anti-fundamentalist campaigns waged by SBS, especially in South Asian communities. For example, we opposed Sikh religious leaders who attempted to take over local schools in Southall using the 'opting out' laws introduced by the Tories in 1988. The 'Save Our Schools' campaign was significant for various reasons. It tested the boundaries of alliance within a broad anti-racist and secular coalition, because SBS had to fight hard (unsuccessfully) to make explicit the school's agenda for the policing of women/girls – the real objective behind the bid to opt out. This agenda was readily recognised by many of the parents, whose views we canvassed, but not by the anti-racist left. So, as long ago as 1991, women in particular were blasting a hole through the assumption that minorities readily identify with their 'faith communities'.

Members of SBS were also active in the anti-communal organisation AWAAZ, and its predecessor Alliance Against Communalism and for Democracy in South Asia, formed in the wake of the destruction of the Babri Masjid by Hindutva forces in 1992. A key moment was the organisation of a public meeting in 1993 in the heart of the Gujarati Hindu population in Wembley. We flew over Mahatma Gandhi's grandson for the meeting, and read out messages of support from well-known anti-communalist Indian actor turned politician Sunil Dutt. It was a particularly poignant moment for me, but also one of the most disturbing: many of the men and women who attended were rabid supporters of the Hindu Right, and their anti-Muslim sentiments and aggression shocked us, as did their denouncement of Mahatma Gandhi as a traitor who had 'emasculated' India by not dealing with the 'Muslim question'.

This experience, amongst others, helped inform my recognition of the role played by Hindutva politics in the Indian diaspora in the construction of anti-Muslim racism. This is as much a product of communal politics in the Indian subcontinent as it is of Western racism and imperialism. For example, Sikh and Hindu religious right leaderships in the UK and US have deployed the same narratives as Hindutva forces in India to create an alliance with the Jewish right against the Muslim 'other'. What this tells us is that any strategy to counter either the religious right or racism in the UK cannot focus solely on the British state or western foreign policies, but must also look at the construction of identities by right-wing religious and nationalist forces in the subcontinent itself.

In the early days of AWAAZ, however, the alliance between SBS and other anti-racists was severely tested by an unwillingness on the part of many in the coalition to address the growing problem of Muslim fundamentalism in the UK, largely because they were also complicit in constructing Muslim victimhood. Muslim fundamentalism was the proverbial elephant in the room.

## FRACTURES AND FISSURES IN WAF

WAF ran out of steam from the mid-1990s for a host of reasons, but mainly because of the depletion of resources and personnel. Most if not all WAF members were holding down full-time jobs and were also full-time activists in other organisations, which made it extremely difficult to maintain the momentum of WAF on a voluntary basis.

Then 9/11, the War on Terror, the London bombings and the civil unrest in English northern cities happened. Not long afterwards the government's policies on cohesion and integration and the subsequent Coalition Big Society agenda culminated in a wholesale assault on the welfare state. At the same time an anti-immigration consensus emerged as we witnessed a backlash against multiculturalism, which was now replaced by multi-faithism. These events revived WAF, although nowhere near to the level of activity we had undertaken in the 1990s. But it has proved much more difficult to maintain WAF this time around, as differences or shifts in political priorities and perspectives have challenged unity within WAF.

We often found ourselves at painful loggerheads with each other as to how to respond to rapidly moving events. It seemed as if the confidence and certainty that we had possessed at the highest point of our early campaigns and in the brilliant WAF journals were knocked out of us. This is a pity, because what we were particularly good at was joining the dots of what appeared to be disparate political, social and economic developments in order to bypass the polarity of the logic 'you're either with us or against us'. Finding an alternative way, however difficult, was WAF's foundational mantra. Perhaps the political landscape has become so difficult to navigate that we are no longer sure of our allies? It would appear that one outcome of the War on Terror and the growth of anti-Muslim racism has been that, for some in WAF, it has become more difficult to confront Muslim fundamentalism while at the same time dissociating from racists and fascists – who also use the language of secularism, feminism, homophobia and human rights to gain their political ground.

One example of these difficulties related to deciding how to intervene in the anti-racist protests against a threatened EDL march through Tower Hamlets on 20 June 2010. Some of us were uneasy about the ways in which Muslim fundamentalist organisations such as the East London Mosque had quietly but effectively monopolised the anti-racist demonstrations. We were alarmed by the Islamisation of the Bangladeshi community and the politics of anti-racism. WAF had many discussions to try and figure out how to show support for the people of Tower Hamlets without conceding legitimacy to fundamentalists – a legitimacy that confers on them the power to define community identity, culture and religion, a power that silences any challenge through fear, intimidation and subjugation.

## OF SECULARISM AND HUMAN RIGHTS

A much more difficult faultline had already emerged earlier in 2010, in the wake of the Amnesty International and Gita Sahgal (a founding WAF member) affair. It proved impossible for WAF members to reach a consensus on how to respond to the issue. For my part, Gita was right in drawing attention to human rights organisations and those on the left who remain silent in the face of the rising danger of all religious fundamentalisms and their murderous and even genocidal tendencies. Of course the human rights of Moazzam Begg and others who are subject to state terror and torture matter, but what matters just as much is the need to see beyond victimhood, when the 'victims' are promoting religious extremism, violence and intolerance towards those they have constructed as the 'other'. One of the central ironies highlighted by the whole affair was the engagement by religious right movements in what has been termed 'double discourse'. They rightly draw on democratic legal mechanisms such as the rule of law and due process to obtain justice, but then deny these very same rights mechanisms to women and other vulnerable minorities struggling for freedom and self-determination. In these contexts, they charge women with adopting 'western values', and seek to erode the principle that human rights are universal, non-negotiable and non-divisible. Taking our cue from WAF during the Rushdie affair, SBS argued that there is another way of looking at human rights, for both the right to security and the right to manifest religious identity – one which does not trade women's rights or those of other vulnerable minorities. In a climate where there is constant attack on the principle of human rights from all directions, we think it is important that we do not vacate the territory of human rights, however flawed, to the religious right or to the state.

Sadly, the Amnesty International affair signalled the end of political unity within WAF. Lack of time and resources, and perhaps other collective and individual limitations, have also taken their toll. It has been very painful to watch the demise of WAF, particularly at this political juncture when the forces of neo-conservative liberalism and religious fundamentalism have become mirror images of each other. The politics of unity that WAF attempted to forge are, to my mind, more needed than ever. The uprisings of ordinary people, but especially women, in Egypt, Libya and elsewhere in the Middle East, and their continuing struggles against religious right politics and Islamist regimes, attest to the power and universality of human rights. Those struggles also highlight the flaws in electoral democracy, which does not of itself guarantee equality and dignity for all.

## CONCLUSION

Politically, I have grown immeasurably from my encounters with the wise, creative and skilled women that have made up WAF over the years. It is an experience that will not be lost, since it has taught me to look at issues and events in a more complex, nuanced and contextualised way. It has also strengthened my goal of working within SBS to find ways of evidencing the folly and danger of not linking the struggle for secularism with feminism and the struggle for women's human rights.

In these troubling times, all we can do is to strengthen our resolve to work with others to forge a WAF-like politics of unity which recognises the need to 'fly by the nets' of race, class, caste, religion, sexuality, nationality and patriarchy: nets which prevent women, sexual minorities, writers, artists, intellectuals and other powerless subgroups from soaring high and finding their own voice.

## NOTES

1. James Joyce, *A Portrait of the Artist as a Young Man*, B.W. Huebsch, New York 1916.
2. I have discussed this case in more detail in P. Patel, 'Shifting Terrains: Old Struggles for New', in Rahila Gupta (ed), *From Homebreakers to Jailbreakers: Southall Black Sisters*, Zed Books, London 2003. Kiranjit published her own story in K. Ahluwhalia and R. Gupta, *Provoked: The Story of Kiranjit Ahluwahlia*, Harper Collins, India 2007. This campaign was also covered in WAF journal number 4, 1992/93.
3. This is part of a statement issued by SBS following the Rushdie Affair. See *Women Against Fundamentalism* Newsletter No 1 November, 1990, p12.
4. Communalism is a term that is specific to the Indian subcontinent. It refers to the construction of a community solely around religious identity and religious conflict. Communal politics is the politics of such a religious community posing as a monolithic bloc in opposition to those perceived not to belong and are therefore constructed as the 'other'.
5. This statement was published in the first issue of the Women Against Fundamentalism journal, No 1, November 1990, p12.
6. For the campaign for abortion rights in Ireland see WAF Newsletter No 1 November 1990.
7. www.womenagainstfundamentalism.org.

# 2. Confessions of an Anti-Clerical Feminist

*Clara Connolly*

These few pages will necessarily be selective, but a much fuller account would still illustrate how pervasive were the twin influences of the Catholic and nationalist ideologies on a young woman growing up in southern Ireland in the middle of the last century.

## CHILDHOOD

I was the oldest of six children born to a senior civil servant in the south east of Ireland. My father, from a large and poor farming family in the west, was able to take advantage of the expansion of education for Catholics, and of the Irish state bureaucracy, to qualify as an agriculturalist. My mother belonged to an established Wexford family: her grand uncle was Solicitor General at the time of the Irish Rising in 1916. But her family had fallen on hard times, and much to her regret, she was unable to attend third level education.

My father was twenty years older than my mother and (as she afterwards told me) taught her everything she knew about sexual matters. For both, contraception was unthinkable, and for my father, abstinence. There was nothing unusual about this at the time. My mother suffered a catastrophic birth in 1951. Her children suspected long afterwards that she had suffered a symphiosotomy without her knowledge or consent. A symphiosotomy is the breaking of the pelvis, preferred at that time in Irish hospitals to a caesarean in such cases as a breech birth. Besides being unsafe for the baby, the after-effects for the mother include difficulty in walking, incontinence and depression. But the then Archbishop of Dublin disapproved of caesarean operations because they allegedly encouraged fewer births. And because of the 'special position' of the Catholic Church as enshrined in the 1937 Constitution, no one in Ireland dared defy the Archbishop in matters gynaecological. The after effects of that traumatic birth cast a shadow on our otherwise comfortable childhood.

As a child I identified closely with my father, as his close companion. But in adolescence I flipped to my mother's side, as I saw her continuing fear of child birth. My changing attitude towards my father coincided with a change of attitude on his part. As they reached adolescence he expected his daughters to lead a more sheltered life, in preparation for future lives as wives and mothers. This was a shock to me, as he had previously indulged my freedom of opinion and manners. Our relationship did not recover for a long time. He wanted me to attend University College Dublin, where I would live in a (very expensive) girls' hostel, guarded by nuns. But I made a last-minute escape to Galway, where I was determined to enjoy my first taste of freedom.

## GENTLE REVOLUTION

I fell in quickly with a group of young Marxists there. This was 1967 – during the wave of radicalisation of university students across Europe and the United States, but a few years before the women's liberation movement reached Ireland. I regret now that I did not have enough grasp of feminism in my early student years to cultivate the friendship of women. But after my convent education, I could not wait to discover the perils of men about which the nuns had so assiduously warned.

Like many in the student movements, we started with reading all the French and German Marxist texts we could get our hands on. Because of the particular clericalisation of Galway University, dominated by Franciscan monks – particularly in the humanities, including philosophy and sociology – we were, first of all, anti-clerical. We invaded their lectures, with reading lists of Marxist and Humanist philosophers, and ran counter-seminars for other students. The counter education that I was lucky enough to experience absorbed me far more than the official curriculum, which I neglected. We occupied the library and distributed lists of banned books, and also occupied the University canteen on Catholic feast days to prevent their closure.

We gradually progressed to events outside the university. For example we supported the campaigns of travellers against the attacks made on them by local residents, when the local council introduced a settlement programme. Hostility against travellers was so notorious in

Galway that it led to the coining of a new word – 'Rahoonery' – after the estate where the attacks took place.

Unlike other student movements of the time, we seemed to have a revolution happening on our doorstep. The Northern Ireland Civil Rights movement, an extension of the Black Civil Rights Movement, began to challenge systematic inequality and discrimination against Northern Irish Catholics.[1] Students in Queens University Belfast founded People's Democracy (PD), a more radical civil rights organisation, which was staunchly anti-sectarian and favoured street politics. For a short time, PD played a significant role in the northern Irish conflagration. Bernadette Devlin and Michael Farrell (co-founders of PD) were our heroes. While 21-year-old Bernadette was busy getting herself elected as the youngest MP in Westminster, PD decided to march to Dublin at Easter 1969. Although it has to be said that it did not set southern Ireland on fire, some of us joined the march. We loved the fact that early PD saw the 'green Tories' in the south as an enemy of liberation, too.

## UP NORTH

For myself, I left the university for a teaching post in Enniskillen, Northern Ireland. I wanted to join PD, so effective in highlighting discrimination and sectarianism only the year before. But although there was a branch in Enniskillen, I could not find them, much to my disappointment. PD was in disarray – I had arrived to join the revolution too late.

It was not until August 1971, just after the introduction of internment in Northern Ireland, that PD came to town. Internment was a disastrous move by the authorities, concentrated as it was on Catholics: such was the outrage that a policy of civil disobedience was proposed alongside marches and other forms of street politics. Now I did get to meet Michael Farrell, but he seemed to have metamorphosed into an Irish nationalist of the kind that the PD had denounced only two years earlier, when they said 'the border is not an issue, civil rights is, and many of our demands in the north are equally relevant in the south'. He now praised Northern Ireland nationalists and republicans – including IRA members. When I questioned him on this switch of allegiance (and the seeming abandonment of their anti-sectarian project) I was labelled an 'armchair socialist from Dublin'. There seemed little room for a cross-border anti-sectarian alliance. My friends and I were very confused and disheartened.

My best friend then was Kathleen, a liberal (and socialist) Protestant who taught with me in the only educational institution in the county which was non-sectarian – with about 60 per cent Protestant pupils and 40 per cent Catholics. At that time the anti-internment marches were sharply dividing the student population. Then came Bloody Sunday, 30 January 1972, when the British army shot thirteen unarmed civilians during an anti-internment march. The shock reverberated throughout Ireland, and was also felt keenly in the college.[2] I was summoned from an almost empty classroom the next morning by a teacher whom I did not know, who told me: 'come to the Principal's office, the Bishop has ordered all Catholics to go on strike'. I wondered in what way I had been identified as 'Catholic': there were eight of us, as I discovered, of a staff of about forty. I offered to let Kathleen know but was told that since she was a Protestant 'it did not concern her'. The Principal wanted us to sign a paper saying we had been intimidated into striking by the IRA. We responded that the issue was not intimidation, and that we could not condone the actions of the British Army. No one signed the proposed statement.

When I reported back to Kathleen, she rushed down to the Principal's office to say she was joining us in our strike. I became alarmed for her, and hurried into the staff room to try to convince at least our friends to join her. I also suggested that, rather than striking (which I saw as divisive), we should ask the Principal to close the school as a mark of respect for the dead. Most of the Catholic students had stayed away anyway (the message had reached them quicker than the teachers). But no one would budge: they gave various uneasy reasons – they were related to Unionist politicians, a family member had been blown up by the IRA, etc.

The repercussions for me afterwards were negligible, but Kathleen was severely punished by her Protestant students for breaking ranks. This episode represented a severe shock to me. I felt suffocated and unable to understand the traps set by communal sectarianism for progressive politics. I began to see that internment, and then Bloody Sunday, had seen off the non-sectarian civil rights movement, and the IRA had stepped out of the shadows to take its place. The constitutional position of Northern Ireland (and the unification of Ireland) became the main issue.

There were a number of small Leftist groups in Belfast and Dublin who had split from republicanism, partly influenced by the potential they saw in the growing militancy of the Protestant working class, which had culminated in the Ulster Loyalist strikes of 1973 and 1974. PD had taken the Catholic working class as its agent of change – and had run into a pro-nationalist dead end. But I did not see the point of flipping a coin and relying on the even more sectarian Protestant working class. Still, I began to understand more fully the assault on democratic rights that the republican project represented. I saw the constitutional issue more clearly: the Protestant majority had the right to decide their own destiny, and the imposition of a united Ireland on the province, by force, was illegitimate. The northern Irish people as a whole should decide: a solution could only emerge by consent – and that seemed a very long way off in 1972. It followed that the IRA campaign was unjustified, and I became (to the extent that I was not already) a convinced opponent of republicanism.

I returned to Dublin a married woman, and discovered that my new status banned me from teaching and other public sector jobs. My GP refused to prescribe the pill, which I had been able to obtain in Northern Ireland, and recommended valium instead. So we emigrated to the UK in 1973.

## EXILE

My first taste of British multiculturalism was as follows: I was offered a Catholic school to teach in by County Hall, while my then husband was offered a place in a Catholic college by Cambridge University. This was presumably meant to make us feel at home – despite the fact that we were determined to run away! What I had learned in the North remained true on the mainland: our names, accents and schooling would continue to define many other features of our personae – including our supposed religious affiliation.

No matter – I enjoyed teaching in that school and caught glimpses of how the Irish church organised itself in the UK. On the run up to a SPUC anti-abortion rally, the local priest came to the school assembly every day to urge the pupils (and through them their parents) to attend. Transport was arranged from local schools and churches. A feminist colleague and I took our own private action: we decided to turn every lesson that week into a pro-choice seminar. The girls did not tell, but something must have leaked out afterwards, because a few months later I was invited to the head's study. There was a pupil who (the head told me) was pregnant and in need of 'advice', which I was asked to help her to find. So I became the school's unofficial abortion counsellor. However, the head's flexibility did not stretch to offering me a permanent post on the staff. 'Regrettably', she said, 'you cannot find a priest to vouch for your attendance at Sunday mass'. Once a Catholic always a Catholic, even if a lapsed one.

By this time, I had become a feminist – influenced by my teacher friends, and I had also became involved in left-wing teacher politics. I edited and wrote for *Socialist Teacher*, and helped to organise a large anti-racist teacher's rally in March 1978, which attracted nearly 3000 teachers. The following June, a secondary school teachers section was established, which published *Teaching and Racism* – a critique of multiculturalism (then popular with progressive local authorities) from a more radical anti-racist position, with a series of chapters on anti-racist perspectives across the sciences and humanities.[3] I wrote the introduction, which criticised multiculturalism as concerned with surface appearances and 'positive images', hiding the fact that not all cultural manifestations are equally progressive. Furthermore, its claim that racism was 'ignorance' and could be cured by 'respect' did not allow the issue of racial inequalities to be confronted directly. The really dangerous element of properly anti-racist teaching, I argued, was that it presented a challenge to orthodox political explanations – 'your activities will not be sanctioned as safe'. Unlike the Anti Nazi League, our group was committed to challenging mainstream racism, not just the National Front or fascism.

Although I was politically active throughout the 1970s, I found myself unable to join any left-wing groups, mainly because of their romantic attachment to Irish republicanism. If they were so wrong on this issue, so close to home, I figured I could not trust their 'anti imperialism' on a wider global scale. I knew from Northern Ireland that the enemy's enemy is not always the friend of progressive politics. For example, I remember arguing in 1979 with Iranian Trotskyists against trusting the Ayatollah Khomeini (whom I instinctively recognised as a dangerous religious patriarch). Tragically, thousands returned home to persecution and death.

## FEMINIST PROJECTS

For the same reason it was also difficult to participate in exile Irish politics, with its assumption of support for republicanism, apart from the Irish Women's Abortion Support Group (IWASG), which I joined in the early 1980s.[4] At that time about 7000 women were crossing the water each year, from Ireland North and South, to have clandestine abortions. IWASG provided a telephone information and advice service (strictly illegal in the south) and made arrangements including booking the clinic and overnight accommodation. In one in ten cases we were able to provide free abortions, or to pay for them by fundraising. The IWASG line telephone number was codenamed 'Imelda' and distributed in Ireland through an underground movement. We would meet the women from the plane or train and accommodate them in our own homes – my daughter knew from a very young age the purpose of these over night visits, and was always tactful and discreet about it. The women were often consumed with guilt and shame, and we were sometimes their only confidantes. I was glad to be involved in this network, and was consistently reminded of the high price paid by its women to keep Ireland a Catholic country (or in the North, a rigidly sectarian one).

Outcasts ourselves from the London Irish community (our advertisements were not carried in the London Irish press, nor were we welcome at St Patrick's Day or other parades), we created our own vibrant community life through fundraising events – with our Spanish sister organisation. What I remember most is the music – Irish ceili music mixed with lively Spanish guitar.

I also joined *Feminist Review* around this time – a socialist feminist magazine editing and publishing the work of mainly academic feminists. I felt at home there too. I was particularly grateful for its cool tone when I stepped headlong into the sex wars of 1980s feminism.

During this period I was still married, and I had had a child in 1982, and I also worked mainly with young single mothers. So I was seen as 'sleeping with the enemy' by feminists for whom lesbianism was supposed to be a moral and political choice. I don't think younger women now can understand the extraordinary personal spite with which these kinds of disputes were conducted. In fact I was emerging from my marriage as a lesbian during that time, but the process was delayed by my own stubbornness in the face of such an onslaught on my integrity.

What's more, despite my anti-racist credentials I was also white, and therefore could potentially be considered racist. Because of this I did not dare openly express views on, or support for, the Asian young women at feminist youth project with which I was involved. To criticise aspects of South Asian family or community life would have been considered racist. This placed the Asian worker in the project in an isolated position. I believed that I could support her dilemmas across 'race' lines, but that was not possible in the hothouse atmosphere of 'identity politics'. I expressed my views on leaving the project in a *Feminist Review* article that underwent many revisions as circumstances changed around me.[5]

## RUSHDIE

The Ayatollah Khomeini's fatwa on Salman Rushdie in February 1989 was a life-changing event for me, as for many of us. I passionately identified with the author – as a dissident, and an irreverent lover of his country and its history.

In April that year I was invited to a conference on multiculturalism in Copenhagen, organised by the Institute of Cultural Sociology there, to present a paper on the feminist youth project I had been involved with. I was not at all sure, at first, what I could say. But I thought I would use the safe environment of a faraway academic conference to express some tentatively critical views of multiculturalism, along the lines of what I had written a decade earlier, as an anti-racist teacher. I also struggled to find a way to introduce another topic on my mind – the fatwa against Salman Rushdie – in a way that would illustrate how vital it was to stand for progressive values, in no matter what context or community. Paul Gilroy was one of the main participants at this conference, speaking on the politics of race and anti-racism in Britain, and I believed that his perspective would be sympathetic. But he and other leftists at the conference, British and Danish, appeared to be completely unsympathetic to Rushdie. I was shocked. And I made instant friends with a Turkish participant – Mehmet Umut Necif – who had attracted death threats because of his daring support for Rushdie in the Danish press. Mehmet wondered if there were pro-Rushdie events being organised by the left in the UK. I would have loved to say 'yes' but I didn't know.

So I made it my business to find out on my return. At *Feminist*

*Review* I heard about a meeting that had been held in March by a group called Southall Black Sisters, of whom I had never heard. Their statement from the meeting – 'Rushdie's right to write is ours to dissent. Community leaders do not speak for us' – rang a bell in my heart. I asked the FR meeting to mandate me to call a forum in support of Rushdie, and invite SBS to co-chair it if they would. They agreed.

In May 1989 'Voices for Rushdie' was launched, which I co-chaired with Gita Sahgal. It was attended by leftists, trade unionists, Labour Party members and representatives of minority community groups – Iranians, Irish, Turkish. Our founding statement included the following: 'no culture or society has a monopoly on the values of pluralism and the right to dissent'.

I remember saying to the SBS members present, 'where have you been all my life?'. The perspective of SBS took my breath away with its boldness, and at the same time it was instantly familiar. As I stated afterwards in an article co-written with Pragna Patel: 'although they spoke from a history and location far removed from mine, I recognised them instantly as expressing a shared understanding of the implications for women's autonomy of cultures deeply influenced by religion'.[6]

There were speakers from Voices for Rushdie at the House of Commons and the Labour Party conference that year, but our highlight was an 'Unholy Night' in Conway Hall: a glorious celebration of blasphemy around the world. We were not able to survive for long, though, because of the differences that proliferated in such a disparate mix of groups and individuals, and the lack of real will on the left to support such a maverick as Rushdie.

## COMING HOME

But meanwhile, SBS introduced me to Women Against Fundamentalism, where I made myself instantly at home. This was a more clearly focused group than Voices: it was a coalition of feminists challenging religious fundamentalism in our countries of origin, and in our communities in Britain. I have written an account of WAF's first year, but here I want to provide some of my own edited highlights.[7]

The first one – exhilarating and terrifying – was our counter demonstration at the 80,000 strong Muslim march against Rushdie on 27 May 1989. This anti-Rushdie march was the first confident demonstration of a community united under the banner of religion rather than race, and a foretaste of many developments to come. It was brilliantly captured in Gita Sahgal's film for the *Bandung File*.[8] What strikes me now about our action was its carnival atmosphere. To disguise our intentions from the police, we pretended we were gathering for a picnic in Parliament Square – we brought food and dressed in our best. Then we jumped up and appeared suddenly on that wall overlooking the marchers, with jaw-dropping effect. That was to be a feature of WAF events, taught to us by SBS – they involved food, fun and songs composed for the occasion (for that one: 'we are women who walk on water').

A second vivid memory is a WAF picket of the Irish embassy in London, around the time of the Irish 'X' case of 1992, which for me was exhilarating because feminists from different backgrounds had come together in a noisy and lively expression of solidarity with Irish women. Based on the 1983 amendment to the constitution giving equal rights to the foetus as to the mother, the Irish Attorney General issued an injunction preventing a 14-year-old girl who was pregnant as a result of rape from travelling to Britain with her parents for an abortion. This caused outrage in Ireland – and the eventual outcome was a lifting of the ban on travel and on provision of information about abortion services abroad. But this simply exported the issue: it didn't resolve it. This became clear in the shocking case of Savita Halappanavar, the Indian woman who died in Galway University Hospital in 2012 after being refused a life-saving abortion. By way of explanation for this refusal she was told: 'this is a Catholic country'.[9]

When WAF was invited to speak in those early days, we tried to stick to the principle of travelling in pairs, from different ethnic or religious backgrounds. This provided surprises for the audience, and underlined our commitment to fight fundamentalism in all religions, not just in Islam (as was sometimes mistakenly supposed). My role in these duos was usually to speak about the privileged role of Christianity in a supposedly secular Britain. My third vivid memory is of travelling with Pragna to speak at an international conference organised by the Helsinki Citizens Assembly (a pan-European human rights organisation) in Turkey in 1992. Our double act was well received by the audience of Turkish leftist feminists whom we met in the women's section of the conference: they drew parallels between the struggle for secularism in Britain and their own dismay at the rise of Islamism in a supposedly secular Turkey.

However we noticed a group of women sitting separately, with a very striking woman in their midst, a Kurdish MP named Leyla Zana. It seemed to us that this group were being side-lined and silenced, and so we approached them. We were immediately struck by the eloquence and passion of Leyla Zana, who spoke to us about the terrible violations of the human rights of the Kurdish people. She herself had been banned from the Turkish parliament. We asked the conference convenor to organise a public dialogue between Leyla and one of the Turkish feminists: it was a conference on human rights in Turkey, and it seemed to us unfortunate at best if the Kurdish human rights issues were to be ignored. This was agreed but proved to be a highly controversial decision. Firstly, the men, who had happily ignored the other women's sessions, insisted on participation in this one. But we refused, and in the end won on security grounds – the Kurdish women told us that the conference was packed with Turkish government spies. However, despite our precautions Leyla was arrested afterwards for what she was supposed to have said at the conference. Secondly, Leyla was forbidden to speak unless she prefaced her remarks with a denunciation of violence and of the PKK. I was forcibly reminded of similar pressures to denounce violence being exerted on Irish campaigns against miscarriages of justice in Britain. I argued successfully, speaking as an Irish woman in Britain, against setting terms on Leyla's entry into dialogue at that conference. Whatever her views about the PKK, Leyla was an MP, and was being silenced in her attempts to raise the legitimate concerns of her constituency. She did not renounce terrorism in her talk, but neither did she use the platform to support it.

## WAF INSPIRATION

My involvement with WAF gave me the confidence to speak in others areas of my life. For example, I returned in May 1992 to University College Galway for a 'gender and colonialism' conference organised in part by old friends – some of them the Marxists from my university days now grown up into professors.[10] To my shock, I found myself involved in quarrels with them from the start! I heard for the first time an articulation of the more sophisticated academic brand of 'anti-imperialism' that was a feature of post-colonial studies. I was disturbed by what I saw of its anti-secularism and anti-feminism: it seemed to treat 'culture' as a 'postcolonial' resource, which in my view served to provide an alibi for gender oppression. In an Ireland convulsed by the 'X' case this seemed to me to be perverse and out of touch with reality – especially that of Irish women. In this I made common cause with Irish feminists. Only my experience of WAF could have inspired me with the mad idea of taking on old friends in public! It says a lot about our bonds of affection that we remained friends afterwards.

In the following year *Feminist Review* decided to produce a special issue on Ireland.[11] I was part of the issue group, which included guest editors from Britain and from Southern Ireland. In a totally unexpected turn of events I found myself leaving *Feminist Review* after the production of the issue. My WAF experience sharpened and focused for me a series of disagreements that emerged in the course of production, the first being about the role of the Irish community in Britain. I argued, without success, for a more nuanced definition of anti-Irish racism, and of the role of the Irish in Empire. Although we had been the focus of hostile racist attention in the 1970s and 1980s, during the IRA bombing campaign, we were not positioned in the same way as Asians or Afro-Caribbeans. Firstly we are white, and secondly we are privileged in immigration terms, being part of a 'common travel area' and of the EU.

I also raised concerns about the tendency among the British left of 'revolutionary tourism' towards Northern Ireland, to which some FR members were not immune. I disagreed with their uncritical support for Irish nationalism and republicanism: Southern Irish feminists are often much more critical. The Northern Ireland 'peace process' was presenting an opportunity for feminists on both sides of the border to learn more from each other, but I felt that within FR this was a missed opportunity.

## ROISIN'S SISTERS

A further highlight for me was an event which, though not a WAF event, was inspired by it. Ann Rossiter and I decided to organise a large WAF-type demonstration on International Women's Day 1997, in solidarity with Roisin McAliskey. Roisin was the daughter of Bernadette Devlin (of sacred memory from my youth), and had had the misfortune to fall in love with an IRA member. She had been arrested on an extradition warrant from Germany, in relation to an IRA attack on a British Army barracks there. (In fact there was evidence that she was in Northern Ireland at the time, which was ignored.) In April 1997, Amnesty International described the conditions under which she was being held in Holloway, while pregnant, as 'cruel, inhuman and degrading'.

Ann and I called ourselves Roisin's Sisters, and decided to use the techniques and resources, and access to the wider women's movement, we had learned in WAF. What we planned was primarily a feminist event, a party as well as a protest. Roisin was very isolated in prison, to the extent that it was taking a serious toll on her mental health, and she had been attacked by other prisoners as a 'terrorist'. So we wanted to show Holloway, as well as the world, the extent of her support, as we believed or hoped that this would alleviate her sense of isolation. So we floated thousands of balloons over the prison, in the suffrage colours, saying 'Free Roisin'. We knew she wouldn't hear the speeches, so we booked the noisiest women's bands, singers and drummers we could find. Through our contacts with Irish feminists and republican contacts with Irish-Americans, we arranged for hundreds of bouquets to be sent to the prison gate from well-wishers from around the world. We arranged for Emma Humphries, only recently released from Holloway herself as a result of a campaign by Justice for Women, to present the pre-agreed number of bouquets of flowers to the prison governor. Bernadette Devlin (now MacAliskey) spoke at the event, as did Roisin's psychiatrist and others campaigning for the rights of pregnant women in jail. And, of course, SBS attended in their usual style, with a song composed for the occasion. Perhaps most moving for me was the beautiful song from a Kurdish women's group – absolutely heart-wrenching in its sadness and solidarity. Roisin was released by Jack Straw from the extradition warrant a few months later, in one of his first acts as (New Labour) Home Secretary. In this the Holloway demonstration had played its part – though there were of course other more powerful advocates, not least her formidable lawyer Gareth Peirce.

Ann – closer to Republicanism than me – also wanted to involve a (mainly republican) Irish prisoners' rights organisation, and I agreed, in recognition of the long and lonely struggle throughout the 1970s and 1980s to highlight miscarriages of justice towards Irish prisoners. But we were determined not to allow them to set the agenda, or to decide the tone or nature of the event. But once they realised that the event might attract a wider audience than the usual Irish protest, they made an attempt to take it over. They wanted the road outside the prison to be lined with the names of every Irish 'political' prisoner, including those convicted of violent crimes. They wanted their own banners, and fiery 'anti-imperialist' speeches. At almost the last minute, we called their bluff. We said we would cancel the event altogether (which would have been difficult) rather than agree to it in this form. They backed down. They subsequently behaved impeccably – no banners and one speech from a woman representative.

I tell that story because it represents for me my own coming to terms with Irishness in Britain. Thanks to the experience of WAF, and the kinds of organising brought to us by SBS, we could find a way to express anger at the mistreatment of Irish prisoners in the UK, on our terms, without allowing such an event to be taken over by sectarian or nationalist politics.

## WINDING UP

The other reason for telling this story is that I was reminded of it later, just before Women Against Fundamentalism finally disbanded in 2012. The debacle of Amnesty International's engagement of Moazzam Begg as main speaker in their anti-Guantanamo tour affected WAF profoundly, especially when longstanding (and founding) member Gita Sahgal was dismissed from her post at Amnesty for speaking publicly about this.

Some WAF members, in her support, drafted a dossier exploring the political history of Moazzam Begg, and of Cageprisoners (the organisation he represents) – which became, in a later draft, a booklet by American feminist Meredith Tax.[12] This argues that Cageprisoners is a public relations organisation for jihadists, and it also describes Moazzam Begg himself as a jihadist.

But the organising group (of which I was a member) could not agree to release the dossier in WAF's name, and this caused great personal upset among some longstanding members. We had disagreed before, and had learned to live with our differences. But this disagreement seemed to go to the heart of WAF, and its message.

Personally, I could not see that Amnesty was wrong to engage Moazzam Begg, a former Guantanamo Bay internee, as a collaborator in their campaign. I do not see Moazzam Begg, or his organisation Cageprisoners, as any differently from the Irish prisoners' rights organisations with whom I had worked (with difficulty) in 1997.

Roisin's Sisters set the terms of that collaboration, and it worked on a strictly temporary and limited basis. They did not preach their proto-nationalist message on our platform any more than I would expect Moazzam Begg to be allowed (if he wished) to preach a pro-Islamist or pro-jihadi message on Amnesty's platform. I believe that in human rights campaigns against injustice of this nature, the political context and the balance of power between the protagonists should be considered.

But I also accept that other WAF members, whom I deeply respect, disagreed with me and still do. I can understand their dismay that WAF, which never hesitated to put gender issues at the centre, while recognising other forms of oppression, would seem to them to show a loss of nerve when it came to the 'War on Terror'. I share their rejection of leftist sanitising of the Muslim Right, for example in the anti-war movement. I just cannot agree with them that a prisoners' rights organisation is the proper target – rather than other self-styled community or religious leaders who support fundamentalist organisations, at home or abroad.

Despite our disagreements, I continue to believe (along with others) that WAF filled a unique place in British feminism, whose influence stretched beyond our numbers and our national borders. It transformed my life and my thinking – and this carries into my current work as an immigration solicitor at an anti-trafficking project, trying daily to redress the balance of power between state, community and the autonomous woman, in her favour.[13]

## NOTES

1. F. O Dochartaigh, *Ulster's white negroes: from civil rights to insurrection*, Edinburgh Press 1994.
2. I have told this story elsewhere. See 'Communalism: Obstacle to Social Change' in *Women a Cultural Review* Vol 2, No 3; reprinted in *The Field Day Anthology of Irish Writing*, vols 4/5, Cork University Press 2002.
3. *Teaching and Racism: discussion document by the ALTARF secondary workshop: All London Teachers against Racism and Fascism*, 1979.
4. A. Rossiter, *Ireland's Hidden Diaspora Irish Abortion Solidarity Campaign*, 2009.
5. 'Splintered Sisterhood: Anti-racism in a Young Women's Project', in *Feminist Review* 36, 1990.
6. P. Patel and C. Connolly, 'Women who Walk on Water', in L. Lowe and

D. Lloyd (eds), *Politics of Culture in the Shadow of Capital*, Duke University Press 1997.
7. 'Washing Our Linen: One year of WAF', *Feminist Review* 37, 1991.
8. *Struggle Or Submission*, made in 1989 by Gita Sahgal for Channel 4's series *The Bandung File*: www.youtube.com/watch?v=zPZ22wBT46Y.
9. H. Mcdonald, 'Abortion-refused death: Hindu woman told Ireland is a Catholic country', *Guardian*, 8.4.13.
10. 'Culture or citizenship?' *Feminist Review* 44, 1993.
11. 'The Irish Issue, the British Question', *Feminist Review* 50, 1995.
12. M. Tax, *Double Bind: The Muslim Right, the Anglo-American Left, and Universal Human Rights Centre for Secular Space*, London and New York, 2013.
13. www.atleu.org.uk.

# 3. Knowing my place – the secular tradition and universal values

*Gita Sahgal*

> We shall not cease from exploration, and the end of all our exploring will be to arrive where we started and know the place for the first time.
>
> T.S Eliot

Where to begin? Maybe by explaining that, while there are some people who have been attracted into WAF because of their experiences of fundamentalism, my experience was the opposite. I grew up in a very secular environment. My family members, of several generations, were not religious in any ritualistic sense; some considered themselves atheist. I come from the family of Nehru, the first Prime Minister of India. Considering how politicians today have to demonstrate their piety and proclaim their religion publicly, it is remarkable that one of the founders of modern India was so ready to challenge religious sentiment and to face down fundamentalists. This is a lesson that cannot be repeated often enough – that fundamentalists were not the winners in the early period of decolonisation. Nehru had a sense of awe and wonder about the world and about the history and traditions of India, but he was, at the very least, an agnostic; and his father, before him, had been impatient of superstition and religious ritual.

As a student, I didn't see myself as following in my family's tradition. I was a rebel against it – being influenced by the politics of the far left and disliking the authoritarian Congress of Indira Gandhi and the Labour government in Britain. What could be worse than these?

I'm not convinced that it is easy to draw a line from personal experience and family background to political activism. It makes me uncomfortable because it seems to suggest that environment and emotion are paramount, rather than reason, ideas and experience. Within my family, the same upbringing has led to people developing many sorts of politics. But there is one important thread through it all, and that is the idea of secularism. For me, it was a foundational idea, and it has become more and more central to my work and thought.

The story of my family is one part of a larger story – of colonial deviousness, and of the struggle for secular and universal values in the fight against imperialism. It was the larger story that I was driven to tell. It was that which led me to become one of the founders of Women Against Fundamentalism.

## MY FAMILY AND INDIAN NATIONAL POLITICS

Jawaharlal Nehru was my great uncle, but my mother always said he was like a third parent to her and a grandfather to me, as her own father had died in 1944 after repeated periods of imprisonment by the British. My mother was a writer, and my father was a businessman. My father was much more conservative than my mother, and they divorced when I was young. As a child I was expected to do well academically, and neither of my parents ever expected me to have an arranged marriage. I grew up with none of the stereotypes one associates with the Indian subcontinent.

I grew up in a household where the dominant influence was of very strong women, although they didn't necessarily consider themselves feminists. My grandmother, Vijaya Lakshmi Pandit (Nehru's sister), had been active in the national movement, and it had shaped her entire life. She had spent many years of her youth in jail, but had also successfully stood for election in a provincial legislature during British rule. After my grandfather's death she continued her political activism, representing anti-colonial India in the US and challenging senior British officials to public debates. She also took a strong anti-colonial and anti-racist vision of the United Nations to San Francisco in 1945, where she helped to lobby for India at the founding of the UN. In 1946, as leader of the Indian delegation, she was the first to challenge South Africa at the UN on human rights issues. In 1953 she became the first woman president of the UN general assembly, and in 1954 she became one of the first women ambassadors in the world.

My grandmother's fight for women's equality was through the nationalist struggle: she was involved in national women's organisations, and saw women's emancipation as part of the national struggle. It was my grandfather who supported feminists – he had marched with the suffragettes in London and believed absolutely in women's equality. He never treated his three daughters any differently than he would have done a son.

My mother, Nayantara Sahgal, is an intensely private person – although her divorce from my father and move to live openly with her lover, a high-level civil servant, was a scandal in its time. She is a novelist, and made a living as a writer and a journalist. The only time she became involved in a political movement was when she supported the JP movement against Congress corruption in the early 1970s. After 1975 she was also a strong critic of the imposition of Emergency rule by her first cousin Indira Gandhi, and she helped to disseminate information about the abuses of that time.[1]

My grandmother remained silent about the Emergency for a time, but then came out against it, and eventually became a representative of the secular camp within the grand oppositional coalition that included Muslim clerics and the Hindu Right parties. In 1977 this grand coalition led to the first electoral defeat of the Congress Party since independence. This was a great victory but it had its price: for the first time it legitimised the Hindu Right as a political power in India.

So, as a child, I had this experience of being very close to power, via my grandmother and great-uncle/grandfather. But later, by the 1970s, my mother's activities led to us being treated as dissidents and largely excluded. However, I wasn't very conscious of all these things when I was growing up. While my mother encouraged me to read the papers, I was a typical teenager and not interested in politics. At the age of sixteen I was sent to boarding school in the UK, as was the tradition in my family. It was a progressive international school – Atlantic College. Afterwards I continued my undergraduate studies in history at SOAS. This is the place where I became politicised.

## BECOMING A POLITICAL ACTIVIST

When I left for school I took with me a sense of cosmopolitan nationalism – as so well expressed in the letters Nehru wrote from prison to his daughter: of being rooted where you are but being aware of what was happening in the world. At school I identified myself much more as a socialist. At SOAS I became involved in leftist student politics, including anti-racist demonstrations, opposing apartheid South Africa and university occupations. I spent my twenty-first birthday on the Grunwick strikers' picket line to support an Asian women workers' struggle. As it was the time of the Emergency in India, I also spent a lot of time disseminating the articles my mother secretly sent me, though I did feel a certain envy of those who were living in India in one of the most germinal moments of its history. Also, the second wave of feminism was beginning to emerge and I went to hear feminists who spoke at SOAS, including one speaker who made a feminist critique of E.P. Thompson, and argued the need to bring women into working-class history.

When I returned to India in 1977 it was at a moment of victory for a mass democratic movement, and the start of the Indian civil liberties movement. My first job was working with agricultural and landless labour on unionisation and land rights. I was also part of a feminist group, Stri Sangharsh, which organised to expose the issue of dowry murders, including through producing a street play on the subject, in which I took part. We performed in neighbourhoods where women had been killed, and worked with their relatives to get them justice. I also started to bring feminist issues to my development work, in spite of the resistance of some of my co-workers, and I organised separate Dalit women's meetings so that women could have access to the same information as the men, and contribute to the same discussions. We also managed to get a big contingent of Dalit women to come along to the first national mobilisation on rape. That was my first feminist victory.

I continued to be active in these organisations until I moved back to London in 1983, after getting married to an Englishman. I was quite happy to move back, although I felt I was leaving behind an exciting life. The activities I'd been involved with during that period in India had set the pattern of my political concerns for years to come.

## FEMINIST ACTIVISM IN LONDON

When I came back to London I met Pragna and other women, and became active in SBS, but my first job was as an advice worker in the Brent Asian Women's Centre, which was related to the Asian Women's Refuge. Here there was a clash between the more conservative board members and us – the radical women workers who wanted to go beyond giving the women personal support and legal and welfare advice, and engage them in political discussions and activities. As a result, we occupied the refuge for months and eventually the two organisations separated.

In 1984, black feminists organised a demonstration in front of the house of Krishna Sharma, who had committed suicide because of domestic violence. This was an Indian technique, unusual in the UK, and it made people nervous. So too did the fact that we invited white feminists from the European Forum of Socialist Feminists and others to join the demonstration. I saw myself as a socialist feminist, rather than as a black feminist, if I needed to put any label on myself. I wasn't opposed to separatist black feminism, but I was always sceptical. Unlike so many of the women I worked with, I had not been brought up in Britain and experienced the sort of racism that destroyed so many people's life chances. Although I've been involved in many anti-racist struggles, I couldn't embrace an identity-based anti-racism.

On the other hand, I was very interested in questions of discrimination and employment, and carried out a research project for the GLC on Asian women workers. I found that it was sometimes hard to distinguish racism from other exploitative work practices. Racism manifested itself in the changing structures of work, rather than in obvious things like name-calling. The worsening conditions of Asian women workers were to do with the attack on unionisation and the increase in privatised and sub-contracted labour. That early work was a life lesson in what later became known as 'intersectional analysis'.

Later, I worked for Channel 4 when it was a radical channel. I got my start on the *Bandung File*, a black current affairs programme established by Tariq Ali and Darcus Howe and commissioned by Farukh Dhondy. I worked as a presenter, then a researcher, and eventually a director. I drew on my GLC research to make a documentary about racism and employment, and I made other films about police brutality and the criminalisation of young black men, discrimination against Bangladeshis in housing in the East End, the riots, and gangs in Southall and their effect on women. I also made films about cinema, writers and music. The first film I directed drew on my solidarity work on the Bhopal disaster with Suresh Grover of The Southall Monitoring Group. We followed the visit of a delegation of Bhopal activists to the UK to meet community activists involved in health and safety campaigns here.[2]

I worked at the *Bandung File* for about four to five years. It was a very rewarding period for me as I was able to draw on my work experience and my politics to say something very new on British television. Discussions of racism today tend to defend religious identity politics. At *Bandung*, we investigated and critiqued racism, but we also attacked religious identity politics. One of *Bandung*'s first films was on the funding of Hindu fundamentalist groups by Labour councils, including the GLC. But the two films that have really survived, and have been shown repeatedly, were those I made during the Rushdie affair. *Hullaballoo Over Satanic Verses* was broadcast on the night of the fatwa issued by Ayatollah Khomeni.[3] It was the last public interview given by Salman Rushdie before he had to disappear from view, and it contained all the themes that I have spent my life engaged in; the right to dissent; the blasphemy debate; the space multiculturalism has made for religious fundamentalists; and the link between organisations such as the Jamaat-e-Islami and the demand for blasphemy laws.

Years later, I had a discussion on the Bangladesh genocide with Ghayasuddin Siddiqui, in which he admitted, for the first time, that he and his mentor had gone to Iran to advocate for action against Rushdie. Although many writers have been threatened and even killed for blasphemy, this global fatwa was unprecedented – and it was not issued because of some sort of 'medieval mindset' in a far off country, but because religious fundamentalists in Britain were determined to create mayhem around the *Satanic Verses*.[4]

The second film was *Struggle or Submission? Women Under Islam* (see below).[5] Its title came from a slogan I had invented with Gerry, an SBS worker, for the march through Southall on domestic violence. It went 'Black Women's Tradition, Struggle Not Submission'. This changed a few times, before eventually becoming a slogan on WAF's banner that read 'Our tradition, Struggle not Submission'.

## FOUNDING AND FILMING WAF

After the fatwa I travelled around Britain speaking about fundamentalism. India had seen many fundamentalist movements and insurgencies – including the Sikh Khalistani movement, and the Hindutva campaign to destroy a mosque and replace it with a temple at Ayodhya. So I was very aware that religious fundamentalist movements had political goals (years later, Cass Balchin reminded us that in stressing the political, we should not forget the emotional and religious resonance of fundamentalist movements).

So, when, in 1989, the Labour Party Women's Section wanted a topic for International Women's Day, Pragna and I suggested that SBS would like to focus on fundamentalism in all religions. Even after the fatwa, religion was a subject of little interest to socialist activists, and its connections to women's rights were obscure. But the meeting was a success, and the resulting solidarity statement on Rushdie became a classic statement of the SBS position; and it was also the basis for a lot of the political work I have done since, including feeding into my thinking in *Refusing Holy Orders*.[6] The statement suggested that we were defending our secular traditions, an important emphasis since most people think secularisation is a product of western thinking rather than having its source in nationalist, anti-colonial struggles. My article conceptualising Asian women's activism as the creation of secular space was an attempt to examine how we did this in practice. Our daily work at the refuge was simultaneously a space for freedom from religion as well as freedom for religion.

These issues were explored in *Struggle or Submission?* The film was researched by Smita Bhide (who had worked at SBS and went on to become a writer and film maker), and the early footage was shot by the South African director Jenny Morgan. Fortunately, for us, *Bandung File* decided to film the first – and most famous – public stand by WAF, a picket against a massive march of Muslim men demanding death to Rushdie and a blasphemy law to protect Islam. But as I was one of the organisers of the picket I obviously could not film it myself. However it turned out later that Jenny couldn't finish the film, so I ended up doing it myself, and filming women working and living in the refuge, who had their own interpretation of Islam – which did not justify fundamentalist threats. As a film director, I felt that secular space and the failure of multiculturalism were the heart of the film. I was not interested in seeing the Rushdie affair as a response to British racism. This seemed to me to be an entirely parochial approach, a sort of comfort zone for professional anti-racists. My views were largely instinctive, based on my Indian secular politics. I wrote at the time that the Rushdie affair had turned me into an evangelist – for secularism. But the investigative work that I later undertook justified the arguments made both in *Struggle or Submission?* and *Hullaballoo Over Satanic Verses*. I was closer to the truth, the underlying dynamic of what was happening, than even I realised at the time, and I am still unravelling elements of the events that occurred twenty-odd years ago. I am glad that those films were made, because the record of what we did has often been muddied and attacked. Another documentary made at the same time for Channel 4, from the point of view of organisers of the march, blamed our picket for the fighting that broke out on Westminster Bridge. Other anti-racists (one later became a pro-Hindutva journalist in India) accused us of standing with fascists, who we were in fact opposing.

WAF was very emotionally important for me. As one of the founders, I felt it brought into focus both my British politics and what I had learned from the values of my family and my socialist-feminist political life in India. I know of no other organisation which tried to stand against all forms of religious fundamentalism. There were some exceptions – anti-communal organisations in South Asia, and coalitions and groups that we established in Britain such as Awaaz: South Asia Watch – but their primary purpose was to oppose Hindutva.

A related issue, which I wrote about for the tenth anniversary of SBS in *Against the Grain*, was about the fallacy of multiculturalism, which first opened the space for conservative 'community leaders', and later led to the promotion of religious fundamentalists by the British state.[7] Since an assortment of pro-fundamentalist academics, SWP members and trade unionists have taken to defending multiculturalism from attacks, the issue is mistakenly seen as a 'left/right' debate. If you are anti-racist and for diversity, you should be pro-multiculturalism. Our critique was developed at least a decade before these arguments. We showed how the Christian character of the British state had opened the way for demands to extend the blasphemy law, put yet more religious types into the House of Lords, and to increase state-funding for religious education run by fundamentalist sects.[8] All this was done in the name of equality, sometimes backed by human rights arguments. A 'multicultural' version of human rights has been used to enhance the role of religion rather than limit religious attempts to control other freedoms. My thinking was developed by WAF's discussions on secularism and religious personal laws, and on Islamisation and the demand for the imposition of 'Shariah law'.[9] We had begun to develop collective thinking in a way that diverged from classical western iterations of secularism, which rely on a removal of religion from the public square while leaving it alone in private. As feminists we knew that law governing the private sphere was crucial to secular values, and underpinned arguments for emancipation and equality. Our position was also informed by a knowledge of colonial governance – which had clearly been adopted wholesale by both the harsh and the well-meaning in terms of the managing of immigrants. Although 'post-colonial' is a term applied to former colonies, it is seldom used to apply to the 'home country'. Perhaps that is because colonial mind-sets still inform everything from protection of vulnerable children to national security policy. Today, the One Law for All campaign has taken on this dual opposition to racism and fundamentalism, and argues for universal values and the prosecution of crimes, rather than a 'post-colonial' pandering to fundamentalists.

## THE WAR CRIMES FILE

In 1994 I went to Bangladesh to investigate crimes committed by the Jamaat-e-Islami. As a child I had read about mass rape in Bangladesh in 1971, but I hadn't realised that the Jamaat-e-Islami political party was implicated in the genocidal war launched by the Pakistani army. I knew it only as a fundamentalist party, involved in Islamicising laws in Pakistan, such as the 'Shariah' introduced death sentence for 'Zina' (sex outside marriage) and blasphemy. During our investigation, which was broadcast on Channel 4's *Dispatches* programme, David Bergman and I worked with a large team of Bangladeshis to expose the role in specific crimes of three British men of Bangladeshi origin.[10] The Jamaat-e-Islami was involved in the massacre of secular nationalists, religious minorities and left intellectuals. This film has had a long after-life as a tool of political mobilisation. Thousands of pirate copies of *The War Crimes File* have circulated all over Bangladesh, and become part of people's mobilisation to demand trials. In the mean time we were also trying to use it in the UK, to campaign for trials of the war criminals living in Britain – a very early example of extra-territorial jurisdiction as part of human rights law.

## THE 1990S UN CONFERENCES

Much of my international activism in the 1990s related to the three big UN conferences – in Vienna (on human rights), Cairo (on reproductive rights) and Beijing (on women's rights). Somewhere along the way I became associated with WLUML (Women Living Under Muslim Laws), who were very central to organising NGO panels at these conferences. I took part as a WAF activist. Walking around the UN conferences I saw so many groups of perpetrators as well as victims of human rights violations. This is where the seeds of many issues of identity politics began to be embedded in the human rights framework. We could see these issues developing, and we were very conscious of them at the time.

After 9/11 and the launch of 'the global war on terror', WAF, WLUML and WiB wrote a pamphlet together, based on a combined public meeting at which I was one of the speakers. It was good to work with other women's networks to try to create a feminist analysis of the coming war and political context that justified neither dictatorship or fundamentalism, militarism or pro-Americanism. That certainly was a good moment in WAF's history, although it became hard for us, in the face of a war, to keep our own positions. Things started to change, including in the wider movement – at the beginning the Stop The War Coalition included good people, our political allies, but it gradually began to ally itself with organisations that were fronts of the Muslim Brotherhood.

## MOVING TO AMNESTY INTERNATIONAL

In 2001 I made a film on forced marriage – the only film I ever made for a government! This was a big success for the SBS campaign on this issue, and we managed to influence national policy. However, you could see the seeds of future problems in the way we were asked to frame the issue. The government wanted us to stress that 'Islam allows choice in marriage', a meaningless statement given that the religious establishment does not 'allow' such choices. They thought that this false narrative would somehow reduce racism. It was clear that most British officials had no concept of a 'secular Muslim', and thought that Muslims were only persuaded by quoting the Qu'ran. *Tying the Knot* – along with *Love Snatched: Forced Marriage and Multiculturalism*, another film on forced marriage, made for a major project on honour crime – showed how government policies had changed, from ignoring the issue to seeing choice in marriage as a human right.[11]

However, it was becoming clear I could not really make a living as a freelancer, so I applied for and was offered the post of Head of the Gender Unit of Amnesty International. The job was completely impossible because I had basically one person working with me, but was supposed to advise an International Secretariat of 400 people, as well as help to set the gender policy right throughout the organisation and all national sections. But I managed to do it anyway, and wrote the framework for the Stop Violence Against Women's Campaign. I had joined at a time when Amnesty was trying to change, and become more 'gender sensitive'. One of the things that I pointed out was that we had to look at the issue of fundamentalism, because we couldn't look at women's rights and violence without taking note of the backlash against women's rights. They appeared to agree but didn't really understand, and were very nervous about this position. Around this time WLUML held a conference about the warning signs of fundamentalism, at which it was pointed out that Amnesty had an extremely bad track record on these issues.[12]

From feminists outside Amnesty, particularly Algerians, I found out that the organisation was in bed with lots of fundamentalists, whom they treated solely as victims of torture. The organisation was also silent, or deliberately had 'no position', on many fundamental women's rights issues. For instance, Amnesty International had 'no position' on abortion, and had not made a clear statement that Zina laws (criminalisation of sex outside marriage) were a violation of international human rights law. The Amnesty network on LGBT rights had won a victory in the recognition that no law should criminalise same sex relationships, but there was no similar lobby of secularists willing to support Muslim women, who were struggling on Zina. I had to chip away at the ingrained reluctance to support struggles that involved challenging fundamentalists. But we did manage to overturn Amnesty's policy of remaining silent on Zina where it concerned heterosexual sex. After I had worked there for six years Amnesty also took a position on abortion. But we were basically civil servants of the movement, so the major decisions were taken in other places, and there were some very conservative national branches.

While I was at Amnesty I also commissioned a paper on parallel legal systems (from Cass Balchin and Sohail Warraich), which was the foundational paper for a big multi-country study on legal pluralism and human rights, in which Cass was the lead researcher.[13] Nira and I also worked with Cass on AWID's (Association for Women's Rights in Development) study of religious fundamentalisms.[14] In this way I managed to ensure that, even though I was constantly blocked at Amnesty International, the work that I started there was carried on elsewhere. After being in WAF, Amnesty International felt like an intellectual backwater on these issues.

## THE MOAZZAM BEGG AFFAIR

To sum up the circumstances of my leaving Amnesty: I went public about Amnesty's relationship with Moazzam Begg and his organization Cageprisoners, a pro-jihadi public relations organisation. It was clear that internal reform would not be possible, given that Moazzam Begg was being taken around Europe by Kate Allen of AI UK. At that time, the Amnesty Afghanistan team was warning of the dangers of talks with the Taliban, but in spite of these warnings by experts on the Afghanistan 'desk', well-meaning white human rights advocates continued to treated Begg like a human rights defender, even though he was nostalgic for the Taliban era.

After I had to leave, Amnesty held an enquiry, which upheld what I had alleged – that they had never investigated Begg, that they had never done their homework on him, and had not exercised 'due diligence'. However, the inquiry – which also did not investigate Begg – cleared him of involvement with terrorism. The inquiry also failed to examine or comment on statements by Amnesty International that supported 'jihad in self-defence', which they characterised as 'not inimical to human rights'.[15] To this day, Amnesty International have not been able to explain why they endorsed Al Qaeda's ideology.

Amnesty approach to women's rights work makes human rights workers complicit with the pro-fundamentalist agenda. My experience shows that 'gender mainstreaming' simply hasn't happened: Amnesty's notion of universality is deeply flawed. It is a notion of equal diversity – here we support some fundamentalists and here we support some women's rights people, and that equals us guarding human rights. Their vision of human rights has incorporated multicultural values into the human rights framework. I should make clear that most Muslims in Amnesty did not hold 'multicultural' views: these tended to be propagated by well-meaning white Westerners and some Western Muslims.

## OPPOSING FUNDAMENTALISTS, NOT SIMPLY FUNDAMENTALISM

The real work I could do on fundamentalism in London was with Awaaz: South Asia Watch, founded after the massacre of Muslims in Gujarat in India by the Hindu right. Awaaz was a coalition to deal with communalism, but we also carried out two key pieces of work mapping fundamentalist organising in Britain. WAF did not undertake any such work: it tended to discuss the shrinking space for secularism rather than actually analyse who the fundamentalists were. Its problem was that fundamentalism was often talked about as an abstract phenomenon. Especially in relation to Muslim fundamentalism, there was a feeling that we were supposed to oppose the general phenomenon without being able to recognise or name a single fundamentalist. It was rather like trying to do anti-racist work while failing to recognise the danger of the BNP and EDL, and not knowing the names of their chief spokesmen.

Awaaz produced an important report on Hindutva organisations in Britain – and campaigned against them – as well as a smaller piece of work mapping Muslim fundamentalist organisations in Britain.[16] But one point of contention in both Awaaz and WAF concerned Tariq Ramadan, who is currently one of the most important apologists for fundamentalism. I took part in a major discussion on state policy and fundamentalism in a 2006 radio programme called *Hecklers*, in which I argued that state policies were assisting the development of fundamentalism rather than otherwise, debating with five people who were mostly fundamentalist, including Ramadan and Begg.[17] It became clear to me after that discussion – and others – that there was a core in WAF who would never challenge the organisations of Muslim fundamentalists.

Meanwhile some kinds of anti-fundamentalist work went on. For a time, some WAF members – Helen, Sukhwant and Clara – were involved with supporting Christian minorities under attack in Pakistan, but I don't think this work was ever sustained. Two other issues that we took up as WAF subgroups were the issues of education and law. I participated in the law group, where we discussed 'Shariah' councils and 'Shariah' tribunals. In striving for complexity, we never took a collective public position for WAF. In fact our most useful contributions were to the One Law for All Campaign, where, after immense hard work, Maryam Namazie and Anne Marie Waters built an important coalition. Cass, who was then Chair of the Muslim Women's Network, didn't like the way this campaign discussed 'Shariah' and didn't want us to join it. But after attending an excellent meeting, both Helen and I argued that we should affiliate to them. I have no idea whether anyone from WAF ever did formally affiliate, but I continued to work with Maryam, who, for me, embodies much of the original spirit of WAF and is a wonderful organiser.

There was a clear blockage in WAF in dealing with Muslim fundamentalism once you actually started naming who the Muslim fundamentalists were. As long as the discussion was on fundamentalism in general, or on issues relating to blasphemy, people were quite comfortable. But once the discussion turned to specific people living in Britain, who were appearing in meetings with political comrades known from other anti-racist contexts, there would be a distancing, and a claim that there was not enough evidence. As I discovered later from working with Bangladeshi and other secular activists, people unwilling to listen to evidence will often say there is no evidence – and then demand more and more of it. Confusion, and finding issues too 'complex', are also used as a way of failing to take a stand.

I am glad that I did not waste time arguing with WAF's organising committee (its only leadership body) about Begg. I was not surprised they refused to do anything. I am also glad, however, that this forced others in WAF to realise what was happening. But some people were so frightened about the potential political reaction in Britain – and so parochial – that they failed to see all those women's movements across the world who were standing up on this issue, particularly those working in Muslim contexts.[18] I had expected a backlash from the pro-jihadi left, but I hadn't imagined that there would never be a public meeting about these issues. Even Pragna, who is a lioness, felt that she couldn't hold a public meeting until there was a publication she could hand out: she thought that 'evidence' would change people's minds. I knew it would not. She and Sukhwant heroically decided to investigate Cageprisoners. They prepared a draft document which went to the SBS board and was agreed. But the WAF organising committee rejected it.

I did not expect to win the argument with Amnesty International about Moazzam Begg. What I did was to set an ethical test, not only for my employers but for everyone. While many WAF women rallied to my defence, and Clara helped find me a lawyer, as a whole WAF was profoundly divided by the dispute. Muslim-identified women and all others willing to challenge Muslim fundamentalist organisations were severely let down. Having fought all my life against the politics known as 'anti-racism', I was brought face to face with the fact that an unacknowledged racialised politics is still alive amongst us.

## THE CENTRE FOR SECULAR SPACE

The Centre for Secular Space was founded by a number of people appalled by the state of the human rights debate and the erosion of secular space. Our first publication, *Double Bind; the Muslim Right, the Anglo-American Left and Universal Human Rights*, was written by Meredith Tax, one of the founders of CSS, and drew on Sukhwant and Pragna's draft.[19] The book clarified many of the underlying political arguments that were used by progressives to promote a 'salafi-jihadi public relations group' (as we described Cageprisoners).[20]

WAF began an interesting discussion on secularism during the 1990s. We were critical of existing secular states, particularly their failures on women's rights and family laws. But we did feel, unfashionably at the time, that secularism was a precondition for equality, and also for religious freedom. That is the position I still hold as we produce material to argue for a new paradigm on human rights.

Neither Amnesty International nor Human Rights Watch has a position on secularism. In fact, a debate between Human Rights Watch and women's rights advocates from the Centre for Secular Space and Women Living Under Muslim Laws and others showed clearly that international organisations were willing to promote Islamist organisations, and to liken women's activists fighting fundamentalism to people such as Geert Wilders. In short, Human Rights Watch made no distinction between Islamists and Muslims.[21]

My experience in WAF shaped much of my life and work. Its failure has taught me much about the difficulties of building an alliance to oppose and challenge Muslim fundamentalism. The past few years have not been easy, but where there was a complete lack of solidarity among old comrades, I found it among older activists across the world and younger ones coming into politics for the first time.

## NOTES

1. The Emergency or Emergency Rule refers to the period June 1975 to March 1977 when the then Indian Prime Minister Indira Gandhi declared a state of emergency after internal political upheaval and opposition threatened her government.
2. The Bhopal gas tragedy in December 1984 at the Union Carbide Corporation plant in the central Indian state of Madhya Pradesh killed several thousand workers and injured around half a million local people.
3. *Hullabaloo Over Satanic Verses*, a film made by Gita Sahgal for the Bandung File in 1989: www.youtube.com/watch?v=cLbx47Nyfio&feature=relmfu.
4. *Bangladesh Genocide: what human rights, anti-racist and peace organisations won't tell you.* Speakers: Gita Sahgal, Dr Ghayasuddin Siddiqui, and

Asif Munier. At SOAS, London, 27 November 2012. A full video of the talk is available to view at: www.youtube.com/watch?v=HKEHLvMQm-0.

5. *Struggle Or Submission* made in 1989 by Gita Sahgal for *The Bandung File*: www.youtube.com/watch?v=zPZ22wBT46Y
6. G. Sahgal, 'Secular Spaces; The Experience of Asian Women Organising' in G. Sahgal and N. Yuval-Davis, *Refusing Holy Orders: Women and Fundamentalism in Britain*, Virago Press, London 1992.
7. G. Sahgal, 'Fundamentalism and the Multi-Cultural Fallacy' in Southall Black Sisters (eds), *Against the Grain*, Southall Black Sisters, London 1990.
8. G. Sahgal, 'The Question Asked by Satan: Doubt, Dissent and Discrimination in 21st Century Britain', in WLUML (ed), *The Struggle for Secularism in Europe and North Africa*, Dossier 30-31, WLUML, 2011: www.law.ucdavis.edu/faculty/Bennoune/files/WLUML-dossier-30-31-v2.pdf.
9. I place this in quotation marks because Shariah law doesn't actually exist.
10. Channel 4, *Dispatches: The War Crimes File*, Twenty Twenty TV, London, 3.5.95: www.youtube.com/watch?v=4A1Ev17ZTAY.
11. G. Sahgal, *Love Snatched: Forced Marriage and Multiculturalism*, Faction Films, London, 2001: www.factionfilms.co.uk/films-for-sale/love-snatched-forced-marriage-and-multiculturalism/; G. Sahgal, *Tying the knot?* Faction Films, London, 2002: www.factionfilms.co.uk/films-for-sale/tying-the-knot/.The major publication to come out of this project was L. Welchman and S. Hossain (eds), *Honour Crimes, Paradigms and Violence Against Women*, Zed Books, London 2005.
12. See A. Imam, J. Morgan & N. Yuval-Davis (eds), *Warning Signs of Fundamentalisms*, WLUML, 2004.
13. International Council of Human Rights Policy, *When Legal Worlds Overlap: Human Rights, State and Non-State Law*, ICHRP, Geneva 2010.
14. Find out more about AWID's *Resisting and Challenging Fundamentalisms* projectat: www.awid.org/Our-Initiatives/Resisting-and-Challenging-Religious-Fundamentalisms.
15. M. Tax, *Double Bind: The Muslim Right, the Anglo-American Left, and Universal Human Rights*, Centre for Secular Space, London 2013, p3.
16. Awaaz: South Asia Watch, *In Bad Faith? British Charity and Hindu Extremism*, Awaaz, London 2004; and *Key Tendencies of the Islamic Right* (copy with author).
17. *Hecklers*, Gita Sahgal, SecularZone: www.youtube.com/watch?v=msX677UYA8o.
18. Global Petition to Amnesty International: Restore the Integrity of Human Rights: http://www.human-rights-for-all.org/spip.php?article15.
19. M. Tax, op cit.
20. Ibid.
21. http://www.nybooks.com/blogs/nyrblog/2012/feb/23/women-islam-debate-human-rights-watch/

# 4. Linking the Local with the Global: The Legacy of Migrant Grandparents

*Ruth Pearson*

## MY PARENTS' ECONOMIC AND POLITICAL STRUGGLES

I was the middle child of second-generation Jewish migrants from Eastern Europe. Both my maternal and paternal grandparents came to the UK around 1900. I am a bit hazy about the trajectory of my mother's family, who came from the Polish Russian steppes, but I learned at her stone-setting that my paternal grandmother's migration to the UK was undertaken as the result of a personal tragedy. She had married my grandfather, an illiterate tailor, when she was about seventeen. But her first child was stillborn, and, according to the rabbi in London, the 'soothsayer' had told the young couple to leave Lodz and go West, which they duly did, arriving in the East End of London in 1902.

Born in 1914, my mother was one of eight children, and lived in extreme poverty in Clapton, where she and her older sister had to sleep in the kitchen of their overcrowded tenement house. Her brothers worked in a number of semi-skilled occupations – one was a taxi driver and another had a number of 'one-arm bandits' in Southend-on-Sea – a reference to fruit machines on the pier rather than the amputated gangsters of my childhood imagination. Apparently, my mother was relatively successful at school but was withdrawn from studies after she broke both her arms while playing netball. Her mother insisted that she had better quit 'before you break your legs'. At fourteen years of age she was apprenticed to a milliner in Hackney. The family observed the Jewish calendars and holidays, but did not regularly attend the synagogue or go to Hebrew classes.

When my mother was about 15 she met my father, and he encouraged her to get more education. So she enrolled in a shorthand and typing course, and graduated top of the class – her prize was a Pitman Shorthand edition of *Dr Jekyll and Mr Hyde.*

My father, who was born in 1912, became a classic aspirant migrant. He had three brothers and a sister – not a very large family for the era, but a challenge for my grandmother, who had to become the sole breadwinner when my grandfather, a tailor, went blind from diabetes in his early thirties. My father attended the Central Boy's Foundation School, where he discovered a faculty for academic work. He was also determined to access the cultural opportunities London had to offer, and for many years my parents kept a box containing their old theatre programmes, regaling me with tales of walking miles across London to queue for gallery tickets to see the theatrical greats of the time. My father won a place to read Chemistry at Imperial College. Although this was supported by a small stipend – 50 shillings a week, which he told me he had to give to his mother – his brothers deeply resented the fact that he was allowed to continue studying rather than being forced to earn money as they were.

My father's intellectual aspirations included politics, and he rejected religion as 'unscientific', convinced by the socialism he found in political rallies and the publications of the New Left Book Club. But growing up Jewish in the East End in the 1920s and 1930s also meant confronting fascism and anti-semitism. Alongside many others, and in defiance of the British Board of Deputies, who advised London Jews to keep away, my parents were involved in the Battle of Cable Street in 1936, when an alliance of anti-fascists, including local Jewish, socialist, Irish, anarchist and communist groups fought off Mosley's British Union of Fascists (also known as The Blackshirts) who were actively protected by a strong police force. By this time my father had changed his original Polish surname to a more Anglophone surname, having been wounded by the sometimes violent anti-Jewish sentiment of fellow students at Imperial College.

My parents married in December 1936 – my mother was 22 and my father was 24. After he graduated, my father got a job in a pencil factory in Long Eaton, Nottinghamshire. My mother was dismissed from her secretarial position at Coty's because of the widely applied marriage bar, which insisted that married women resign their professional or administrative posts to take up their 'proper' place in the home.

In Nottinghamshire my parents joined the Independent Labour Party, which at that time boasted the participation of people who were later to become important leaders in the post-war Labour Party, such as Barbara Castle the Chair and Fenner Brockway. Brockway was a lifelong pacifist, socialist and anti-colonial activist, and became our local Labour MP in 1950 when I was growing up in Slough; my mother remained on friendly terms with him until her death. By 1937 Brockway, along with other former pacifists, decided that armed struggle was necessary to defeat the fascists led by General Franco in Spain. He helped organise an ILP contingent of partisans to fight alongside the republicans – but remained Chair of the Central Board for Conscientious Objectors throughout the war.

When war broke out in 1939 my father, now a qualified industrial chemist, was sent to the ICI's explosive factory in Ardeer, West Scotland, where my older brother was born in 1943. In 1945 he was redeployed to a research post in the ICI's Paint Division in Slough, where he developed new varieties of Dulux paint. I was born in December 1945, and my younger brother in 1947.

## MEMORIES OF A SECULAR CHILDHOOD

My upbringing in Slough involved no contact with the Jewish community apart from some family friends from Central Europe, and a couple of Jewish members of the local Communist Party. My father was at one time active in the Co-operative Society – and my mother found her political place as a key organiser and long term Chairwoman of the local Co-operative Women's Guild. We did visit family in East London quite regularly, and occasionally participated in the Seders they invited us to, as well as family bar mitzvahs, weddings and funerals – though none of these took place near home.[1]

There was a lot of political debate at home, and my father increasingly moved towards a pro-Zionist position, particularly after 1967. But until that time active politics was led by my mother's anti-nuclear activities – she was, I think, one of the original Committee of 100 signatories, and as the route of the Aldermaston march went through Slough, she – and I – became heavily involved in CND. Successive Easters saw us hosting Robin Cook over night – his parents and mine had become friendly while the family was in Scotland. And through Fenner Brockway (MP for Slough from 1950 to 1964) we met other Labour politicians, including Antony Crosland.

My own views were directly influenced by my parents' politics and educational aspirations, which they saw as key to class mobility and success and acceptance within the UK professional classes. After we moved to the 'smart' side of town in about 1953, my mother, characteristically, befriended the first and only Asian woman to move into the street. The neighbours were aghast. Someone apparently thought 'if she likes them she can live with them', and placed a notice in the local newspaper advertising a flat to rent at our house which read 'Coloured family preferred. £5 per week. Children welcome.' In response families came from as far away as Birmingham and Coventry. We invited them in, gave them tea and took them round the house to convince them that this was a hoax. I recall one West Indian couple saying 'We knew it was too good to be true but we had to come and see – just in case'. The incident made a lasting impression on me, and I remembered it when I later read about how at this time immigrants were included in the labour market but excluded from the housing market.

I passed the 11-plus exam and went at the age of 10 to Slough High School for Girls, a traditional single-sex grammar school founded in 1936. There I was allowed to be different, not so much because I was Jewish (the headmistress inevitably called me Rachel rather than Ruth, but no other concessions were made) but because I was 'intellectual' and interested in politics. An excellent history teacher, Miss Raikes, encouraged my rather stroppy rebelliousness, fostered my role in the debating society (which included defeating the neighbouring Eton College), facilitated my participation in the Christmas conferences of the Council for World Citizenship at Westminster, and encouraged me to apply for Oxbridge. I was offered a place at New Hall (now Murray Edwards) College and went up in 1964.

## STUDENT YEARS – EXPLORING ISRAEL AND ZIONISM

I had been a member of the Young Socialists from about the age of fourteen, and tried to follow this kind of politics when I got to Cambridge. I felt intimidated by the Islington set and those who were clearly destined for political roles in the Labour Party. But for the first time I met other young Jewish people and became interested in the political issues of Israel and Zionism rather than in religion. In the summer of 1965, at the end of my first year at university, I applied for a travel scholarship from an organisation known as JET – the Jewish Educational Trust, whose purpose was purportedly to offer non-Jewish young people the chance to visit Israel and experience first-hand the transformations and political and social life of the country. JET agreed that my knowledge of Judaism was so slight that I was eligible for the scheme and in August 1965 I set out – with about twenty other students – in a propeller-powered plane from London to Tel Aviv (via Cyprus). I worked on a Kibbutz, met a range of Jewish and Arab Israelis, and visited the major cities and resorts. But if the purpose of the trip was to induct me into Zionism, it failed. When we returned we were each obliged to write an article for the JET magazine about our experiences. Mine dealt with discrimination against Sephardi Jews, particularly from other Middle Eastern countries, and I think – though I may have invented this – the organisation refused to publish it.

## ... AND FEMINISM

During my years at Cambridge I had no engagement with feminist politics. When I later became a post-graduate student at the University of Sussex I was still maintaining that feminism was for other women – those who had not had the educational and professional opportunities open to me. I only faced up to the folly of this when a fellow student challenged me about the ways in which my mobility, security and presentation were compromised when travelling. I had to admit I had been the victim of two stranger attacks while an undergraduate, which had seriously interfered with my undergraduate studies.

## INTERNATIONALIST AND SOLIDARITY POLITICS – AND LATIN AMERICA

But I had brought with me to Sussex a more internationalist, anti-imperialist outlook, having been involved in a Mozambique/Angola solidarity group in London, and having also been on the fringes of some 1968 cultural and political activities, as well as burgeoning opposition to large-scale urban redevelopment in London. I had also worked for a project that was part of Fritz Schumacher's Intermediate Technology Development Group, and had travelled to Nigeria at the end of the Biafran War. When I returned to London I had been keen to further my knowledge of international development, not least because, like many of my generation, I considered that the interesting struggles and changes were happening in the post-colonial world. So I went to the University of Sussex to do an MA in Development Economics in 1971, and stayed on to do a PhD on technological dependency. I was aware of the socialist triumph in Chile under Salvador Allende, but with some prescience decided there were enough would-be European socialists in Chile, and focused the field work for my doctorate thesis on Argentina.

My time in Argentina – only nine months between January and October 1974 – was crucial in terms of my later political activism. The CIA-supported military coup in Chile had taken place on 11 September 1973 (Chile's 9/11), an event that led the way to the dark decade of military despotism and neo-fascist politics in South America. Peron returned to Argentina and became President for the third time, but died of a heart attack in July 1974, and was succeeded by his third wife, Isabel Peron, and her military advisors. Against this backdrop I attended my first feminist conference in Buenos Aires, and got drawn into feminist debates with sociologists and economists. When I returned to the UK in October 1974 I became heavily involved in supporting Chilean refugees – who had been permitted to enter the UK only after the election of the Labour government, since the Heath government had recognised the military regime under General Pinochet. I also participated in Marxist reading groups, and became a member of an important grouping of academic feminists who were questioning the male bias and absence of gender analysis in international development – the so called Subordination of Women group, which was focused on the Institute of Development Studies and the University of Sussex.

My Sussex days were interrupted by accompanying my partner, Rhys Jenkins, to Mexico for a year in 1976 – just after the Conference on the Status of Women held in Mexico City in June 1975 to coincide with the UN's International Women's Year. Mexican feminism was flourishing in the wake of the 1975 conference, and I became an active member of two or three feminist study and political groups in Mexico City, alongside notable Mexican feminists such as Marta Llamas and Lourdes Arizpe. In 1976 I published an article on domestic violence in one of the first issues of the Mexican feminist journal *fem*.

During my year in Mexico I undertook some research on the *maquiladora* industry, the term used to describe the growing phenomenon of international firms locating South of the US/Mexican border where they employed 'cheap' Mexican women to process labour intensive manufactured goods for re-export to the US and elsewhere.

My academic interest switched from technological dependency to women's employment in the global economy, where it has remained firmly lodged ever since.

Before I returned to the UK I was contacted by an Argentine woman, Laura Bonaparte, whom I interviewed at length in Mexico City. She gave testimony concerning her daughter Noni, who had been a member of the Monteneros, and had 'disappeared' in 1975. Through family connections, Laura had pursued a case of habeas corpus against the military, and had discovered her daughter's mutilated body alongside some thirty others in an unmarked mass grave in the suburbs of Buenos Aires. I returned to the UK determined to publicise this case, only to discover that the British left were not interested. A well-known journalist at the *Guardian* told me that this was not news – unlike the six white nuns who had been raped in Rhodesia in the early months of 1977. Laura Bonaparte later lost another daughter and two sons to the 'dirty war' in Argentina. She became a founder of the Madres de Plaza de Mayo and has spent her life fighting against the horrors of fascism and military dictatorship. She, like the Chilean women in Britain who gave testimony about sexual abuse and the torture of women after the coup, had a profound impact on me in terms of understanding the importance of women's agency in the struggle for human rights.

## MAKING FEMINIST AND SOCIALIST POLITICS IN THE PROVINCES

I returned to the UK at the beginning of 1977 and went to live in Norwich, where Rhys had a job at the University of East Anglia, and we had two children over the next four years. Feminism in Norwich was also on the rise, indicated by the establishment of a women's refuge in 1974, only the third in the UK, for women fleeing domestic violence. I was succumbing to the burdens of motherhood and finishing my PhD, but was rescued – just in time I think – by the Subordination of Women collective (SOW) which had been organised during my absence in Mexico. I attended meetings in London, where, with my long term collaborator and co-author Diane Elson, I studied the way international capital was targeting young docile women, and wrote the first draft of what was to become our hallmark article, 'Nimble fingers make cheap workers' for presentation at the SOW conference held in Sussex in September 1978.[2]

This conference was a landmark event. Sixty feminists and activists from around the world – half from the global South – attended, and its academic impact is reflected in the two edited volumes published from the conference: *Of Marriage and the Market* and *Serving Two Masters*.[3] After dinner one evening, we were treated to a session organised by Nawal el Saadawi, who wanted to know from each of us how we became a feminist. To this day I remember the fusion of personal and political stories much more clearly than the academic debates. A Peruvian woman married to a Protestant priest recalled how she had cut up her husband's clerical collars – thus preventing him from performing his duties – in response to him forbidding her to go out to work.

In 1978 I got a job teaching economics A-level in a Catholic secondary school. The head was a progressive nun – my first real contact with 'Christian women'. When I agreed to take the job she asked me not to undermine the Catholic values of the school. So we made a bargain: I agreed to this and she undertook to respect my values. I was also a member of a small political group which we called 'the Norwich Socialist Group', as well as (re)joining the Labour Party in Norwich.

But my political interest centred more and more on feminism. Unlike in metropolitan London, where the political disagreements between radical and socialist feminists led to fierce debates, and tendencies for each to be active in different spheres, the small size of Norwich meant that the whole spectrum of feminists were active in campaigning and initiatives about women's sexuality and against violence, as well as about economic and social opportunities. In 1980, with two other women, I set up the Norwich Women's Studies Collective. Our first focus was on women's health, which led some five years later to a fierce but ultimately successful campaign to establish a Well Woman Clinic, to offset the scarcity of women GPs in the region, as well as to reflect the burgeoning women's health movement. Two things about this stand out in my memory. The first was the cross-party alliances – one of the Tory members of the Health Authority which ultimately had to approve the proposals told the public hearing that '[a]s far as I can see women in Norfolk get a better service from their vets than they did from their doctors'. The other concerned strategy. We carried out a large-scale questionnaire survey, and also encouraged women to write in to support this initiative. At the crucial meeting the Chair had the casting vote, which he used in favour of financing the clinic. He said he had been very influenced by the large number of letters he had received from members of the public, and chose one to read out – which he said had been a clincher for him. This letter was from a man who was writing on his wife's behalf: she was 'too shy to visit the doctor about "women's complaints"'. When we went to the pub to celebrate the victory a fellow campaigner took me aside. 'You know that letter the chair read out', she said proudly. 'I wrote that!'

The Women's Studies initiative continued for three or four years, and we studied women's rights and the law, art and therapy, literature, sport, politics and the difficulty of voluntarily opting not to have children. We set up a Women's Health Information Service (WHIS) to support women using the well-woman clinic; and we agitated successfully for funds for a Women's Centre, and subsequently for WEETU (the Women's Employment, Enterprise and Training Unit), which campaigned for innovative services to support women's economic opportunities, and survived the changing political fortunes and fashions for twenty-five subsequent years. Others set up a Rape Crisis Centre, and many continued to work with the women's refuge. And we went to Greenham to 'embrace the base' in 1982.

I also tried to maintain a participation in London-based feminist groups – I was part of the socialist feminist CSE's Sex and Class discussion group. But it was difficult to get to London for meetings, especially when I had small children, so I increasingly confined my activism to local organisations. But I continued to follow my internationalist path, teaching a wonderful Open University Third World Studies course, and organising the summer schools for that course which were held annually at UEA in Norwich. In 1989 I was appointed to a lectureship in Development Studies at UEA, teaching economics and gender analysis of development, which has continued to be the main focus of my academic work.

The demographics of the university community at UEA were different from those prevailing within the mainly white city of Norwich, and I was involved in mobilisations against racial abuse as well as various feminist groups within the UEA and in the city. I remember one Iranian student at a women's discussion group declaring that the holocaust was a Zionist myth, making me aware of the ways in which history and social narrative are constantly reconstructed to reflect particular ideological positions – a view which was reinforced by my contact with younger feminist academics particularly in the literature department.

## LINKING WITH ANTI-FUNDAMENTALIST POLITICS

It was these contacts that led four of us to decide to go to Ealing to attend an International Women's Day meeting jointly organised by Southall Black Sisters and the Southall Labour Party on 9 March 1989, entitled 'The resurgence of Religion: What price do women pay'. The other three were Lakshmi Holmström (part of the Asian Women's Writers' Collective and now a well-known translator, broadcaster and expert on Indian women's writing), Fadia Faquir (a Jordanian/British novelist who was the first PhD in Critical and Creative Writing in the UK) and Nalini Vital (a development economics PhD student from India). The other three had first-hand knowledge of the dangers of religion from the South Asian and West Asian context. Fadia was concerned about the role religion played in curtailing freedom of speech. Nalini had lived through the invasion of the Sikh Golden temple in Amritsar in 1984 and the prolonged communal violence between Hindus and Muslims in Ahmedabad in 1985, in which minority women were targeted and suffered hideous atrocities.

On 14 February 1989, between the announcement of the SBS meeting and the date it took place, the *fatwa* against Rushdie was pronounced. So at the Southall meeting, as well as local Asian and Irish women talking about the ways in which the rise of religious power had impacted on their lives, a statement was drawn up by those present, including the four of us from Norwich, in support of Rushdie. This led to the establishment of Women Against Fundamentalism in May 1989. The text of the letter of support, which was also published in the *Independent*, began 'We are women of many religions and of none', and made a clear statement of respect for women's religious beliefs and practices, alongside a stern determination that religious power and hierarchy had no role in dictating the private or public life of women or men. For me, this political initiative – to bring together feminist activists to take on the insidious power of religious leaders to dictate to women – brought together my activism concerning women and feminism in Britain and also my internationalism.

Having been there at the birth of WAF in London I struggled with maintaining a consistent level of presence and activism, given my location in Norwich and the demands of my job, family and other feminist activities. In July 1989 I hosted Nawal el Saadawi, who came to UEA and gave a lecture on 'Fundamentalism and Arab Feminism'. In the wake of the 'Rushdie Affair' the University was very nervous about having a lecture with fundamentalism and feminism in the same breath, and forbade me to advertise it widely or to make press statements. Interestingly, the literature department, who later became big supporters of Rushdie, were not interested in or supportive of this endeavour. I introduced the issue of religious fundamentalism into my teaching, and wrote an article for a German political magazine entitled 'Feminism and Fundamentalism in Britain', which was reprinted and widely disseminated in an Open University Women's Studies textbook.[4] I also made a point of attending as many of the big WAF meetings in London as I could.

At a meeting on women and fundamentalism in an international context, the case of Rabia Janjua made a big impression on me. Rabia Janjua was a Pakistani national who had been forced to marry her rapist to avoid *zina* charges. He fled to the UK and sponsored her to join him, but he didn't regularise her immigration status. She then suffered continuous domestic violence and finally evicted her husband, who subsequently denounced her as an illegal immigrant. SBS had done a very effective job in preventing the immigration service from deporting her immediately. At this meeting, Gita Sahgal and Pragna Patel argued that if she was sent back to Pakistan she was at risk of persecution under the *zina* laws, and that she should be granted asylum in the UK. It took me some time to realise that my limited notion of political persecution needed to be expanded to encompass the ways in which women as a gender were denied citizenship and protection from their natal state – and this has informed my analytical understanding of migration and citizenship ever since.

In 1996 I went to the International Institute of Social Studies in the Hague, and in 2000 moved to a Chair at the University of Leeds, so my contact with WAF over these years was sporadic, though I signed up to the email list. But I remained in touch with WAF, and when I was on the Board of Management of AWID (the Association of Women's Rights in Development based in Toronto) I put them in touch with activists in WAF – resulting in a very productive joint global project on 'Women and Fundamentalisms'.

## WHERE WE GO FROM HERE – REFLECTIONS ON WAF AND ITS LEGACY

Through WAF and other work, I became interested in understanding religious institutions as social/political actors. Religion is the architecture of many people's lives and communities, and in many countries it is the mosque or the church that offers support in times of crises or disasters. I developed an understanding of the ways in which women's options were circumscribed by the nature of the religious and political institutions available to them. When I was in Ethiopia in 1991, I met the minister who headed the women's affairs office in the transitional government; she maintained very strongly that the new government could not work with any woman who had been involved in REWA – the women's organisation set up by the Dergue government- and was deaf to my protestations that, in the absence of a broader civil society, women had no other option if they were interested in pursuing women's empowerment. By the same token I could understand why so many women worked with religious organisations in many different circumstances and contexts.

In recent years I have become concerned that WAF's commitment to 'women of many religions' as well as 'of none' was becoming lost in translation. I was aware that some former WAF supporters, particularly black feminists, had left the organisation in the 1990s, angered by the lack of understanding or support for minority women active in churches in London and elsewhere. I also worried that the arguments for secular public life ignored the fact that for many individuals and academics the term 'secular' carried a double meaning – not just a separation of religion and state, but also the absence of religious beliefs and practices. I was increasingly concerned that WAF was representing a particular kind of metropolitan debate and politics. At WAF's twentieth anniversary meeting held at SOAS in November 2009, I was particularly alarmed by a discussion about the teaching and text books used in teaching religious studies in London schools. An Asian male teacher from West London, who tried to argue that there were a range of materials and approaches being utilised in teaching comparative religions, was shot down by the speaker, not defended by the chair and was so visibly upset that he left the meeting immediately. This, it seemed to me, reflected a disrespect for alternative voices which was the very opposite of what WAF was established to defend.

The reasons that propelled me to go to the 1989 meeting are still there and I continue to support WAF's aims and struggles to adapt to changing geopolitical and national contexts. I still adhere to intersectional politics, however, and am persuaded that some religious institutions can be progressive and that we ignore this at our peril. The original WAF analysis about religion as power at different levels, including gender subordination, still stands. I still consider that WAF, as a collective initiative to challenge the price women are paying for the political rise of religion, is sorely needed. But I wonder what the appropriate organisational form is to forward this project at the present time. I continue to engage academically with this issue and I published an article in 2008 questioning the ways in which the 'religious turn' in development thinking had forged partnerships which had turned their back on any commitment to prioritise women's equality and gender justice in development policy and practice.[5] But in the rush to 'religiosize' identity that has been a feature of the post 9/11 landscape, the task is to challenge stereotypes of minority groups in the UK and elsewhere, rather than feed them. In recent research I have undertaken about South Asian women workers who have been involved in industrial disputes in London over the last thirty years – from Grunwick to Gate Gourmet – I have become conscious of the fact that in many political, academic and policy circles women's identities are increasingly being defined solely in terms of religion rather than class, ethnicity, or employment status; indeed much of this discourse is a work-free zone, ignoring the centrality of paid and unpaid work for minority women.[6] The political challenges of fundamentalisms are enormous, and WAF – or any successor organisation – needs to be able to present a sharp analysis of the gendered nature and impact of these processes without over-determining women's identity in terms of religion.

## NOTES

1. A 'Seder' is a ritual meal that marks the beginning of the Jewish Passover holiday, which celebrates the liberation of the Jews from slavery in Pharonic Egypt. 'Bar Mitzvahs' are the religious and social celebrations of Jewish boys' transition to manhood at the age of thirteen.
2. 'Nimble Fingers Make Cheap Workers: An Analysis of Women's Employment in Third World Export Manufacturing' (with D. Elson), in *Feminist Review*, Spring 1981.

3. K Young (ed), *Serving Two Masters: Third World Women in Development*, Allied Publishers, India 1989; K. Young, C. Wolkowitz and R. McCullagh (eds), *Of Marriage and the Market: Women's Sub ordination In International Perspective*, CSE Books, London 1981. Republished by Routledge in 1984.
4. 'Feminism and Fundamentalism', in *Hard Times*, Berlin No.42 December 1990; reprinted in Linda McDowell and Rosemary Pringle (eds), *Defining Women: Social Institutions and Gender Divisions*, Polity Press 1992.
5. Ruth Pearson and Emma Tomalin (2008), 'Intelligent Design: A Gender Sensitive Interrogation of Religions and Development', in Gerard Clarke and Michael Jennings (eds), *Development, Civil Society and Faith-based Organizations: Bridging the Sacred and the Secular*, Palgrave MacMillan, Basingstoke 2008.
6. See www.leeds.ac.uk/strikingwomen.

# 5. Gods and daughters

*Shakila Taranum Maan*

## INTRODUCTION

I have always been, and continue to be, surrounded by religion in every guise. This presence is much more acute within my family life, and choosing my battles has become an art. I grew up in a small Sunni Muslim family which has grown in numbers over the years, garnering a powerful voice through religious expression, sexuality, caste, class and sect. Since my youth I actively sought to challenge and shut out these voices. I grew up thinking I had no role models, but writing 'Gods and daughters' for WAF has helped to show me the countless women, including my mother, who have shaped me and most crucially, that being and working in Southall has made me who I am.

## INHERITANCE

'A celestial bull makes day and night', explained my mother. 'When it's time for night to come, it tosses the earth onto its horn on the left and there it spins for the entire night and when day is to come, the bull tosses it back on to the right horn and we have day'. My siblings and I sat in silence as my mother decided to help us with our homework on planetary systems. She truly believed what she was telling us about how day and night occurred.

My mother, Akhtar Sultana, was married to my father at the age of twelve. My father was eighteen. She would tell me and my older sister about her wedding day which she had thought was the festival of Eid. She and her friends were dressed up in shiny clothes embellished with gold and silver lace; she looked the best. While she was playing with dolls and clay toys in the street, my grandmother called her in to join witnesses and the local Maulvi, as my grandfather read the Nikah on her behalf. My mother used to laugh when she told us this story. 'Technically, I am not married to your father ... But my father is!'

My mother grew into an extraordinary woman despite her far from adequate education. Her school comprised rooms full of sand for chairs, and slate and chalk for paper and pen. She learnt basic Urdu with sentences like 'Billi ko Kuttey sey pyaar hai' (the cat is in love with the dog). She picked up fantastical tales, and was taught that those born into any royal family were placed there by god. She rarely lost her temper, but when I would discuss opium-ridden kings and princes of the Moghul Empire she would be deeply hurt, and would refuse to speak to me for the rest of the day. She knew the birth dates of all of the queen's children and often wondered whom Prince Charles would marry. She learnt the Quran in Arabic, not knowing what the passages meant. She later studied Urdu, reading in translation the Quran, Bible and Torah. This enabled her to debate with some authority with visitors of various religious denominations. Although born a Sunni Muslim, she found herself embracing Sufism in her quest for understanding Islam.

I remember as a child going with her to a Zikar in Shepherds Bush, where the congregation would get into a pitched frenzy, with children present as young as seven years old. Adults and children sat, with heads swaying side-ways refusing to collide, entranced by prayer and devotion. Had she been alive today, she would have found it hard to exist in the Wahhabi Islam that has now gripped my family, let alone amongst the majority of Sufi sects in the world today, particularly now that the global influence of Chechnyan Sufis has spread so rapidly since the collapse of the Soviet Union. From the late 1990s, the failure of the secular struggle for independence from Russia left Chechnya in the control of fundamentalist Wahhabism, led by the Saudi Emir Khattab. This dramatic and rapid change in Sufi Islam then snowballed into the surrounding regions such as Pakistan, and inevitably Britain.

My mother had a very turbulent life and perhaps never found any happiness. She suffered the partition of India in 1947 and walked from Ludhiana to Lahore with my grandfather and her younger sister and brother. My grandmother was left behind in Ludhiana protected by a Sikh family, and was later united with her family in Lahore. My mother lost her younger sister on the long walk to Pakistan, and they were only reunited when she was found by my grandfather in 1973.

After her marriage, my mother left her village in Toba Tek Singh to join my father and her in-laws in the small fishing town of Nanga in Kenya on the banks of Lake Victoria. It must have been a frightful journey, not knowing what she would be facing or what was expected of her. What she found was an indifferent husband and in-laws who practised an austere Islam. Her father-in-law earned money through his fishing boats and spent it on building mosques across Kenya and Pakistan.

In Kenya our relationship with Africans was very different from that of other Asian families. My great grandfather and his brothers had worked alongside Africans building the railways. Africans were seen as equals. Many of the men from my grandfather's generation had married African women. My father grew up with mixed-race cousins. Later, when my mother and father lived independently, they also mixed with Hindus and Sikhs, creating lifelong friendships. My mother's journey into tolerance had roots in the Partition of India, and her understanding of humanity was made concrete as she grew into a young woman in Africa. This personality trait came in handy many years later, when the turbulent expulsion of Ugandan Asians had a domino effect on Kenya and Tanzania, forcing many Asian families, including ours, to flee. It was then that my mother moved, for the fourth and final time, to England.

My siblings and I were all born in Kenya, but my sisters were both sent from there to Pakistan to live with our maternal grandmother and learn how to be gentle ladies, whilst my brother and I lived in Kenya and were brought up on Enid Blyton and the *Beano*. Ironically, I can put my sense of equality down to reading *Beano* and seeing rows and rows of English houses where it seemed all families lived sheltered and protected lives. What I saw in Kenya was the opposite of this.

Arriving in England on a cold March day in 1973 changed everything for us. Our understanding of racism became much more acute as *we* were now the hated targets. Joining my mother's brother, who had settled in Yorkshire, was our first introduction to a British Pakistani community. I found it strange that women would not leave the house without covering their heads. Streets surrounding ours were full of Pakistani families, and the only white people I came across were in my class at school.

My mother didn't know what to do and whom to befriend. Her disastrous attempt at making friends with a neighbour led her into a deep depression. Within a few weeks of being in England, she put on her lilac sari, her bead necklace and her silver heels and went to visit our Pakistani neighbours, only to be told that what she was wearing was inappropriate and non-Islamic. My mother said nothing. She swallowed the insults, came home and went to bed. There she lay for months, until our father came to take us away to London, to a small West London suburb called Northolt, on the border of Southall. My mother's misery only increased, as the family continued to experience misfortune, racist attacks and poverty.

My father found what little work he could, but the lack of money led us into a life of squalor and cramped accommodation, sometimes with only one bedroom for the whole family, other times in filthy houses surrounded by racist thugs whom my mother would dodge on street corners. Poverty is a great leveller. Trying to keep some semblance of sanity, my mother would invite in anyone who came to the door selling god. She would stop her work as a machinist and order us to make tea for a Jehovah's Witness or a Mormon while they discussed the pain of Christ.

**DISSENT**

I come from a long line of dissenting women. Amongst other things, my grandmother, Halima Mangat, was well known in her village for the following story. Halima loved her afternoon naps, and one hot summer afternoon she had taken her nap later than planned. Her day had gone badly. She had no money to pay her workers because of the devastating effects of the Iran/Iraq war on her trade in selling oranges. Neither she nor Wahed, a bonded labourer that she favoured over her own son, could think of any plans to solve the cash flow issue. To top it all, her son had decided to return home drunk and abuse the workers. She normally woke before the evening prayer, but since on this day she had slept later than planned, she was rudely awoken when the call to prayer sounded out from the mosque's newly installed speakers. She immediately dispatched Wahed to cut the leads. This battle went on for some months, until finally Wahed was caught in the act, and this left my grandmother no choice but to confront the clergy herself – who eventually bowed to her wishes. We later learnt that she had threatened to withhold her farm produce, which would have forced the village to buy from outside at a higher price! This episode was remembered fondly by villagers even after my grandmother passed away.

I did not want the suffering of my mother's life and the crushing of her creative flair. I did not want an arranged marriage or any kind of marriage. There were no positive male role models in my life, so marriage or relationships were off the books. I didn't want to have children as I felt that there are too many people in the world and I would adopt. These views inevitably led to confrontation in the family when my mother was trying to arrange my marriage – arguing against this course became very difficult. But my need for artistic expression superseded any other needs. Setting up theatre groups, and writing and directing plays central to my struggles, became a dominant focus. I had left school in 1978 with no qualifications, and started working in a supermarket populated with racist co-workers – which was challenging. Nevertheless, it was good to be in a job and contributing towards bills and rent. The uprising of 1979 in Southall changed all that for me. Watching the events of 23 April 1979 unfold on television, I was determined to be a part of the change and resistance.

The Southall uprising came as no surprise, as people were very angry, and keen to shed their passive skins. I wanted to be in Southall the next day, but my father didn't want me to go, despite my protests. I welcomed the uprising, and saw strength in a group of people who had for too long been reduced to mere shadows. My experiences of being at school in Northolt, a predominantly white area that Asians didn't venture into much, had left deep scars. The bussing in of kids from Southall into Northolt schools hadn't helped my situation.[1] The white kids reacted to being 'swamped', while the Southall kids were tough and could fight back – whereas I was targeted and beaten up by gangs of white kids on a regular basis, but was unable to reach out to the Southall kids.

Moving away from Northolt and into the largely South Asian area of Slough brought relief for the family. Although our financial situation did not improve, violence and hostility from the outside world did cease. My mother enrolled me into a local madrasah, but my experience thus far had left very little space for belief in god. My mother, however, had been battered in her daily life and was suffering a terminal illness. She sought solace in god and prayer, and she began to identify with the Pakistani community, striking strong friendships with women who helped her when she suffered physical, emotional or financial crisis. From time to time they helped her find work as a machinist working from home.

The presence of the National Front in Southall had also angered Asian communities living outside the area. I saw change occur around me, from my father to other Asian families. I sought any opportunity to be in Southall because I wanted to change my world. I had set up a theatre group in Slough for writing and directing plays dealing with race (for instance, *Spirits* was based on a relationship between a Rasta and young Sikh girl, and *Rani* was a play about a Pakistani singer, who was also a prostitute). This work led to some recognition amongst British Asian artists, and in 1980 I was offered work as a community arts co-ordinator by the National Association of Asian Youth (NAAY) based in Southall.[2]

This was a good opportunity for me to seek out The Monitoring Group (TMG, then known as the Southall Monitoring Group). TMG is an anti-racist organisation that had become synonymous with the uprising of 1979. I can clearly mark 1980 as the time of the beginning of my political work. Seeing Asians rise and fight, and my own desire for that voice, was a dominant force that took hold of me. Joining TMG later led me to Southall Black Sisters, with whom I developed a very deep emotional link. I saw in them a group of like-minded women, looking to create a just world, and believed that the only way to do this was through direct action, step by step, measure for measure. As my involvement with Southall Black Sisters grew, I came to understand their work, and saw a lot of what my mother had experienced being reflected in the stories of the women who came there for help.

Both TMG and SBS were pivotal in forging my politics and world view. At this time, my creative work was centred on writing for my street theatre company as well as working with musicians and visual artists from India and Pakistan. Unity was at the forefront of my work. I felt safe being in Southall and the days of dodging Paki-bashers on the pavements of Northolt were becoming a distant memory.

In 1982 I left the NAAY set-up for the Southall Asian and African Caribbean Arts Collective (SAAAC). I had wanted to create a space which brought together black artists (Asians and African Caribbean). This political identity was directly influenced by the political perspectives of SBS and TMG; it pushed further the standard celebration of multiculturalism, and fulfilled the need for an outlet which went beyond Indian classical dance performance, bhangra gigs and theatre productions from the subcontinent. Rather, I wanted to create a space in Southall where local artists could develop creative work that reflected their experience. At SAAAC I was able to explore visual art, ceramics and street theatre, and I was also able to develop my political banner making, which I did for local groups like SBS and TMG among others. Later on I also made the first WAF banner that was used at the demonstration in Parliament Square in 1989.

During this time, in Southall and across Britain, I saw an unprecedented outpouring of political and artistic expression, creating an environment in which activists, directors, novelists, actors and musicians were reflecting and creating original and cutting-edge work. Inspired, my work at SAAAC and in street theatre took me into council estates and high streets, and to the visualising of stories of domestic violence and self-defence, with themes such as the differential sentencing of women who kill.

All that changed in 1984 following the assassination of Indira Gandhi and Operation Blue Star in India. The storming of the Golden Temple reverberated globally. In Southall, the police intensified its stop and search operations, seeking out Sikh terrorists and agitators. Mistrust and suspicion became the main architects within communities, and the rot set in. Sikhs became disconnected from British Asian communities and forged their own groups. Years later we would see separate Sikh schools becoming a powerful presence in and around Southall. These divisions were compounded and further entrenched when in 1989 Khomeini's fatwa on Salman Rushdie led to mass demonstrations and book burnings. This time I felt it even closer to home. I openly supported Rushdie but this was tolerated and never fully challenged. At family functions I was ignored. Occasionally I was teased with the line 'ask her, she knows where he is!'

The Rushdie affair and WAF protests set in me a seed of courage and dissent. Although my involvement with WAF was brief, the impact was profound. Here was a group for me, which seemed to be so concentrated on challenging fundamentalist religion and the ways in which it affected women and our communities at a local and global level. Listening to these incredibly articulate women helped me to place my point of view. Culture, tradition and religion were a point of debate at SBS, which we challenged on a daily basis through casework. At WAF, religion and the ways it affected women and society were the focus. I felt an enormous strength and freedom to explore difficult issues within my own work. Although I did not stay, WAF's presence and what WAF achieved through its direct challenge to the book-burners was enough to give me permission to question religion within my work.

The Rushdie affair has had a profound effect on my family. They have become much more insular, seeking out an Islamic identity and embracing the dictates of Saudi Arabia's Wahhabi Islam as the true Islam. Other forms of Islam and non-believers are casually referred to as 'Kafirs' (non-believer). On a day-to-day basis, more young women are wearing the hijab and young men are taking to another level the meaning of living by the dictates of Islam. The feelings of persecution are immense yet discriminating against others is constant and the contradictions are stark; misogyny, homophobia and religious intolerance are the main components of an Islam that is being projected under a liberal guise. At one point, one of my family members came under a great deal of pressure from her son to adopt the hijab. She resisted this by stating that her rights as a mother superseded his as a son. Some young women in my extended family have chosen to wear the hijab and are creating their own expression, but are coming under pressure to conform to a 'respectable' form. Their construction of the headscarf is seen as a form of abuse, yet these are colourful creations, and indeed statements which are immediately noticeable. Paradoxically, these creations are worn with figure hugging shirts and jeans – and thereby ignore the purpose of the hijab!

## EXPANDING AND TRANSFORMING MY CREATIVE WORK

Through my work in the 1990s I began to articulate a different voice, another strand of opposition. Mainstream theatre and cinema at that time seemed impossible to penetrate: there were great difficulties if you didn't fit in, which made it impossible to step outside the confines of either a racist or multiculturalist stereotype of being Black or Asian. My heroes at the time were the far more radical Black Audio Film Collective. I followed their work religiously; *Handsworth Songs* in particular was a source of inspiration.[3] Hanging on to everything they produced, I tried to emulate this in my work. My decision to study film and venture into working as a researcher and producer in television had its roots as much in the Black Audio Film Collective as in my father's film club in Kenya and my mother's love of Hindi films.

My father would get 16 mm prints of films from India on rent that he showed at his film club, and we would also see Hindi films in the cinemas of Kenya, and neighbouring Uganda and Tanzania. For us, Hindi film was a way of seeing ourselves on the screen. Cinema was one passion that I shared with my mother. In Kenya, Hindi cinema was her only reference point as an Asian woman. Every Wednesday our local cinema ran a 'Ladies Only' screening; and sometimes she would see two films in a day. These were opportunities for her to check out the latest fashion, leave the cinema with her friends, visit the fabric shop, buy up material and visit the tailor; and by the end of the week, she and her friends would be fashioned into movie stars.

I looked to Hindi cinema for visual references because that is what I knew. It was only when I studied cinema later, in my mid-twenties that I learnt about types of cinema other than Hollywood and Hindi Cinema. I combined this source of references with the inspiration I took from my political campaigning and from the Black Audio Collective to produce dissenting and more challenging work. For my graduation film, I made a short film entitled *Ferdous* (Arabic for Paradise). This was a brief and lyrical film that explored the Quranic law on homosexuality. Later I was funded by the Arts Council to make *A Thousand Borrowed Eyes*, a portrait of the dancer Nahid Siddiqui, who evolved Kathak Dance in Pakistan and Britain and went on to forge an international repertoire of Kathak dance, infusing it with Islamic mythologies. In theatre, I continued experimenting, and *Not Just An Asian Babe*, which I co-wrote with Parminder Sekhon, helped me forge courage in my writing. Parminder had already set the scene with the characters and had written twenty minutes of the script when I was called in to direct, but she was concerned about its length, and asked me to write more material with her. Working with Parminder was extraordinary. She helped me draw out characters which would otherwise not have been tackled. Together we researched and created memorable characters, and the play debuted at The Oval Theatre. It centred on two prostitutes working in the heart of Southall for a businessman running a strip club. His lovers included Roshini, a transvestite, and Julie, a young Sikh girl looking for stardom on cable television. Into this set-up steps Nasreen, a young Muslim girl from Ireland, who accidentally falls into the life of vice.

Nasreen was a fascinating character for me, for which I drew on all the stories I had heard of young girls in madrasahs and the neighbourhood. I also looked to popular and classical traditions of the ways in which prostitutes were seen in the subcontinent. Alongside being shunned and ostracised, prostitutes were also seen as the custodians of etiquette, poetry and wisdom – and this appealed to me. So in our story Nasreen inadvertently became Julie's teacher, and her contradictions riddled the play. I focused in on her desire in her darkest moments for dialogue with Allah, and turned these dialogues into challenges, in the way that the Hindus and Greeks challenged their gods. At the heart of Nasreen's discourse with Allah was the sexual abuse she suffered by the trusted family Maulana:

> Nasreen:
>
> I was looking for you.
>
> (Laughs) Even in summer time often the front door got jammed, me pushing and Maulvi Saab pulling from the inside. The force of our daily battle would make the holy text slip between my fingers, straight into the blue bells of your paradise. Except your bells have no sound. I heard you … your feet turned and walked away from me, slowly at first and then they became a thunderous gallop blowing up all sorts into my face until I became a speck of dirt in your Dominion.
>
> He moved his hand on to my bare right shoulder and said that here sit my good angels. These angels write down all that is good about me.
>
> He moved his hand across my breasts. I was freezing. The radiators were not working. His chapped hand played a while. I remember it clearly because he had discovered a small hair growing in the brown of my nipple. He pulled it out, then he moved to my left shoulder.
>
> He looked deep into my terrified eyes and said, 'Nasreen, this is the Angel who writes all your bad doing, your evil doings. Just as there are the seven heavens there are also seven sins. Many of them deadly'.
>
> Just as I thought it was over he looked into my eyes again, saying, that I was deep like the ocean. And then all of a sudden he took his eyes away from mine and said that my gaze had become evil.
>
> He lifted his Caftan, pulling out his belt.

Turn around Nasreen.

It started to snow.

So he looked at my left shoulder and flicked my sins off it. The angels had written all the things down in their book and my evil deeds were being collected. Just as his were; I saw it in his eyes. How he hated being born in the wrong sect. If only he could bask in the glory of Muharram and weep for Hassan and Husain, beating his body with chains and swords, for that was the true path to God. He did not have the courage to go to the other side.

For *Bhavni Bhavai*, directed by Ajay Kumar, I created a tableau exploring the ritual of the death of a beloved, in the act of being washed before burial. Ajay incorporated this into a full-length play, but more was needed to make it work. He wanted to explore the notion of the outsider, the untouchable, a Dalit. For this, the most logical place for me to go was to Southall Broadway. I performed the Outsider's character one cold February morning, when I walked naked on the street. It was an extraordinary experience. At first I was ignored until people got over the shock of my nudity. My character was a woman who was vulnerable, disturbed and in need of protection. The difference between how the men and women reacted to me was startling. The women were deeply concerned about my well-being and spoke to my minders asking if they knew me. They were worried I would catch cold and I should put on some shoes. The men on the other hand became very hostile. As I was in character, I was not aware of what was going on around me. I had sat down outside a shoe shop close to a butcher's shop, which was unfortunate. All I heard was an axe-wielding butcher telling me to 'get off the pavement bitch'. As we didn't manage to film this performance, we decided to risk it and went further down the street. This time the performance was interrupted by a group of Black male converts to Islam on a day trip to Southall. We managed to film the scene, but Parminder Sekhon – who was the official photographer and also the driver – had been busy buying her Amla hair oil, and only turned up in the nick of time to have me bundled into her car for a speedy getaway!

The last work I created was *The Bride*, which explore the Two Year immigration rule, through which women were often left at the mercy of husbands and in-laws. The aim was to provoke. The performance involved a naked and bloodied and bruised bride being brought on to the stage, with a Union Jack stuffed up her vagina, strands hanging out. She then filled her mouth with another piece of the flag, gagging herself into silence, taking it out of her mouth intermittently. She placed herself between two pillars, cling-film wrapped around the pillars, emulating a nice neat little package. Her wedding attire was strewn across the floor, and the bridal bangles were all that remained on her body. She sings throughout the performance, lamenting 'Aina akhian vich pavan kiwain kajla, akhian vich tu vas da' (How can I adorn my eyes with black kohl when it is you who lives in my eyes).

## BACKLASH

The camaraderie and collective nature of these productions were shattered when some years later Gurpeet Bhatti, who had played Nasreen in *Not Just An Asian Babe*, wrote the play *Behzti*, which was to be performed at the Birmingham Repertory Theatre. The play included scenes of rape and murder taking place within a Sikh temple, and was disrupted by the Council of Sikh Gurdwaras, headed by Sewa Singh Mandla, who initiated a demonstration supported by both moderate and extremist Sikhs. Death threats, kidnapping, violence and intimidation were the order of the day. Mandla and his gang said they would allow the play to go ahead if there were 'minor' changes to the script – but this included the demand that the play should not be set in a Sikh temple. After an emergency meeting of the theatre management, and discussions between the local Sikh community, West Midlands Police and the Commission for Racial Equality, Birmingham Repertory Theatre decided to cancel the show. In my view, this was a significant turning point for the British Asian theatre fraternity. I tried to organise an artist-led protest in defence of Gurpreet, but found that I could not get anyone to attend other than a close friend! This was too close to the bone for fellow artists, and after receiving abusive messages I was excommunicated from the fraternity. There were rumours of secret meetings held at the Arts Council discussing how to deal with 'difficult' and 'controversial' work coming out of the British Asian community, and whether the work should be vetted before it was given funds etc. A public meeting was held at Tara Arts where prominent theatre producers showed their true colours and disgraced themselves by aligning with Khalistanis. The most shocking part was that producers who had supported the Sikh protesters outside the Birmingham theatre Rep were given a platform to speak. So much for freedom of speech! After an enforced hiatus, Gurpreet survived a very difficult ordeal and went on to produce more outstanding work.

## CONCLUSION

Perhaps if I had stayed engaged with WAF, I would have shared the difficulties that I faced as an artist, particularly when I chose to challenge the Khalistani attack on Gurpreet's play *Behzti*. At the time, I wanted my protests to be purely an artist led demonstration, but in retrospect, it would have been far more effective to have had broader support involving WAF and SBS. But we have to live with our mistakes. The *Behzti* episode crystallised the dangers that we, as artists, feared. No more cutting-edge and challenging work came out for years, and some would argue that this is still the case as far as British Asian theatre and cinema is concerned. A faith-based attitude to social relations is fast fragmenting and distorting the history of Asian theatre in this country. We are living in a creative whitewash, where disjointed and separate religiosities are given free hand. With little or no challenges to this world view, it is influencing artistic expression and community life, cementing conservatism, denying the voice of dissenting and subversive artists – and enabling racism, homophobia and misogyny. Having come out of a creative tradition that seeks to provoke the audience, I now find myself self-censoring my work. As attitudes harden, the work of dissenting black and BME artists seldom sees the light of day. The fragmentation and splintering of religious groups has strengthened the right, and the conservative elements within and outside of communities, forcing many of us back out to the margins.

## NOTES

1. 'Bussing' refers to the daily dispersal of minority children to schools outside the area. It was part of the implementation of the 'Boyle Law', which came about because white parents in Southall complained about the high percentage of Asian students in local schools. The legislation stated that no more than 30 per cent of pupils in any one school would be of Asian or African Caribbean descent.
2. The National Association of Asian Youth was set up to bring together Asian youth organisations in the UK. They established a bookshop as well

as cultural and educational activities that influenced a generation and played a pivotal role in the 1979 uprisings.

3. The Black Audio Film Collective was founded in 1982 by undergraduates in Sociology and Fine Art: John Akomfrah, Lina Gopaul, Avril Johnson, Reece Auguiste, Trevor Mathison, Edward George, Claire Johnson and David Lawson. They created a distinctive visual and political voice that changed the face of documentary making film in the UK during that period. Their film *Handsworth Songs* explored the civil disturbances that occurred during October 1985 in the Birmingham district of Handsworth and also in London. These events were marked by unprecedented violence, culminating in the tragic death of Joy Gardner, an elderly black woman, and a white policeman, Keith Blakelock. The film won seven international awards including the BFI John Grierson Award for Best Documentary.

# 6. Intersectional contestations

*Nira Yuval-Davis*

Recently I took part in the 'Silver Action' live performance at the Tate Modern.[1] During this discussion with other ageing feminist activists, I was asked what made me into an activist. It occurred to me then that it was my experience in the Israeli army, when, as a naïve and sheltered eighteen-year-old middle-class Israeli Ashkenazi Jew, I was transformed from promising 'officer material' into a 'low security' private doomed to work as a typist in the army headquarters garage for the duration of my two years service. During my military service I had encountered the Israeli policy towards 'Israeli Arabs', as the Palestinians with Israeli citizenship were known then. I had also learned about class and ethnic differences among Israeli Jews and encountered extreme sexism and sexual harassment. Most of all I had come face to face with oppressive arbitrary authority and learned that I couldn't stand it.

These experiences eventually brought me to the libertarian left. My clash with the army authorities was not my first meaningful act of rebellion, but it was the one that led me to cross significant social and political boundaries, and set me on a path that eventually drove me to the outer bounds of the anti-Zionist Israeli left and then eventually to become part of a transnational socialist, anti-racist and anti-fundamentalist feminist 'global village' – and, of course, to WAF.

But maybe I should start at the beginning.

## GROWING UP

I was born in a small town outside Tel Aviv and from the age of four I grew up in a co-operative housing estate that was located – both geographically and socially – at the heart of north Tel Aviv. It was an exclusive housing estate to the extent that only members of the Histadrut (the umbrella organisation of Labour Zionist parties) were allowed to own a lease there. My father was the son of a Rabbi who had become an ardent socialist Zionist in Lithuania. He migrated from Lithuania to Palestine in the early 1930s and joined a kibbutz, where my mother joined him after some months, travelling there from Alitus, their home townlet. Unlike my father, my mother didn't like living in a collective, so when the kibbutz members pressurised my father (who had previously worked in a bank) to work on the finances of the kibbutz rather than in agriculture – which was considered then to be the 'real' pioneering Zionist work – he gave in to my mother's insistence and moved to Tel Aviv to work on the finances of the co-operative movement attached to the Histadrut. I always associated my father with the development of hegemonic Labour Zionism: first he worked with the co-operatives; then, at the age of fifty, when they had all transformed into capitalist companies, he passed an accountancy exam and continued to work with the same companies. But when he was in his seventies, the growing Americanisation of Israeli society meant that everyone in his field needed to learn English and computing. The hegemony of the old Labour Party was weakened, and my father became marginalised at the same time. A few days before he died, at the age of 76, on the day that Israel invaded Lebanon in 1982, he whispered to me that in his worst nightmares he wouldn't have dreamt that the utopian society he had helped to build would turn out the way it had. It was the first time we had talked politics since the stalemate of our shouting matches shortly after the 1967 war.

But these developments were still far away when I was growing up on the housing estate. All the children on the estate formed strong peer groups. There were about ten boys and girls around my age. Since I was a 'newcomer', and slightly overweight, I was bullied, and experienced what it was to be an outsider. My mother, who couldn't hide her disappointment that I had inherited the 'solid' figure of my father's family rather than her beautiful slender frame, nevertheless encouraged me to fight back against the bullies. She told me to call my main nemesis, a thin girl called Mimi, a 'raisin'. It didn't seem to have much of an effect at the time, but years later, when we were teenage friends, Mimi confessed how much this had hurt her. I felt bad on both our accounts, and probably became sensitive to 'hate speech' issues from that moment on.

The bullying stopped after a few months, mostly when the children of my age group discovered that I could read them the stories in the books, while they could only view the pictures. I suppose this is how I became a 'bookworm' – it provided me with an escape into a fantasy world and also gave me some kind of social acceptability.

In fact my two main rebellions as a child and teenager were associated with books.

The first occurred when in the eighth grade (aged around thirteen) we were taught the stories of the Yiddish writer Mendele Mocher Sforim (also known as 'Mendele the book peddler'). I wrote a passionate attack on the author because of the very negative way he described the diasporic Jews of Eastern Europe. I was already sensitive to anti-semitism. It was around that time that the sole surviving Jew from Alitus came to Israel and told my parents about the massacre of Jews there – they had been led into the local forest, forced to strip, then shot, and had then fallen into the huge holes in the ground that Soviet prisoners of war had dug. Many years later in the Jewish museum in Vilnius I saw a report about my grandfather who, as the local Rabbi, had supported the members of the community until the last moment. Just one survivor, who was a teenager at the time, had survived, because his grandfather had covered him with his own body and kept him safe from the bayonets that German and local Nazis stuck into the bodies after the shooting in order to ensure there were no survivors. When he regained consciousness this boy managed to escape and sought the help of local peasants who had done business with his wood merchant father. Eventually he found himself with the partisans in the forest. My mother's family had been closely associated with the partisans – her cousin had led the revolt in Vilnius ghetto before escaping it and leading the Jewish partisans' brigade in the woods. He did not survive the war, but there is a huge monument in his memory at the Jewish cemetery in Vilnius.

Returning for a moment to the stories by Mendele, I did not know the whole picture then, nor realise that the Zionist discourse about the need for the Jews to be 'normalised' actually involved the internalisation of stereotypical anti-semitic discourses. Nevertheless, I could not accept what seemed to be a cruel mockery of the same people who were mass murdered by the Nazis and their assistants, all of whom were from the same localities that Mendele wrote about. My teacher was impressed by my effort, but needless to say was not really affected by my 'rebellion'. Nor were the other children. However, retrospectively, this was an early starting point for my dissociation from the hegemonic Zionist discourse.

My second rebellion had more effect on my life. At the age of fifteen

I read Ayn Rand's book *The Fountainhead* and was completely 'converted' – though not to the neoliberalism for which she's mostly known now (when I eventually read *Atlas Shrugged* I could not accept its praise of greed). But *The Fountainhead* told me that the majority is not always right, that it is all right not to conform to your peer group, or any other social and political collectivity. Rand's book showed me that I could choose not to be part of 'the herd', but to find my own way towards self realisation. I decided to leave the Labour Zionist youth movement (the 'United Movement') that I was part of; I decided my future would not be in a kibbutz, which symbolised for me this kind of conformist social grouping. This decision made me lonely for a while, but then I found alternative ways of socialising. I became active in an organisation called Youth for Youth, which, among other things, allowed me to meet Israeli Palestinians of my age group, as well as severely disabled children from Tel Aviv slums. I suppose this was some kind of preparation for what could be called an intersectional analysis of Israeli society.

Another form of socialising I started to take part in led me to think explicitly that I wanted to become a sociologist 'when I grow up'. I was taken by a classmate to what was known as a 'salonic society'. This was the way teenagers who were not part of any formal youth organisation used to socialize. A core group of boys would incorporate their girlfriends into the 'society' – and also some of their friends, in order to even up the numbers. Every weekend we would meet at a party at one of the teenagers' homes and dance some version of ballroom dances. (No Hora or any other folk dancing for us!) Those who are interested in social network theories would be fascinated by the way girls moved from one 'salonic society' to another, while the boys mostly stayed in the same one. What fascinated me was that, unlike in the youth movement, there were no clear written rules, and yet unwritten rules were as rigid: girls had to be asked to dance by the boys; once a couple was 'going out' there were certain regulations on what they could or could not do with others, and so on. I thought I should study sociology to understand how such unwritten group norms worked.

## MILITARY SERVICE, UNIVERSITY AND MY PROCESS OF POLITICISATION

I never became a full member of any particular 'salonic society' because I could never internalise or take seriously their unwritten rules and regulations. Nor did I fall in love with any of the boys, although it was the first stage of my sexual experimentation. I hankered after wider and further horizons and read existentialist literature about the 'outsider'. I often hitchhiked to the desert, which I loved, and tried to get into the 'bohemian' circles that used to sit in cafe Kasit.

And then, when I was eighteen and newly graduated from high school, it was time to undertake military service, like the rest of my peer group. I was among fifty girls in one unit at the basic training camp trying to adjust to our new military uniform, learning how to 'square' our bedding so as not to get punished, training to dismember our personal guns whilst blindfolded. What was most insulting to me was that we were not only forced to march and run in straight lines, but that while doing so we were forced to sing!

After a few days, however, I gave in and became part of the organic whole of the group. I sang and even invented new words for the old songs (a talent I never had before or since), I stopped reading, increased my smoking and was looking forward to going on the officers' course for which my sergeant seemed to think I was destined. Since my sister had become an officer ten years earlier I accepted the sergeant's verdict.

While waiting for this course to start, I was sent to work in the office of the Military Governor who gave permits to Israeli Arabs who wanted to travel out of their villages. It was thought to be a wonderful place to work – you didn't even need to wear the army uniforms! However, at the end of my first day in the friendly office, the commander casually asked what I thought of the military government of the Israeli Arabs. Naively I replied (as the good Ayn Randist that I was) that it didn't seem fair to me. I explained that it was clearly a case of collective punishment aimed at every Arab, rather than only at those deemed to cause reasonable suspicion of threat to the security of the state.

The following morning I was casually sent to the field security office and did not emerge from there until after a full month of investigations and on-going attempts to make me accept the necessity of military government. They discovered that I had a communist female friend and a Palestinian boyfriend (whom I had met during one of the Youth for Youth trips), and I discovered that I actually agreed with my off-the-cuff remark about the military government.

So this is when I was moved off the path leading to the officers' course and directed to low-security rank to work as a typist at the army garage. At the garage I came into contact with issues of class, ethnicity and sexual harassment (I was the only one there who actually finished high school, and the majority of the other soldiers – not the officers – were of Mizrakhi, not Ashkenazi origin). I tried to study in the evenings at the university, but my officer, who on some days would send me to the campus with his chauffeur, on other days would stop me from going and force me to clean the glass top of his desk again and again. After a year of this I got completely fed up and applied for alternative civic service for the second year of my military service (an option open to women, but not men, on 'conscientious and religious grounds'). They agreed for me to live and work in a border co-operative farm, Neot Hakikar, in my beloved desert near the Dead Sea. This was in 1961, and I spent a year living in a place which had more dogs and horses than people, with the first generation of hippy volunteers, and undertook hard physical work in the kitchen and the fields. It was during this year that I discovered a shocking fact: that I had more in common with people who were not Israeli or Jewish (I had never met anyone outside these two, largely overlapping, human categories before) than with the people I had grown up with. My feelings of claustrophobia from living in Israel, this small militarized society with absolutely opaque borders, also started to grow.

However, my mother's first bout of ovarian cancer stopped me from joining my hippy friends when my service ended, and the following year I found myself at the Hebrew University in Jerusalem, studying Sociology and Psychology. At first I was disappointed because the sort of people I met on campus were the same ones I had met during high school, from whom I had wanted to escape. But then things started to change. I was part of a small group of students chosen to work as research assistants even though we were still second-year undergraduates. I will never forget the thrill of writing my first interview questions and conducting my first fieldwork. Through working on this research project about the national identity of Israeli Jewish teenagers, and later on the first Israeli sociological study on Israeli Arab teenagers, I met new kinds of Israeli Jewish people. These were Israelis who had not grown up on Labour Zionist housing estates, some of whose parents had not migrated to Palestine/Israel for ideological Zionist reasons, and were trying to promote what we would now call human rights.

My first tentative political involvement with some of these non-Zionist, non-Labour people was within the League Against Religious

Coercion. Only orthodox religious personal laws are recognised as binding for Jews within the state of Israel, and the League was calling for applying instead civil laws. [2]

Then I met Uri Davis, who eventually became my first husband, while he was on hunger strike against the confiscation of the lands of three Palestinian villages in the Galilee in order to build a new Jewish city there (Karmi'el), part of the 'Judaization of the Galilee' programme. His was the first such act of public protest in Israel. I joined that campaign, and also a campaign against the military government (following on from my opposition to the military government of the Palestinians whilst I was in the army), and became a 'political activist'. Uri was given an eight-month jail sentence for going into the confiscated lands, which were officially under military authority. He was the only Israeli Jew (unlike many Israeli Arabs) to be punished for this 'crime'. When he finished this sentence he moved in with me in Jerusalem and some months later we got married. When the military government was lifted in 1966, so that Israeli Palestinians could move freely in the country, and no more Palestinian lands were confiscated, we naively thought that we had 'won'.

Then came the 1967 war.

## THE WAR, MATZPEN AND LEAVING ISRAEL

Uri was then a pacifist and did not serve in the army so we spent the war in Jerusalem, helping to look after frightened children in air shelters, a couple of blocks away from the border with Jordan at the heart of the city. After two days of non-stop military music on the radio, during which we waited for the Jordanian army to step into the shelter at any minute, the news of the scale and speed of the Israeli victory started to filter through. I was called out of the shelter by the research director of the project on adolescent Israeli Arabs. We had just finished the pilot study of the research and did not yet know the major identity changes that were going to take place among the previously isolated (since 1948) Palestinian citizens of Israel. Indeed, one of the sharpest changes we found when we carried out the 'official' research after the war was the sudden re-emergence of the title 'Palestinian', which had hardly been used by the research participants before the war. At the same time we found the almost complete disappearance of the previously popular title 'Israeli' from any self-labelling.[3]

Another facet of our research was to compare the school curricula in Jewish and Arab schools in Israel.[4] The director wanted a couple of us to have a look and analyse the school curricula of schools in Gaza and the West Bank that had just become 'available'. While studying these, I was shocked to learn that the children in Gaza were being taught the infamous fabricated and anti-semitic text *The Protocols of the Elders of Zion* as part of their school curriculum!

When the war was over, it was also shocking to join the human river of Israelis who crossed the border to East Jerusalem. With the exception of the sea front, we had been surrounded by hermetically sealed borders since 1948, so we could not avoid feeling a sense of liberation from actually being able to cross borders. It is fascinating that, from then on, whenever I was travelling to the university, I noticed the walls of Old Jerusalem as if these had become physically nearer after the borders were opened. Except, of course, that they were not 'opened' or 'liberated'; they were conquered and occupied. And very quickly that made all the difference. While most Israelis continued to be drunk on a sense of victory – and one that seemed miraculous to those who were not part of the Israeli political, military and intelligence machine – we were meeting with intellectuals in the West Bank and discussing strategies of non-violent resistance to the occupation. The women were very receptive. The men, at that time, thought that the best way was 'zumud' (holding on) – refraining from any open act of resistance to avoid giving the authorities any cause to uproot people from the territories – so that their continued existence and reproduction in the territories would prevent the Israelis from annexing that area.

During the first local elections after the war, Uri stood as the first candidate on a list called Peace for Jerusalem – which carried the paradoxical message to the annexed Palestinians of East Jerusalem that they should boycott the elections rather than vote for the Peace for Jerusalem list. We used the election campaign to stage symbolic acts of protest, such as leafleting in the centre of West Jerusalem while using a loudspeaker in a car to 'announce' to the local inhabitants that archaeological discoveries important to the Palestinians had been found under the square: therefore the local Israeli inhabitants should evacuate their homes in the same way that the Palestinians who lived near the Wailing Wall had had to do in East Jerusalem shortly after the end of the war. This was the first time I was involved in an action in which the police actually saved our lives from the raging crowds. The second time this would happen to me was at the 1989 WAF demonstration – but this was still many years in the future.

Some of the people who worked with us in the election campaign were members of the Israeli Socialist organisation Matzpen (Compass). And they also then became the subject of my MA dissertation. Matzpen was a small anti-Zionist organisation started by some dissident members of the Communist Party, and at that time it had become the magnet for all those in Israel who were attracted to New Left ideologies, from Trotskyites to anarchists. I was always proud to have predicted their eventual political splits. Nevertheless, in addition to the fascination of becoming engaged in ethnographic fieldwork and meeting some of the most interesting people that I had ever met in Israel, sitting in on their series of seminars also meant that I was exposed to another history of the Zionist project, one which has been completely invisible in the Israeli official and informal discourse. This was not the projection of Zionism as a national liberation movement that saved Jews from anti-semitism and 'rootless' diasporic existence, but the projection of Zionism as a settler colonial project, with devastating effects on the local Palestinian population. This was a historical process that started at the end of the nineteenth century and continued in post-1948 Israel (via the military government and confiscation of lands from Palestinian citizens of Israel), and it was gaining extra momentum through the post-1967 occupied territories.

As Uri and I were finishing our MAs, Uri was invited by the American Jewish Peace Fellowship to give a lecture tour about the conflict, and we both felt it was time to continue our studies abroad and gain a broader global experience. However, I never imagined when I left Israel towards the end of 1969 that, except for shorter or longer visits, I would never go back to live there, and would settle first in the USA and then in London, as a 'permanently temporary' diasporic.

## THE USA AND THE DIFFERENT FACETS OF MY RADICALISATION

Touring the USA and its Jewish communities made me realise that the versions of Jewishness I came across in Israel were only a small selection of the contested varieties. For many American Jews at that time, resisting the war in Vietnam was the right way of being Jewish (which they saw as following the moral code of the biblical prophets). One did not need to choose between only two versions of Jewishness, as in Israel: either being an occupying Israeli or following a racist and sexist ultra-Orthodox version of Jewishness. This is when I decided to look at the many different political and religious movements of radical American Jews that existed between 1967 and 1973 for my PhD dissertation. Through this I became increasingly engaged with the new social movements of the time and became more politically radical. Along the way, I spent one month at a Japanese corporation in Tokyo (learning to use a Japanese method to teach Hebrew to American children in Boston while we were studying for our PhDs), and this made me a socialist. Also in Boston, I underwent two miscarriages and then had a baby with a husband who wanted to save the world (actually, only the Palestinians) but disregarded the people around him. This made me a feminist. I put my foot down when Uri wanted us to move to live among the Palestinian refugees in Lebanon, whom he wanted to lead to the 'promised land'. I thought, firstly, that the Palestinians did not need Uri to lead them – they could do it themselves; and, secondly, that I had not detached myself from the nationalist camp of 'my' side to join another. While in the USA I learned to appreciate living in a pluralist society.

We had been turned down by Brandeis University because of our politics, and Uri had been inspired by radical anthropology while studying at the New School for Social Research in New York. So, while continuing to live in Boston, Uri commuted to New York, while I started a distance learning PhD at the Hebrew University in Jerusalem. After I refused to move to Lebanon, we reached a compromise in moving to London instead – at least half way towards the Middle East – and I joined Uri in London after I had finished the fieldwork for my PhD, towards the end of 1973, with our six-month-old son, Gul. Just one year later I had become a single mother, part-time PhD student at Sussex University, and a sociology lecturer at Thames Polytechnic in London.

## A SOCIALIST FEMINIST SOCIOLOGIST IN LONDON

It took me many years to fully appreciate the cost to me of my second displacement (after leaving the USA) – and even more the cost to my son. I was in London with no family, 'community', or, initially, any close friends. However, politically and intellectually it was an exciting place to be, though in a very different way from living in the USA. I did not find a radical spiritual Jewish community, but I became part of an anti-Zionist Israeli network (many of whom were associated with Matzpen, and which later also included my second husband Alain). As part of its political activities, this group, together with socialists from different Middle Eastern countries, published the journal *Khamsin* (after the desert's hot wind).[5] Together with a couple of others I started to work on the gendered character of the Zionist project.[6]

However, I did not want to be engaged only in exile politics. As I was living in London I thought it was important for me to become engaged in local anti-racist, anti-sexist politics. One important group I became engaged with was WING (Women, Immigration and Nationality Group), with whom I worked on a book that analysed the sexist and racist facets of British immigration and nationality laws.[7] This was an extension of the theoretical and political issues I was studying in relation to Israel, Palestine and Jewishness. Another area of engagement for me was the CSE, which, though it had started life as an annual Conference of Socialist Economists, then expanded to include many other socialist academics, including myself.[8] For a while I also joined the editorial board of their journal, *Capital and Class*. I was also involved in CSE's Sex and Class study group, which is where Floya Anthias (whom I already made friends with as a colleague at Thames Polytechnic) and I really 'discovered' each other and started our long-term academic co-operation.[9] Both of us wanted the group to take on issues of race and ethnicity and not just sex and class, but at that time (the early 1980s), CSE were not interested. When we published our article on 'Contextualizing Feminism: Gender, Ethnic & Class divisions' in 1983, even the editorial collective of *Feminist Review* were not sure what we were talking about.[10] It required the mobilisation of black feminists who edited a special issue of *Feminist Review*, some of whom eventually became permanent members of the editorial collective, to bring racism into the heart of the British feminist agenda.

However, this black feminist agenda was at the same time quite exclusive. Only women of African, Caribbean and South Asian origins were accepted as 'Black' at the Black feminist conference. As non Blacks, Floya and I were rejected as 'bona fide' anti-racist activists. However, this was also when I met Gita and then Pragna from Southall Black Sisters, through which I was exposed to a different kind of anti-racist feminism and found my long-term political allies.

## SBS AND WAF

I first came across Gita at a London meeting of the European Forum of Socialist Feminists – another organisation I was involved in. In complete contrast to the policies of the Black feminist conference, she brought with her an invitation from SBS for all feminists, of whatever racial and ethnic origin, to participate in a forthcoming SBS march through Southall which, inspired by the practices of Indian feminists, would culminate in a demonstration outside the home of a local man whose wife had died as a result of domestic violence. Unlike many other Black feminists at the time, SBS did not assume that if white feminists were involved they would automatically dominate. SBS had the confidence to lead a wide solidarity movement. A few years later, this political strategy led them to invite us all to join in founding Women Against Fundamentalism at the height of the anti-Rushdie campaign.[11] It was this political strategy (that I have talked about elsewhere as 'transversal politics') which has been so important to my political activism since the 1990s.[12]

In WAF we were what some of us eventually theorised as 'intersectional' anti-racist, anti-fundamentalist feminists from different ethnic, national and religious origins, rebelling against our own communities as well as hegemonic and state discourses and policies in law, education and other arenas of public life. It was through WAF that I also got to know and work with similar feminists in other countries such as the networks Women Living Under Muslim Laws and Catholics for Free Choice. Over the years I was able to co-operate with many of these women and other global feminist activists in various NGO forums at United Nations conferences, within international women's initiatives such as AWID, and in an international women's delegations to investigate the gendered violence against Muslims in the Gujarat.[13]

WAF was so important to me as a space for discussing and analysing what was happening both in the UK and globally, that when WAF had its 'remission' periods I organised a series of monthly meetings in my home, where around the kitchen table (and the vegetarian soup that I challenged myself to cook differently each month) we could continue our discussions. Currently, it is through the Centre for Research on Migration, Refugees and Belonging (CMRB), which I direct at the University of East London, that I co-organise (with the Gender Studies Centre at SOAS) a series of symposia on related issues.[14] I see these symposia as a continuation of my WAF activism.

Yet the political agenda of WAF has always only been partial for me. I was in a minority position in WAF because its political agenda was never extended, as I would have liked, to include ethnic, racial and national fundamentalisms. Given my political formation as a political activist around the Middle East conflict, I felt that limiting the political agenda to only religious fundamentalism could only reflect part of the picture. For years I worked (and taught) on the intersectional interface of gender and citizenship, ethnicity, nationalism and racism as well as fundamentalism. In my most recent book, I integrated all of this into a theoretical framework of the intersectional politics of belonging.[15] However, a theoretical integration, complex as it is, is easier than a successful political intervention in practice. With the growing local, regional and global crises of neoliberal governability and governmentality, the need for an integration of these strands is greater than ever. The danger of being overwhelmed by it all and sinking into political paralysis is also much greater. I ache over the failure of WAF to make more effective interventions during a time when the need is so great, and over the bitter political arguments that eventually brought the activities of WAF to a halt. This book reflects my personal and political desire to appreciate the importance of WAF-like politics, but also the need to better understand its limitations.

These days I'm involved in a research project about borders and bordering – as forms of boundaries of belonging and obstacles for bridging solidarities, but hopefully also as providing the context for their transgression – and transformation.[16] One tries not to leave behind the politics of hope.

## NOTES

1. See blog post S. Lacy, 'The relationship of the crystal quilt to silver action' (2013):www.tate.org.uk/context-comment/blogs/suzanne-lacy-silver-action-performance-recreation.
2. N. Yuval-Davis, 'The Bearers of the Collective: Women and Religious Legislation in Israel', in *Feminist Review*, No 4, 1980. For current state of affairs see N. Yuval-Davis, 'Symptoms of Crisis? Religion and women's rights in Israel' (2012), published by *Open Democracy*: www.opendemocracy.net/5050/nira-yuval-davis/symptoms-of-crisis-religion-and-women%E2%80%99s-rights-in-israel.
3. N. Yuval-Davis and Y. Peres, 'Some Observations on the National Identity of the Israeli Arabs', *Human Relations*, Vol 12, No 3, 1969.

4. N. Yuval Davis, Y. Peres and A. Eherlich, 'National Education for the Arab Youth in Israel: a Comparative Analysis of Curricula', in *The Jewish Journal of Sociology,* Vol 12, No 2, 1969.
5. https://libcom.org/library/khamsin-journal-revolutionary-socialists-middle-east.
6. See N. Yuval-Davis and D. Hecht, 'Ideology without Revolution: Jewish Women in Israel', in *Khamsin*, 6, 1978, pp.97-117; and Yuval-Davis, N. 'The Jewish Collectivity and National Reproduction in Israel' in *Khamsin,* Autumn, 1986.
7. WING, *Worlds Apart: Women Under Immigration and Nationality Laws in Britain,* Pluto Press, London 1985.
8. http://www.cseweb.org.uk/.
9. For example, we co-edited *Woman – Nation – State*, Macmillan, London 1989; and we co-authored *Racialised Boundaries: Race, Nation, Gender, Colour and Class and the Anti-Racist Struggle*, Routledge, London 1992.
10. With F. Anthias, 'Contextualizing Feminism: Gender, Ethnic & Class divisions', in *Feminist Review*, No 15, November 1983.
11. See G. Sahgal, and N. Yuval-Davis (eds), *Refusing Holy Orders: Women and Fundamentalism in Britain*. Virago Press, London 1992.
12. For example see the last chapter of N. Yuval-Davis, *Gender and Nation*, Sage Publications, London 1997; and 'Human/Women's rights and feminist transversal politics', in Myra Marx Ferree and Aili Mari Tripp (eds), *Transnational Feminisms: Women's Global Activism and Human Rights*, New York University Press, New York 2006.
13. See the report by International Initiative for Justice, *Threatened Existence: A Feminist Analysis of the Genocide in Gujarat*, IIJ, Delhi, December 2003: www.onlinevolunteers.org/gujarat/reports/iijg/2003/.
14. www.uel.ac.uk/cmrb/.
15. N. Yuval-Davis, *The Politics of Belonging: Intersectional Contestations*, Sage, London 2011.
16. http://www.uel.ac.uk/cmrb/borderscapes/; http://www.euborderscapes.eu/.

# 7. My life as an activist

*Hannana Siddiqui*

I was a co-founder of Women Against Fundamentalism in 1989. Although in recent years I have been less active due to other work commitments, I still believe that the role of WAF in fighting the rise of religious fundamentalisms is as crucial and urgent as ever.

## EARLY LIFE

I was born in Pakistan in 1962 and came to the UK when I was about five years old. My parents came to the UK because they wanted us to have a better life and a good education. I have four brothers and one sister, all of whom were born in Pakistan, with the exception of my younger brother.

My father came first, in the 1960s, to look for work. In Pakistan my father was a teacher. He liked writing and said that he had translated some James Bond books into Urdu. He also read books on philosophy and poetry. So I suppose he was from a lower middle class background. However, he did not have the qualifications required for teaching in the UK, so he worked on the buses and trains, whatever job he could get. He believed in Islam but he was not a strict practising Muslim. My mother was a housewife and looked after the children. She also believed in Islam, but did not practice everything. She wore traditional Punjabi dress, not the hijab.

Initially we lived in Oxford, but about a year later we moved to Middlesbrough, where my father had obtained a job in a steel factory. It was a totally different kind of environment in the North East. At primary school in Oxford I had not spoken English well, but had picked it up fast. By the time I moved to Middlesbrough I could speak English – but I could not understand the local accent.

In the Indian subcontinent, the British education system was regarded as the best in the world, but my own experiences were somewhat mixed.

I had a co-ed comprehensive school education, largely in Middlesbrough. There were not many ethnic minorities in the school at that time and I was conscious of the difference. There was a lot of blatant racism, at school and outside. White people would call us 'Pakis', and sometimes they were quite aggressive. We could not walk down the street without offensive words being used against us. Racism was direct and real. People would throw stones or abuse. I also remember that I had to pass an all-white Roman Catholic primary school every day on my way to high school, and the children would shout racist abuse at me. On one occasion, a white boy in my school harassed me after I suggested that Jesus must have been dark-skinned as he lived in the Middle East. I did and did not enjoy school. I was academic minded, but never felt that I learned enough. The school did not have any ambition for its pupils to go to university, certainly not the best universities. My father was also unhappy with the school. He would often complain, and once even wrote a letter to the papers to criticise changes to the science curriculum.

## POLITICAL CONSCIOUSNESS

My feminist consciousness developed early, although I did not use the word at the time. My father wanted his children to conform to certain traditions. For example he wanted us to read the Koran – but he did not force us when we refused. And we all had to go home for lunch, so that we would eat halal meat – although this did break down later on when we went to sixth form. He also expected me, as a girl, to cover myself and wear 'modest' clothing, and, although I was allowed to wear Western dress, I had to cover my legs. I was not allowed to wear a skirt, unlike my younger sister, who was treated as a child. I was regarded as an adult and had to set the example. I was also not allowed to cut my hair or look pretty in any way, as this might corrupt me. My parents were anxious that I would go wild and have boyfriends, and bring shame and dishonour on the family. My friends were mainly white, and they had more freedoms to go out than I did.

My father was the patriarch. My mother was also traditional, but not as strict. I never questioned the power relations between my parents because I had never personally witnessed any abusive behaviour. However, I had heard that my father had been abusive towards my mother in Pakistan, and that she had even left him for a while as a result. The abuse stopped when I was born. Although my father once slapped me when I said I wanted to be an actress, a profession he regarded as 'morally loose', I witnessed no physical violence.

All of my siblings were expected to conform to some extent, but the boys had more freedoms. Unlike them, I was not allowed to go on school trips. When I questioned this, I was told that was just the way it was. There was also pressure to marry. My eldest brother had a white girlfriend, and that caused arguments. He refused to have an arranged marriage. He eventually left home to go to Leeds Polytechnic. He did not come back and eventually found work in London. My second oldest brother had an arranged marriage to an Asian woman. By then my father had become an electronic engineer and worked at Comet, and my second oldest brother set up a shop selling electronic equipment with my father's help.

But although some Asian families did not want to send their daughters into higher education, my father wanted me to go to university, even if it meant going to London In fact, when I went to university – to the LSE – I had decided to go to London partly to get away from home. My sister and two younger brothers were at home, looking for work or studying, when I left. Then my father suddenly died when I was about nineteen or twenty, and over a period of time my mother and brothers moved to London, while my sister found a job working in a homeless shelter in Leicester. My mother, who was still looking after my younger brother, was on benefits. Later, when he grew up, she stayed on benefits for medical reasons.

In the early 1980s, at sixth form, I was involved in a little anti-racist and anti-fascist work against the National Front. Generally, however, at this stage, I was not politically active. However, in my personal life I was rebellious. I refused to have an arranged marriage. When my father died this pressure disappeared, and after university I did not return home. At university, in about 1983/4, I was involved in feminist campaigning to demand a woman's room, and I also became a member of the Labour Club. I joined the Labour Party itself after leaving university. I saw myself as a socialist, and believed that in this way multiple inequalities could be addressed, including those based on race, gender and social class.

## AFTER UNIVERSITY

After completing my degree, I wanted to get into work. I wanted to be active and get things done. I was living with my partner who I had met at university. He is white. We have now been together for thirty years. My mother wanted me to marry an Asian man, preferably a Pakistani Muslim, but when I failed to do that she wanted me to marry my partner. When I failed to do that, she eventually gave up. My partner's mother was a single parent and a seaside landlady. People from all over the world would lodge with her. She was happy about the relationship and did not expect us to marry.

My partner and I shared a politics which saw marriage as a traditional institution, oppressive to women. We thought we could be happy co-habiting. We are to marry now, however, partly because of financial reasons and the right to make medical decisions as the official 'next of kin'. Also, we have mellowed in our politics. Marriage is fine as long as it is based on equality. Marriage now feels like an expression of commitment and love. We did not have children – not by choice, it just did not happen. I was lucky to lead the life I did as it was based on choice. My partner was not threatened by my feminism. I think he found it politically exciting. He works for a trade union now. We were both active in the Labour Party, but we left when we became disillusioned with New Labour. He became more active in the trade unions, while I got more involved in black feminism.

I graduated in 1984 and started to work at a homeless charity, Housing Advice Switchboard, where I first met Gita Sahgal. When I arrived there, many of the black workers were accusing the white workers of racism. As a socialist I did not agree with the way in which they were applying rigid boundaries that did not acknowledge other forms of oppression. It was the identity politics of the 1980s that created a hierarchy of oppression, and dictated that black women were at the bottom. But if you were a middle-class black woman you might be better off than a working-class white man. Life was complicated, and being from a particular race or gender does not make you the most oppressed in comparison to someone less well off. Gita and I were allies. We shared a similar perspective and opposed the black workers, particularly as they victimised some of the workers, both white and non-white. A group of us eventually resigned at the same time. That job lasted only six months, but it was radicalising. I felt my sense of politics was not as crude as the anti-racist politics of the time. There were also other things at play, such as personalities and power games – which used the 'race card' to silence opposition.

After about six months of unemployment, I got a job as a Race

Relations Officer at Lambeth council. My role was to investigate allegations of racial harassment on council estates. Even though Herman Ouseley was leader of Lambeth Council at the time, I felt we were not dealing with issues such as institutional racism. And we were certainly not allowed to be involved in making policy. We were not even allowed to produce any publicity material to tell council tenants that we existed, so that they would know who to complain to about racism. It was seen to be a sensitive issue. Having race relations officers was controversial because some people did not want the council to be seen to have a problem with racism, while others thought it was just being 'politically correct' and wasting money. Also, there was a lot of power politics involved.

In 1986, I got a job at the Asian Women's Network, which was an umbrella body for Asian women's groups. I really wanted to work with black women, which is why I applied for a job there. I became the co-ordinator of a team of four. The network was funded by the Greater London Grant Scheme (GLGS), now called London Councils, but it only survived for one year due to funding cuts. It was during my time there that I started to work with Southall Black Sisters, through supporting their campaigns.

## SOUTHALL BLACK SISTERS

I started working for SBS as a youth worker in September 1987. This involved working with young women, in support groups, and with advice and casework. Pragna Patel was a worker at SBS and Gita Sahgal was on the management committee. Meena Patel had joined a few months earlier. Rahila Gupta also joined the management committee shortly afterwards, and Shakila Maan and Muneeza Inam were involved in the wider group membership.

By 2000 I had become a joint co-ordinator with Meena, and this meant undertaking management, casework and campaigning. Pragna became pregnant and decided to leave SBS to study law, but in 2009, when we restructured SBS, she returned as Director. By then, I wanted to go part-time and to study, so I decided not to become a Co-Director, a position that was offered to me. As Meena and I have both worked full-time at SBS for twenty-five years we became senior management. I am now head of policy, research and fund-raising. Since SBS is a small organisation, at times with only two or three workers, we were often pushed to our limits. However, it has also been rewarding because not only do we help women with their individual problems, we also create social change. SBS is a political organisation – and more radical than many others. So I feel lucky that I have been able to be an activist at work. It has made my job exciting, but it has also meant hard work with long hours. One of the earliest campaigns by SBS on religion took place in 1991, when we prevented the establishment of separate Sikh schools in Southall, on the grounds that they bred communalism and indoctrinated girls.[1]

## WOMEN AGAINST FUNDAMENTALISM

SBS usually organised activities for International Women's Day, and in 1989 the women's section of the Southall Labour Party approached us to hold a joint event. Gita suggested it should be on religious fundamentalism. Although hesitant, the women's section agreed to the subject matter. The meeting was entitled 'The Resurgence of Religion? What Price do Women Pay?' And we also issued a statement in support of Salman Rushdie, who was attracting worldwide criticism from Muslim fundamentalists who wanted to ban *The Satanic Verses*. Following this meeting, WAF was formed – something which seemed to occur naturally and organically. It attracted SBS members and women from wider networks, from different racial and religious backgrounds. This was when I met many similar minded women, including Clara Connolly, Nira Yuval-Davis, Cynthia Cockburn, Estella Schmidt, Anne Rossiter and Julia Bard. Sukhwant Dhaliwal also worked for WAF at one time, before she came to SBS as a youth worker. I remember having several meetings, often on Saturdays, where we thrashed out our aims and objectives. We agreed the overarching aim of tackling all religious fundamentalisms, with a particular focus on women's rights; and we defined religious fundamentalism as the strict interpretation of religion for political ends, which does not allow for doubt or dissent. We called for secularism as a means to protect the rights of believers and non-believers alike, which meant disestablishing the church and having a truly secular state and secular spaces. Like SBS, WAF recognised the concept of multiple and later intersectional discrimination, and had a critique of multiculturalism.

The Rushdie Affair in 1989 became both a symbol and a catalyst for growing religious fundamentalism and stronger orthodox religious identities in the UK and across the world. SBS and WAF sensed this change both within our work, but also in our lives. I noticed that for some time prior to this, some of my brothers were turning increasingly to religion, going to mosques, for example, or upholding conservative traditions by accepting or even wanting arranged marriages. There was more tension between them and myself and my sister when we challenged their views on religion and marriage, although now, with age and experience, both sides have mellowed – particularly as we have seen both arranged and love marriages flounder or survive, and have developed either a more spiritual, agnostic or atheist outlook on life.

For decades, SBS were accused of 'washing our dirty linen in public' and undermining the anti-racist struggle because of our campaigns against domestic violence within Asian communities. To counter this, we supported white feminist campaigns against domestic violence in the wider society: SBS did not want to concentrate on just Islam and Asian communities. We made alliances in WAF in order to acknowledge our common experiences of the patriarchal use of religion to oppress and control women, and also to counter accusations that we were fuelling Islamophobia. We were also critical of 'hierarchy of oppression' approaches, which placed the rights of minorities above gender. We demanded that we must fight racism and sexism simultaneously, and for secularism, to guarantee human rights for all.

The defining moment for WAF was the 1989 counter-demonstration we held against Muslim fundamentalists who organised an anti-Rushdie demonstration in London: we clashed at Parliament Square. The anti-racist and anti-fascist groups supported the Muslims, and some in the BNP – who believed in the right to separate development – also supported them, while other BNP members attacked them. Meanwhile women from WAF were physically and verbally assaulted by both fascists and fundamentalists. We shouted slogans like 'religious leaders do not speak for us!' and the SBS strapline, later also used by WAF, 'struggle not submission!' Ironically, the police, whom we have often accused of sexism and racism, protected us on that day.

## MATURE MULTICULTURALISM

Before the late 1990s, conservative community and religious leaders argued that 'cultural sensitivity' required that there should be no state interference in their communities, in order to promote good race relations. Under multiculturalism, the community was self-policing when it came to addressing problems such as domestic violence and forced marriage. SBS wanted more state intervention – it was the only way of protecting and empowering women. But this 'hands-off' approach by the state did not change until New Labour came to power in 1997. The then junior Home Office Minister, Mike O'Brien, was an advocate of 'mature multiculturalism'. In an unprecedented debate on forced marriage, he argued that 'multicultural sensitivity is not an excuse for moral blindness';[2] and he set up the Home Office Working Group on Forced Marriage. For the first time in British history, government was being critical of cultural relativism. The momentum for this change had come from a number of sources, including decades of campaigning by the BME women's movement and SBS's critique of multiculturalism.

The joint Chairs of the Home Office Working Group, Baroness Uddin and Lord Ahmed, had strong religious, Muslim identities, and worked closely with Muslim groups. I was also selected to be a member of the Working Group, partly because of my Muslim background, and it appeared that others were also there to represent different faith groups, including a Muslim women's organisation. When I challenged Mike O'Brien he denied this, and stated that members were chosen because of their expertise – although many of these groups or individuals had no track record of tackling forced marriage. The initial approach of the Working Group was to go to mosques and temples with the aim of working with religious leaders to educate the community – rather than be seen as being heavy-handed. I argued that the state had a responsibility, and we had to reform social policy and practice in order to address forced marriage, which meant exposing the community 'warts and all'. However, members of the Working Group advocated mediation as a solution to the problem. I disagreed with mediation as a dangerous practice, because it placed women under pressure to reconcile to abusive situations at home without challenging the abuse itself. I felt I no option but to resign from the Working Group. However, before I did this, I managed to get into the Working Group report the recognition that forced marriage was an abuse of human rights, and the need for the state to act. This was the first time government had recognised harmful practices as an abuse of human rights, and their own responsibility to address the needs of BME women. And I also successfully opposed the recognition of mediation, and later religious arbitration, as an example of best practice in the government's forced marriage guidelines for professional agencies.

After 9/11, multiculturalism was accused of fostering segregation and terrorism. Social cohesion was promoted as the main way of engaging with minority communities, and tackling Muslim extremism. Although dressed up as integration, social cohesion was mainly about assimilation, demanding that minorities adopt core 'British' values. It blamed minorities, particularly migrants, for terrorism, asserting that they were holding onto or importing 'barbaric' value systems, including traditional practices like forced marriage, and aimed to 'resolve' these problems through more immigration controls. SBS resisted the use of racist immigration laws, ironically justified in the name of minority women's rights.[3]

## RELIGIOUS ARBITRATION

In 2008 alarm bells rang when the Muslim Arbitration Tribunal (MAT) stated publically that they are resolving problems of forced marriage and domestic violence through making rulings that are enforceable through the Arbitration Act 1996.[4] This was confirmation of a long-held belief that parallel legal systems were being used within minority communities, and that they were extending beyond their practice of granting religious divorce to rule on other issues, where the 'solution' was to mediate and reconcile women back into abusive situations at home. While some women do want the Sharia courts to pronounce religious divorces, they often prefer to use informal mediation by family and community elders to resolve other family problems, and they also may eventually need to turn to the state for protection from abuse.

The MAT announcement indicated a growing confidence on the part of religious groups in their enforcement of their rulings on abuse within the family, bolstered up by feeling themselves to be supported, or accommodated, by the state. I have heard of cases where the courts are refusing to rule on forced marriage cases involving victims with learning disabilities without hearing from abusive fathers who claim Sharia law as giving them decision-making powers over their children. In one case, I had to give expert evidence where a father invoked religious laws to claim right of custody over his daughter, whom he intended to force into marriage when older. While this problem has been evident for some time, these cases show how religious groups were gaining ground with the state. On one occasion I asked the Association of Chief Police Officers if there was any truth in MAT's statement that they had managed to discontinue criminal proceedings in some cases. In response the police said that they had found no evidence to support the claim. However, one police officer told me that the police are turning a blind eye to the problem. I also raised this issue with Home Office officials. They stated that the government did not support religious arbitration in these types of cases. However, I recently heard that Home Secretary Theresa May had organised meetings with groups – to which we were not invited – to discuss religious divorce, which again raised alarm bells. What role does a secular government have in pronouncing religious divorce, or even in ensuring the procedures are 'fair' to women?

In 2012, Baroness Cox introduced a private members bill to prevent the Arbitration Act from being used by religious courts to uphold their rulings. But although SBS supported reform of the Act, we did not agree with the legal content of Baroness Cox's bill, or with the Christian Right sentiment of the politicians involved. The bill was not supported by the government, which has been careful to be critical of Muslim extremism, but not of multi-faithism – even though this contradicts their assimilationist policies on culture and 'race'.

While religious tribunals are one way in which communities are seeking to exert increased control over women, another is the growth of organised networks of 'bounty hunters', who track down women trying to escape from abuse or forced marriage. In the 1990s, SBS supported Asian women in Huddersfield in their fight against these bounty hunters. However, few BME women's groups feel confident or safe in speaking out, particularly where women face growing vigilante action on the streets by young men, as witnessed in Tower Hamlets in 2013.

## WOMEN'S GROUPS

In 2006, New Labour set up the Muslim Women's Advisory Group. Soon afterwards I was asked by the Women's National Commission (WNC) if I would support the Advisory Group and contribute to a report (entitled *She who Disputes*) they were writing on Muslim women with the Muslim Women's Network. I refused to do so because I did not identify in religious terms, and I did not see the need for such a group. WNC had not thought about the political implications of making demands for women's rights determined by their religion rather than their race or ethnicity. Although Islamophobia or anti-Muslim racism is a problem, they did not recognise the commonality of experience of minority women which cuts across religion, such as domestic violence, forced marriage, honour-based violence and racism. I also wanted to ensure that the demands we make for minority women's rights are not compromised by conservative interpretations of religious belief. I wanted to use the secular framework to prevent those with more power and control from imposing their particular religious doctrine or interpretation on black feminist demands. For example, I was concerned to hear that faith-based women's organisations advised mediation and reconciliation as a solution to violence against minority women.

Some white feminists and people from minority groups working on violence against women and girls (or VAWG) do not understand SBS's rejection of religious fundamentalism. It is something they have only started to deal with recently – as in 2011, when they were concerned at the takeover of the government's tender of services for trafficked women – previously run by the feminist group Eaves (called the Poppy Project) – by the Salvation Army. This shocked the VAWG sector. Unlike WAF, these feminists had not until now realised the full implications of the impact of religion on minority women. (This was in spite of the SBS legal victory against Ealing Council in 2008, when the Council had attempted to cut its funding for specialist services for minority women: issues of religion in the social cohesion agenda were raised, but not fully appreciated by the sector.) SBS does not receive the support it needs when tackling faith-based mobilisations at VAWG sector meetings and forums. When SBS argue with faith groups, other groups keep quiet. Some agree with us silently, but not openly: the fear of being labelled as anti-Muslim and racist silences criticism. I particularly noticed this during the debates on Muslim Asian men's sexual exploitation of white women in Rochdale.[5]

It is also difficult to get the government to acknowledge the impact of religious fundamentalisms on women. I have raised it at Home Office working groups, but there is a failure to engage with it unless it is about Muslim extremism or in other countries. I have also raised it with the Opposition, such as with Vera Baird, Chair of the Labour

Party Women's Safety Commission, but the issue was not discussed in their final report. Religious sensitivity now prevents state action to tackle VAWG. Which begs the question of whether we should now be talking about 'mature multi-faithism'?

## KEEPING OUR LEGACY ALIVE

I do not feel burnt-out because, although it is hard and difficult work with many obstacles, particularly in the current recession, there are also many rewards. Successes in casework and reform in policy and practices, such as the introduction of the domestic violence immigration rule and destitution domestic violence concession, on which I have worked consistently for twenty years at SBS and as Chair of the Campaign to Abolish No Recourse to Public Funds, are rewarding.[6] We are helping to save and transform lives. The London 2012 Olympic slogan was about inspiring a generation through sport. I think we have been inspiring a generation of black feminists. There appears to be a fourth wave or revival of feminism taking place at the moment, with the young becoming more active, supported by older feminists, although many are still not organising against religious fundamentalism. It is a life-time struggle.

What is of concern is the move towards stronger conservative religious identities, particularly amongst young men, but also young women. Even some Muslim feminists put on the veil when we struggled for so long to take it off.[7] I understand the need for spirituality and a sense of belonging. I am no longer an atheist, as I was in my more rebellious youth. People do change and grow. I also understand the need to express religious belief, but there has to be genuine free choice. Women do not always have free choice when religion is imposed upon them. We forget that the pressures can be rooted in social and cultural conditioning within patriarchal structures, where powerful community and religious leaders impose their interpretations on others. Sometimes a strong religious identity is a political statement rather than a personal belief – a statement against racism and deprivation, and a reclaiming of identity. It is also important to think about symbolism, however, and the veil, for example, is a historical symbol of female oppression. I think when Muslim feminists adopt the veil they are letting other women down. I do not agree with the French position where the veil is not allowed in public at all – that is too extreme. But what does the veil represent? It cannot be just about piety, as it has a much wider social and political meaning in society. It is funny now how veils have also become a fashion statement, when you see a design and colours. I even saw one woman wearing a hijab with a union jack on it during the London 2012 Olympics. This seemed to me to be a contradiction in terms, but it does also represent a dual identity, of being British and Muslim.

When I receive letters, calls and emails telling me that I have let down the Muslim sisterhood, I ask the senders, in response, what they are doing for Muslim and other women who face sexual oppression. Are they not letting them down by assuming we all have free choice in determining our identity, beliefs and lifestyles? Our actions have a reaction – they can liberate or oppress women. As a child I was not allowed to express myself, in case it set a bad example to my sister. As rebellious women, the legacy of SBS and WAF is to set an example, so that women can be inspired to act and gain their freedom from oppression.

## NOTES

1. See S. Dhaliwal, 'Orange is not the only colour: young women, religious identity and the Sikh community' in R. Gupta (ed), *From Homebreakers to Jailbreakers*, Zed Books, London 2003.
2. *Hansard*, 10 February 1999, *House of Commons Adjournment Debate on Human Rights (Women).*
3. See H. Siddiqui, '"It was written in her kismet": Forced Marriage', in R. Gupta, op cit; see also H. Siddiqui, '"True Honour": domestic violence, forced marriage and honour crimes in the UK', in Y. Rehman, L. Kelly and H. Siddiqui (eds), *Moving in the Shadows*, Ashgate, London 2013.
4. A. Taher, *Revealed: UK's First Official Sharia Courts*, 14.9.08. Times Online: www.timesonline.co.uk/tol/news/uk/crime/article4749183.ece.
5. See www.telegraph.co.uk/news/uknews/crime/9570189/Jack-Straw-Pakistani-community-must-face-up-to-grooming-scandal-following-Rochdale-case.html.
6. See H. Siddiqui, 'Ending the Stark Choice: domestic violence or deportation and destitution?' in *Safe*, Women's Aid magazine, forthcoming.
7. See H. Siddiqui, 'Letter to Christendom', *Feminist Review*, No 37, 1991.

# 8. Learning to question

*Julia Bard*

I was born in 1950 in London. My parents were children of immigrants from Russia and our family home was traditionally Jewish – observant but not very orthodox. My mother came from a big family who were all very close. My father's family was smaller but much more religious.

Every Friday night we had candles and prayers, but my parents were completely opposed to Jewish schools. They didn't think Jewish people should be segregated from everyone else. They would also travel by car on a Saturday – but not if any of the community were watching. My sister and I accused them of hypocrisy, and that was a source of a lot of rows in our family.

My father had been in the army during the war, and was away in North Africa and Italy for five years. Looking back on it, I can see that he was in a pretty bad psychological state during my early childhood, but this wasn't talked about at all. He was already thirty by the time he volunteered to join the army in 1939, and had just established his solicitor's practice. I think the army was a horrendous experience for him, and when he came back he had to start his career from scratch, at the age of thirty-six. Establishing himself was important, because his own background had been very insecure, financially.

My mother qualified as a dentist, which was unusual for women then, and she had worked as a school dentist during the war. But my sister was born very prematurely in 1945, and they were frightened that she wouldn't survive, and after that Mum never worked again. We thought this was terrible, and tried to persuade her to go back to work.

My father had been a Labour councillor during the 1930s in Hackney. He was right-wing in some ways but left-wing in others, and very class conscious. He was very aware of his working-class roots and never voted Tory. My mother's family was strongly Zionist but also left of centre. Politics was discussed constantly in our house. Discussed is a polite word for it – we shouted and screamed. My older sister would run out of the room and slam doors, leaving me facing two furious parents. I used to get very upset. I learnt a lot about the boundaries between permitted and forbidden arguments, and how power is used to silence uncongenial ideas – a lesson that I think a lot of younger siblings internalise early on in life.

The 1950s were very conformist times. There were massive changes: the welfare state had come into being and, having come through the war, people wanted to settle down and have everything in its place. But children don't allow you to have everything in its place. Our battles were a mixture of political disagreements and resistance to the pressure to conform, which I think came partly from our parents being the first generation to be born in this country. We were expected to conform to some idea of Englishness but without abandoning our Jewishness – to be respectable, not to stand out, and to be economically secure but not ostentatious.

## ESCAPE FROM RESPECTABILITY

The most formative influence for me in my teens was *Habonim*, a socialist Zionist youth movement.[1] I went on my first *Habonim* camp when I was eleven, and enjoyed the relaxed, non-conformist atmosphere, where what you did mattered more than how you appeared, and where girls were taken as seriously as boys.

That was where I learnt my socialism. Some people came from quite wealthy backgrounds but most didn't, and a lot were from poor, working-class homes. That mixture was very significant, and so was the socialism. When we went to camp everybody shared their money. Some people really objected to that. They'd say: 'I've brought £5. I'm not putting in £5 when somebody else only puts in £1!' We had to argue that out, justify and explain it, and deal with ideas about co-operation and egalitarianism. The fact that it was mixed sex was also very important to me because my secondary school, which I hated, was a girls' school. So *Habonim* was my social home and my spiritual home, and it also gave me the beginnings of a political education.

At that time Zionism gave me the confidence to be Jewish in a way that wasn't that awful smothering, conformist, bid for respectability

– to look English in the English world and keep your Jewishness private. The main aim of the movement was to go to Israel and live on a kibbutz. I thought that an agrarian life in a community where everybody was equal was a good thing (and, in principle, I still think that). We spent our holidays in Israel, and I spent time on different kibbutzim. To me, as a teenager in the 1960s, it felt really free.

I first started to part company with *Habonim* when I got interested in Yiddish music, and a friend gave the family some Yiddish records. My parents spoke Yiddish but I didn't. My father used to sing Yiddish songs, and I felt really at home with this music and I explored it and learnt about it. I borrowed an accordion from *Habonim* and brought it home and learnt all these songs – but I kept it hidden. The diaspora and its languages, particularly Yiddish, the language of European Jews, were seen as backward and negative in Zionist circles. We were taught that diaspora was exile and inevitably led to the Holocaust. The picture we were presented with of diaspora Jews was that they had gone like sheep to the slaughter and nobody fought back. I only learnt the real history – of resistance, courage and common cause with non-Jewish antifascists – much later on.

## DIASPORA DYNAMICS

I didn't know anything about the Holocaust until I was ten or eleven. My parents didn't tell me anything about it. Then a friend lent me a fictional account of a concentration camp. I was devastated. The bottom dropped out of my world. But I didn't recognise at the time how close it was – it was in about 1961 and so was very recent history. The Holocaust was talked about quite a lot in *Habonim* but mostly in terms of exceptional heroics – the Warsaw Ghetto Uprising and getting out through the sewers, and, of course, salvation in 'our own country'.

My parents were ambitious for me and sent me to a school that was very pressurised. I started to drown in it almost immediately and was very unhappy. I felt out of my depth in terms of my social class. I was very aware of that. I felt enmeshed in all these hidden, unspoken social rules – which I couldn't ask about because I would be seen as stupid, and which I couldn't figure out because everyone else had been brought up in a different world from me.

About a third of the students were Jewish, but I discovered later on that the school had a quota and wouldn't admit more than a certain number of Jews. I was really appalled when I realised that because I couldn't imagine sending my own children into any institution that had a racist admissions policy. But I think lots of organisations had quotas then and maybe people just accepted it.

About half of the Jewish girls came from a different class background from me. There was some anti-semitism, though not so much from the girls as from a few of the teachers; and I wasn't aware of racism against the black girls. I think class trumped ethnicity. If you were an upper-class Indian girl headed for medical school you were okay. And if you were from a bourgeois German Jewish background you were fine. But if you were *ostjuden* (Jews from Russia or Poland) like us, you weren't. I remember one of the more anglicised Jewish girls referring to families like mine as 'fried fish Jews', because we ate Jewish food rather than English food. But I think the white working-class non-Jewish students also felt like outsiders.

Being marginalised on the combined basis of class and ethnicity undermined me considerably. I'm certain that my English teacher was an anti-semite, and so was the German teacher – we used to share lurid stories about her supposed Nazi past. Both of them were astonished when I achieved high marks in exams, and nevertheless convinced me that I was hopeless at writing and languages. As a result I ended up studying science, which I was actually much worse at, but which wasn't so culturally loaded against my background.

I dropped out of *Habonim* in my last year of secondary school – 1967-68. During the Six Day War, in June 1967, I had been envious of the people in *Habonim* who volunteered to go to Israel. But I wasn't old enough – fortunately, as it turned out. After the 1967 war, though, I began to question what was happening. Even my parents, who were convinced Zionists, were critical of the expansionism and the attitudes of a lot of Israelis to the Palestinians in the newly occupied territories.

Before the Six Day War we used to go to the top of the YMCA tower in West Jerusalem and look across the no man's land which sliced through the centre of the city, at the soldiers on the Palestinian side, with their guns glinting. When we went in 1967, soon after the Six Day War, we walked over there. A lot of our Israeli friends told us not to go because it was dangerous, and came out with racist rhetoric about 'the Arabs' – which we ignored. We stayed in the YMCA in East Jerusalem, and I think my attitude towards Israel started to change then.

## NEW START, NEW HORIZONS

The following year I went to York University and became involved in wider left-wing politics. I deliberately chose York because there were very few Jewish people there; I consciously avoided applying to Manchester or Leeds or anywhere with a big a Jewish community, where I thought I'd be drawn back into the suburban life I wanted to escape.

York was a new university and quite radical. The anti-Vietnam war campaign was still going on and student vanguardism was growing and being theorised. A little group of us came together because we couldn't stomach joining any of the political organisations that were operating on campus. One of these was IS, the International Socialists (forerunners of the Socialist Workers Party), who were good activists but suffered then from the same thing they suffer from now: the twin affliction of the party line and veneration of leaders. Then there was another Trotskyist group, the Revolutionary Socialist Students Federation (RSSF), which had a more intellectual approach – at least that's what I thought, because I didn't understand half of what they said! There were some Communist Party members and Maoists and various others, but we didn't like any of them much. We did want to educate ourselves, though, so we set up a little group that we called Icepick, and we started to develop a libertarian socialist politics. We read and discussed Marxist literature, and we also engaged in quite outlandish activism, including street theatre, and we wore brightly coloured boiler suits. The more orthodox left groups thought you had to wear your Sunday best if the workers were going to take you seriously.

The one big industry in York was Rowntrees, the sweet factory, which was very paternalistic. Everybody said how much they looked after their workers because they gave them flowers on their wedding day and that kind of thing. And we used to say, 'but look at the wages, look what happens if you want to leave – you can't. There's nowhere else to go.'

We were trying to develop a politics which was Marxist but had a libertarian thread running through it. Second-wave feminism hadn't really arrived yet, but one student at the university used to stand up at union meetings and make feminist demands. We all thought she was right really, but rather extreme. By the time we were out the other end, though, in 1971-72, feminism was growing, and all the women who had been in Icepick became – and still are – feminists.

I also got involved with a group of students who were working with the local Traveller community to challenge the terrible prejudice against Travellers in York. And during my first year, in 1969, we had a big protest against Enoch Powell's visit to York at the invitation of the Conservative Association.

I was always very assertive about being Jewish, but I hadn't sorted out my ideas terribly well about Zionism. I was quite afraid of examining it, because it had been so tied up with my identity. But there was a lot of discussion about Israel and Palestine amongst my political friends.

My first battle with fundamentalism was at Leeds University, where, after graduating from York, I went to train as a biology teacher. It was a great relief to be studying education after being trapped in a biology degree for three years. I had a big battle with a Christian fundamentalist on my course, who didn't believe in evolution and thought he had a right and a duty to teach creationism – to me, as well as to his pupils.

## SAVED BY SECOND-WAVE FEMINISM

After teacher training I worked as a secondary school teacher in Scotland, and then taught at a primary school in London. Then I met my first husband, an Israeli who was working in Zambia. Partly because he was an old friend of my sister's, and partly because my parents were deliriously happy that at last I was going out with someone Jewish, we got married very quickly, and I joined him in Africa.

I taught in a primary school there, too. Most of the pupils were Zambian but there were also expatriate children. I had responsibility for music, and I taught them songs from all over the world. I was the first teacher ever to sing African songs with them. Before that they'd been taught the same awful British songs that we'd learnt when I was at junior school: 'The Oak and the Ash', 'Men of Harlech' – that kind of thing. I can't imagine what they made of them. I used to be very pleased to hear the kids after school, walking down the road singing, in harmony, the Swahili song, *Malaika* (Angel), and the Hebrew song, *Ma Tovu Ohalecha Ya'akov* (How goodly are thy tents, O Jacob).

Apart from the teaching, I was really miserable there. I couldn't stand the racism of the expatriate community I'd landed up in, the privilege of the elite, the abject poverty of most of the Zambians, the corruption. Zambia is a beautiful country. The weather is perfect all year round. It should have been like paradise. But its economy and potential for self-sufficiency were destroyed by colonialism. It was a very politicising experience for me.

Then we went to Israel, which was even more politicising. I loved learning the language. My first teacher spoke beautiful, perfectly grammatical Hebrew, but she was incredibly right-wing, so I learnt fast how to argue back. I went to some meetings of a feminist group in Tel Aviv, which met in a library, so I had access to a lot of feminist literature. I read Marilyn French's *The Women's Room* and Ann Oakley's *Housewife*, which helped me articulate some of the problems I was facing both in my marriage and in Israeli society. We also had some anti-Zionist Argentinian friends, who had landed up in Israel to escape the Junta. They were very critical of the occupation, and that helped me to think straight about the situation. But what I hated most when I was in Israel was the corruption that I encountered in every aspect of Israeli life. Perhaps because I'd been so idealistic about the country as a teenager, that was the thing I really couldn't stand.

We used to agonise in the feminist group about how important it was to meet with Palestinians, but I didn't meet any politically in the two and a half years I lived there. Menachem Begin was elected during this time – it was the first defeat for Labour since the establishment of the state, and a lot of people were very shocked. Then Sadat came from Egypt to talk peace – it was a very exciting time politically, but my personal life was becoming more and more unhappy.

The sexism was much more overt than it was in Britain, and, although there was a sense of freedom in the way people behaved, it was actually very conformist, because people poked their noses into other people's business in a very outspoken way. They'd say, 'Why are you wearing that?' 'Women shouldn't do this!' 'What's your salary?' 'How much did that sofa cost?' Your life is exposed.

When I left my husband, a neighbour warned me to get out of the country quickly because a common tactic was for aggrieved partners to invoke the powers of the Rabbinical Court to stop their spouse from leaving. Luckily I took her advice and caught the first plane the following morning, because that's exactly what my husband tried to do. The Rabbis could have forced me to stay in the country for six months, claiming that they were trying to effect reconciliation. In practice, you have to pay them off in order to escape. That's one of the realities of life in a state where religious institutions have political power.

## CHALLENGING ORTHODOXIES

When I returned to Britain I joined *The Leveller* – a cutting-edge, radical magazine. There were ongoing battles on the editorial collective between the feminists and some of the men – including a massive argument about the Iranian revolution and the impact of the Ayatollahs. *The Leveller* was socialist, feminist, and had quite an anarchist element to it, and was trying to break boundaries on the left. For example we had a whole issue about rape, and how the left does or doesn't address sexual violence, and we raised issues that have proved to be still relevant today.

I was interviewed for the magazine about what it was like to live in Israel as a socialist, a feminist and an anti-Zionist, but there were people on the collective who said that we shouldn't give space to a person who had lived in Israel, whatever their politics. I remember knowing that that bid to stop publication of the interview was motivated by anti-semitism, and I started to discuss some of those fault lines within the left. *The Leveller* survived for two or three years after that, and then I went to work on a women's magazine and trained as a professional journalist.

Coming back to London at the end of the 1970s, I had been appalled to see the *Jewish Chronicle* saying that Jewish people shouldn't get involved in the Anti-Nazi League because it was full of anti-Zionists. In the mid-1980s I discovered people in the Jewish Socialists' Group (JSG) who were actively challenging that injunction. At my first JSG conference there was a discussion about diasporism – the importance of fighting for the validity of your community as a minority wherever you are in the world, and arguing against the centrality of Israel in Jewish life. Even though I wasn't a Zionist, I hadn't quite escaped the centrality of Zionism and Israel. I think a lot of anti-Zionists still see Israel as central – it's like the other side of the Zionist coin. But this was something else; in Yiddish it's called *doikayt* (here-ness): having rights and fighting for them here and now.

The JSG also had a different historical perspective, which demonstrated that, apart from short periods, Jews had survived and at times thrived as a diaspora people. After so many centuries, that 'minorityness' is woven through our culture and way of life, so it was actually the idea that we needed to be a majority in 'our own' country that was an aberration. The Jewish Socialists' Group described itself as non-Zionist rather than anti-Zionist, to indicate that no Jewish community anywhere in the world should prioritise their needs over those of others, or dictate a political agenda. So although Israel/Palestine is an important aspect of the group's politics, this is in the context of a campaign to challenge the supposed Zionist (and religious) consensus among Jews, both in Israel and the diaspora. I felt I'd come to a place where I could explore that politics and relate the Jewish experience to the experiences of other minorities and of the wider society.

I met David in the group in 1984 and we got married the following year. Then I persuaded the group that we needed a magazine – partly because of my experience on *The Leveller*, which had been produced co-operatively. So we started producing *Jewish Socialist*, a magazine that was diasporist, non-Zionist, which explored minority politics but didn't have a party line.

One issue we wrote about in the magazine was circumcision. We did quite a lot of research both into the medical aspects and into the religious imperative to circumcise. We faced the accusation that questioning this ancient custom was anti-semitic, but that accusation is often made in an attempt to silence dissent, and this overlaps with the politics of Women Against Fundamentalism. We insisted that we had the right to explore this issue, which was about an abuse of power, and to argue that children had a right to be advocated for by parents who had access to all the facts.

## FIGHTING OUR CORNER

In the early 1980s I was involved in the Jewish Feminist Group as well as the JSG. I was critical of the people in the group who emphasised Jewish spirituality and focused on the place of women in Jewish law, because I thought this was avoiding more urgent political issues in the community. There was also an unproductive emphasis on identity politics. People would preface their interventions with things like: 'Speaking as a Jewish disabled lesbian …', implicitly casting anyone who disagreed with them as discriminatory, anti-semitic and homophobic. The question of Israel was often at the heart of it, with this tactic being used as a device to create the image of a Zionist consensus.

To break out of our sense of being cornered and silenced by the twin conflicting assumed imperatives that as Jews we had to be Zionist but as feminists we had to be anti-Zionists, a few of us set up the Jewish Feminist Publications Group. We produced a pamphlet that still makes interesting reading called *A Word in Edgeways*, which also reflected debates within the JSG about Zionism, anti-Zionism and anti-semitism. When I came into the group there was a battle going on between people who wanted to focus on 'left-wing anti-semitism' and people who didn't automatically see expressions of anti-Zionism as anti-semitic.

That was all part of my political thinking when I had my first encounter with WAF. I was in a three-woman klezmer band which was invited to play at a very early WAF event in 1989. Somehow, this cultural expression of our diaspora identity as a non-religious, feminist band that was quite pioneering culturally seemed just right for this occasion.

I became involved immediately in WAF, which seemed to dovetail with my Jewish socialist politics – partly because the women in WAF came from such diverse backgrounds, but mainly because of their not seeing minority communities as monolithic and homogeneous. Being with people who were dissident within their communities in such a progressive way, who were uncompromising about their anti-racism and were also demanding and fighting for the right to question religious imperatives seemed to fit very well with the JSG's perspective.

I also felt that WAF was a context in which we could explore a dynamic, progressive, changing notion of identity, and think about the role of religion in all communities – not just minorities. People in the group were very courageous about challenging the Catholic church, for example, or the Sikh or Hindu leadership, in situations where dissent was dangerous. The danger is sometimes physical, sometimes social and sometimes psychological. There was a very strong sense of mutual support among the women. We did have some quite profound disagreements, and I think there were fault lines that we never managed to bridge. In some cases we agreed to live with our differences but there have also been unresolved arguments, and conflicts that have been uncontainable.

For example, we haven't managed to forge a common understanding of the War on Terror and its aftermath. There are some women who think that there's no way the war in Iraq and Afghanistan can be progressive, and others who believe that the West could and should intervene to defend human rights there. I don't think it's an easy question, especially as things are getting worse again in Afghanistan, Libya, Syria ... but I don't think naked, greedy, globalised capitalism is going to protect anybody from anything. And if the West is in Afghanistan, Libya and Syria, the motivation is going to be to do with the arms trade and oil, not with protecting human rights.

One manifestation of that disagreement was for us to be drawn more and more into a focus on Islam and Muslim fundamentalism, whereas I saw the real strength of WAF as its overarching analysis of fundamentalism in all religions. Up until then, we had always been very sensitive to the pressure to focus primarily on Islam, and we hadn't allowed it to happen.

For example, when the *Sunday Times* interviewed a group of us, we repeatedly said that we were talking about Hinduism, Judaism, Christianity, Islam and all other religions, and that we *don't* use 'fundamentalism' as code for Islam, but they still published a piece that was all about Islam (though we did get an apology from the newspaper). But I felt that over the final couple of years of WAF's existence, we were being inexorably drawn into a focus on Islam – partly due to the idiotic antics of elements in the anti-racist movement who are unable to understand that defending Muslims (or anyone else) against racism doesn't commit you to defending oppressive and sometimes murderous fundamentalist ideas. We had the political analysis to broaden the debate, but we didn't have the political organisation to sustain it in the way we had done in the past.

During the time that WAF was flourishing, I felt I could contribute a dissident Jewish perspective. My dissent grew from being in the heart of the Jewish community. I don't consider myself an outsider and I won't be made into one. So, for example, I was critical when Jonathan Sacks became Chief Rabbi, because I knew that he was going to divert the community in a fundamentalist direction – according to WAF's definition of fundamentalism as a modern political force. He was chosen because he was supposed to be an intellectual, a Cambridge graduate, a modern person – and a modern fundamentalist.

At the same time WAF has enabled the JSG to develop a secularist perspective that isn't the same as atheism. It understands the role of religion in people's lives, particularly in minority communities, and the complex, shifting manifestations of cultural identity. And it also understands that communities are diverse and conflicted, and are not represented by religious leaders. WAF enabled the JSG to share experiences and campaign with people from other religious and ethnic groups, and to understand clearly that the political challenges we faced in the Jewish community were not unique, and that we could build relationships and act together with others.

I think that WAF's real problem at the end was that world politics and world economics have shifted, and fundamentalism in WAF's terms has become a less central threat than it was. It continues to threaten life, liberty, justice and equality, but the balance of power has shifted. Previously, capitalism and the military economy had a symbiotic relationship with different manifestations of fundamentalism, including Christian fundamentalism, but as that relationship has crumbled, poor and oppressed people across the world can see that what they are up against is vicious, violent, neoliberal capitalism. Some of them try to challenge this through religious channels, without seeing a contradiction between imposing one set of ideas for another, from above.

Muslim fundamentalists benefited from this in the short term in the Arab Spring, partly because they were experienced and well organised. However, having ridden to power on the back of a massive popular demand for democracy, their own anti-democratic politics not only weakened their own position but also undermined the whole opposition movement's chances of preventing the return to power of the brutal military regime.

## CONCLUDING REMARKS

It seems to me that fundamentalism is not in such a healthy state as it was, and it's clearer now that it's not homogeneous. So, for example, Saudi power is not the monolith it once was, and it doesn't have the hegemonic potential that it had a few years ago. WAF didn't seem able to adapt to this complex and fast-changing situation. We didn't have the resources, the political organisation or the structure to keep up with all of that.

One of the unresolved issues was the problem of seniority. Women who were in the group from its very early days developed a sophisticated analysis, but we didn't have mechanisms for transmitting that, with the result that newcomers felt like outsiders. That applied even to people who were not political novices, who came from longstanding political backgrounds. That's not just a social and personal problem, it's a political problem that we never addressed effectively, and it partly accounts for why we stopped developing as a political force.

Some of the friendships I've made in WAF have been very profound, partly because of the subtleties of the politics and partly because of the years spent discussing our differences and teasing out our analysis. I think it was the right decision to close it down because it was becoming unproductive and quite damaging in some ways to some, if not all of us. WAF wasn't a place where we could be creative or politically useful any more, but most of us are active in other political contexts, and I'm sure that we will continue to challenge fundamentalism and other oppressive forces together in the future.

## NOTES

1. Habonim, which means 'The Builders', was a Labour Zionist youth movement with branches in many countries. Its central ideal was to prepare and send young people to live in Israel on kibbutzim, agricultural settlements organised on socialist principles.

# 9. Activist listening

*Georgie Wemyss*

In 1989, when WAF was formed, I was living in Bangladesh, studying the Bengali language. The story of why I was there and how those accumulated experiences contributed to my initial interest in WAF forms the first half of this narrative. In the second half I discuss how my engagement with the political debates and analyses of WAF formed and continues to frame my political outlook and everyday life.

## POSTCOLONIAL RURAL ENGLAND: GENDER, RELIGION, EMPIRE, CITIZENSHIP

My first memory of gender inequality is trivial, but it made a big impact on me. I was five years old and sharing a bedroom with my two sisters when my father burst in to say that our mother had just given birth to a boy. In the same breath told us that 'we can now have a train set'. I was confused about the link between 'boy' and 'train set'. Sure enough, a few years later my father and brother had their trains, by which time I had other interests, developed through the 'traditional' gender roles of most of my extended family. That early memory has stuck with me because it was much repeated by myself and my sisters, and was also taken up by my grandmother, who, for as long as I can remember, called herself a feminist and an agnostic. My teenage discussions with her about feminism and religion – on which we tended to agree – were also arguments about class and racism – where we started from very different standpoints.

My maternal grandmother was a strong-minded woman, born in 1900, the only child of an admiral in the British navy who always made it clear to her that he had wanted her to be a boy. After the 1914-18 war she had hoped to go to university, but instead had accompanied her father on an assignment to the Caribbean. Marriage to an officer in the British army followed, and in 1931 a posting with him to

India, where my mother was born – at the height of the British government's violent clampdown on the Indian independence struggle. My grandmother told me about the restrictions placed on her movement as a British army wife, and how she tried to circumvent them 'to meet Indians'. But she didn't speak to me much about British colonial rule in India or her husband's military role there. Rather, I heard her romantic views of the Mughal dynasty, and her contradictory deliberations over the British empire's global 'civilising' role.

My grandmother's feminism developed when she joined the Women's Royal Naval Service (WRNS) at the beginning of the 1939-45 war. My grandfather was in the army, their house in London was requisitioned, and their children were sent to a 'boarding nursery' out of London. She was posted in various locations, and I was impressed when she told me about a campaign in which she was involved, pressurising for WRNS to be paid the same danger money as the men. She retired as a Chief Officer at the end of that war, and was one of my few female relatives who had been in paid employment – and the only one who referred to herself as a feminist.

Her struggles with religious ideas and practices evolved when she lived in Germany after World War Two, while my grandfather was working there. During my childhood she talked to me about Bergen-Belsen concentration camp, and her experiences of attending war crimes trials in Hamburg. She became close to Monique Lefevre Duclos, a witness at the trials who, when active in the French resistance had been caught by the Nazis in 1941, and had survived four years in concentration camps. Monique's recounting of her experiences affected my grandmother greatly. She told me that afterwards she could never believe in a Christian god or conform to institutionalised religions, and her debates were always around the relative merits of agnosticism and atheism. She would attend weddings, christenings and funerals, but whenever I was with her she would share with me her astonishment at the beliefs that others seemed to hold so unquestioningly. Untypically of others from her 1970s home counties social milieu, she had close Jewish and out gay friends, and through her relationships my horizons expanded.

I was christened into the Church of England, my parents had intermittently sent me to Sunday school, and as a family we would occasionally attend the local church. However, the death of my sister when I was ten led me to question religious belief. She was a year older than me and had suffered for several years with a terminal illness. She died suddenly at home while my younger siblings and I were staying with friends. I was given the news by my friend's mother and didn't speak to my parents until a week later, by which time the funeral had taken place without any children present. When I returned home my family were incapable of discussing what we had experienced, and neither the church nor school made any attempt to support me, which left me emotionally isolated but free to reach my own understandings of the meanings of life and death. My encounters with the church decreased and I started to question its role. When in the presence of men wearing dog collars I felt like the boy observing the Emperor's new clothes, and began to be aware of the power that they acquired through their status as ministers of religion. Although critical of the church, however, I remained accepting of the religious beliefs of relatives, who, I could see, derived personal strength from them.

The 1960s and 1970s rural England that I was part of was overwhelmingly white. Encounters with issues of 'race' and racism were largely filtered through music, the media or my own family's colonial histories. It wasn't until I left home that I began to understand the debates about 'race' and struggles against racism. I was, however, much more aware of the slipperiness of national identity.

When I was seven, my father attempted to renew his British passport and found out that he was a citizen of Mauritius, a newly independent country in which his family went back five generations, but which he had never visited. He was not automatically entitled to full British citizenship. In a panic reaction to the Africanisation policies in newly independent East African states, the Labour government had passed the 1968 Commonwealth Immigrants Act, which sought to prevent the migration of East African Asian British passport-holders to the UK by refusing right of entry to those who had not themselves been born in the UK and whose parents had also not been born there. Since my father had been born in colonial Ceylon (Sri Lanka) and his father in colonial Mauritius, he remained Mauritian until he was able to prove his entitlement to Britishness through other means. In 1972 the arrival of thousands of Ugandan Asian refugees with British passports in the nearby RAF airbase underlined further the shifting nature of nationality. These events aroused my curiosity. I wanted to find out more about how and why, in the nineteenth century, Scottish people had settled around the Indian Ocean and Indians in Africa, so that gradually I began to understand how we had all ended up in twentieth-century England.

Even before my father's loss of citizenship, the British nation had confused me. I was aware of being Scottish even though we all had English accents and never visited Scotland. The family tree included Scottish surnames of people who had left the country and built their lives in England and the colonies. Like many expatriate Scottish middle-class sons, my paternal grandfather had joined the Indian army, and I was used to seeing pictures of him in his uniform turban with Indian soldiers, and hearing about his first world war experiences in Mesopotamia (Iraq). My father's mother would talk about her experiences of housekeeping on the tea plantation that my grandfather managed between the wars in Sri Lanka. They said that the family was Scottish, and yet they had spent their lives in South Asia and England.

## SOUTH ASIA: COLONIALISM, POVERTY, POWER

I was the only one of my female siblings and close cousins to go to university. The egalitarian perspectives of some of the teachers and peers at my co-educational comprehensive school gave me the confidence to make my own choices, and to travel and move to London.

After earning some money I spent four months travelling in India and Nepal, via Kabul. A typical gap-year tourist, I was shocked by poverty and challenged about British colonial history. While I was in India, Margaret Thatcher was elected in Britain, Ayatollah Khomeini was establishing power in Iran, and the Soviet Union began deploying its military in Afghanistan – all events that I was trying to make sense of as I embarked on an Anthropology and Geography degree at UCL. The degree gave me theoretical frameworks for political understanding and analyses of my life experiences of gender, religion, 'race' and colonialism, and this led to me wanting to learn more empirically. So after graduating I volunteered for fourteen months on a small health project based in a leprosy and TB hospital in Santhal Parganas (now in Jharkhand State), India.

Whilst remaining ignorant of much of the big picture of Indian history and politics, in India I learnt about how power operates in complex ways at the micro level. I was immediately aware of the multiculturalism and multilingualism of the area, and over time I found out more about the relative power of different categories of people, of group leadership and communal politics. Most people were extremely poor, working on other people's land; and the most populous of this group were Santhals, who were mainly Christian and/or followed their pre-conversion beliefs. The area was also populated by poor and 'low caste' Hindus and Muslims, as well as Hindu Marwari business families, a local NGO, and various foreign and Indian Catholic and Protestant missionaries and middle-class professionals, including a high caste Bengali schoolteacher and doctor. The longer I spent there, the more I realised my ignorance and powerlessness in relation to the complex and violent environment in which I was living. Events that I could have no control over – including discovering that the distribution of leprosy and TB medication was being used to control patients politically, and observing the brutality of a foreign-aided female sterilisation camp – led me to decide that in future I would work in London in an environment that I would understand, where I could be active so as to change from within.

## BRICK LANE: RACISM, PATRIARCHY, VIOLENCE

I returned to the UK, and, not knowing what to do but having learnt basic Bengali in India, I started volunteering with a Bangladeshi women's group in East London; and after a few months I found paid work as a youth and community worker, working mainly with Bangladeshi girls and women in Brick Lane. At the time the Thatcher government's neoliberal economic and neo-conservative social policies were sharply experienced by all sections of the population of East London. The Bangladeshi population, which had roots going back to seafarers employed by the East India Company two hundred years earlier, was growing as the closure of factories in the north of England led to many migrant workers relocating for work in London. Fears of increasingly restrictive immigration laws led the men, who predominantly worked in the restaurant and tailoring trades, to bring over their families from Bangladesh. Overcrowding, homelessness, high unemployment, too few school places, ill health and inadequate health facilities, racist violence and discrimination – all these were issues that local people from diverse backgrounds and organisations were facing and struggling against.

After the racist murder of Altab Ali in 1978 and continuing violent attacks, young Bangladeshi men had established many organisations that ran activities for youths and campaigned on multiple fronts. In addition, Bangladeshi women were initiating projects to tackle the domestic violence, forced marriage, and prohibitions on further education that were being experienced by Bangladeshi women and girls. The politics of identity were becoming more dominant, and as a white woman with an awareness of historical colonial power structures I was negotiating my way through arguments about racism and sexism and becoming involved in anti-racist campaigns; at the same time I was supporting young women who had been physically and psychologically abused at home but were ignored by social services – which did not want to become involved in Bangladeshi 'family issues', either because they did not care or because they feared being labelled racist for taking issue with what they interpreted as religious or cultural norms. For example, in one case a fourteen-year-old girl was kept out of school by her father who wanted to send her to Bangladesh to get married. The school did nothing because the pressure on school places meant that her place could go to someone else, and the social worker decided not to interfere after meeting and agreeing with the father. Another young woman wanting to study beyond sixteen was told by a white teacher that it was pointless since she would in any case get married soon and stay at home.

It was at this time that, as a youth worker, I heard of the work of Southall Black Sisters in West London. In a complex and politically heated context, their analysis and practice was invaluable in supporting women who were, for example, victims of both domestic violence and racist immigration laws, or of forced marriage and racism in the education system. In the 1980s police and social services' responses to Bangladeshi women's reports of domestic violence were either disbelieving or non-existent, and many women from East London received legal advice, counselling and referrals to Asian women's refuges through SBS.

I wanted to be able to communicate better with women newly arrived from Bangladesh so I attended Bengali language evening classes. In late 1984, my teacher, Abdul Momen, a community worker from Camden, asked the class to support the occupation of Camden Town Hall by homeless families. A Bangladeshi woman and her two children housed by Camden Council in an unsafe Bed and Breakfast hotel had been killed by a fire. Two days later, twenty homeless families living in other dangerous hotels occupied Camden Town Hall, demanding that they and another sixty families should be rehoused immediately. For four weeks men, women and children ate, slept, prayed, studied English, played and negotiated with politicians in the council chamber and adjoining offices, until their demands were met. Along with others from East London, I visited the occupation and helped to deliver curries cooked in Spitalfields. This was my first experience of direct action and I was inspired by the success in achieving their goals of whole families, including women who spoke little or no English.[1]

## BANGLADESH: FRIENDS, FLOODS, FATWA

After several years of youth and community work I left the job in order to complete a teaching qualification, after which a friend and I planned to learn Bengali properly by enrolling at the Bangla Academy in Dhaka. We arrived in Dhaka in July 1988 as the city and three quarters of the country were becoming submerged by the flooding rivers. Through Bangladeshi friends we had made in London, we soon became involved in packing chapattis that were distributed to people stranded in the rising floodwaters. We went out in boats to nearby villages where women and children were crowded together on roofs. The desperate scenes that my family in Britain responded to on the TV news seemed to fit the stereotypical image of Bangladesh as being a country of natural disasters and overpopulation. However, when I was living there I was becoming more aware of the continuing manifestations in the country of the political conflicts that had led to the 1971 genocidal war and the creation of the politically secular Muslim majority state. The month before the floods, in an attempt to strengthen links with oil-rich states, the President, General Ershad, had amended the constitution to make Islam the state religion. Since the mid-1970s the Saudi government had been making loans and donations for an Islamic university, while religious centres were also reliant on Saudi aid, and thousands of men depended on manual work in the Middle East. Flood relief activities reflected this political background, with well organised camps being set up by the Islamist party Jamaat-e-Islami and its student wing the Chatro Shibir. For their part communist and secular political parties also organised flood relief; and President Ershad ensured that he, his wife and the army were all filmed distributing aid.

During the nine months I spent in Bangladesh I developed lasting friendships with students from rural areas living in Dhaka (including my future partner). From them I learnt about the violent conflicts between Islamist and secular students in the universities, and I read about and listened to the personal experiences of survivors of the 1971 war. I was shocked by the photographs and many documented cases of mass murder and rape in Dhaka and Sylhet. Visiting friends' families in rural areas I was told stories about how the war had sometimes been used as an excuse to settle old scores, so that Muslims who had posed no threat to the Pakistani army had been murdered by their Bengali Islamist allies in isolated villages, and how the army itself had torched the straw roofs of village houses from which families had fled, taking with them only their copy of the Qur'an. I met Hindu families who had stayed in Bangladesh after the disappearances and murders of some family members, and the fleeing of others to India. They insisted that they would never leave their homes and childhood Muslim friends. I also learnt about people's passion for the anti-colonial hero Kazi Nazrul Islam, whose Bengali poems and songs synthesised Hindu and Muslim traditions of universal humanity.

Whilst I was in Bangladesh, Salman Rushdie's *The Satanic Verses* became big news when it was banned in India and soon after in Bangladesh. Male and female student friends were also talking about the iconoclastic Bengali writing by feminist doctor Taslima Nasrin, who several years later became the object of a similar fatwa. Between February and April 1989 I was visiting friends in China, where seismic forces were building in the months before the protests in Tiananmen Square and so I was not aware of the aftermath of the death sentence against Rushdie until I returned to Bangladesh. Here, unsurprisingly, reactions to the fatwa depended on the political position of the person in question.

## TOWER HAMLETS COLLEGE: MULTICULTURALISM, IDENTITY AND AUTHENTICITY

When I returned to East London I set about trying to get a job in the about-to-be created Tower Hamlets College. Through contact with SBS I started attending WAF meetings, where I began to understand about the common characteristics central to modern fundamentalisms associated with different religions. Through the discussions, combined with reading and reflecting on my experiences in Bangladesh and Tower Hamlets, I was developing an understanding of religious fundamentalisms as authoritative political movements that achieved power through their claims to purity and authenticity, the control of women's minds and bodies, and the repression of dissenters.

WAF's political analysis was framed by experiences of both racism and fundamentalism, which helped me in identifying how the multiculturalist policy focus on religious needs and representation had taken attention away from the violent racisms and poverty experienced by many students. During the 1980s and 1990s Bangladeshi and Somali people of all ages and genders continued to experience violent racism in Tower Hamlets, particularly in the east of the borough where the college was located. Together with members of the local Law Centre and Homeless Families Campaign, I had been involved in the weekly door-to-door collection of statistics of racist incidents on Poplar housing estates, in order to support the rehousing of families to safe areas.

As a youth worker in Brick Lane I had been involved in campaigns on behalf of children who did not have school places, and I was concerned about the interrupted education of young people who had migrated to the UK, and had then been obliged to change schools frequently due to temporary housing or racial violence that made some routes to school unsafe, or because their families had been put in hotels across London. The Inner London Education Authority had under-invested in further education in East London, and the new college was a significant initiative, which I wanted to be part of. As a qualified teacher and youth worker I was employed in both capacities. The newly appointed senior management team was made up of dynamic and committed white women (some of whom described themselves as socialist feminists) and one white man. They all had experience of working in the multicultural inner city, but not of the political nuances of Tower Hamlets.

Looking at the plans for the new building – an extension to part of an existing college building on Poplar High Street – I noticed the incorporation of separate men's and women's prayer rooms into the design, as well as a chaplaincy and 'female only base'. Unlike the primary and secondary sectors, in which there is a tradition of Voluntary Aided schools, there is no custom of religious institutions running state-funded institutions in further education, and so this central presence of rooms purpose-built for religious activity was something new. It appeared that the religious needs of students were being prioritised over other diverse needs and identities. I also found out that some earlier proposals had suggested that the entire college should be divided into men-only and women-only sections. The final plans were a compromise between different interest groups, and reflected a policy framework of multiculturalism that privileged homogeneous religious identities over other complex – and sometimes conflicting – ones.

The struggles over the college extension resembled the contests in Bangladesh between those who wanted a secular education system and those who preferred either a greater presence of Islam in state schools and/or a parallel Islamic system of education. Secular government colleges in Bangladesh were usually mixed, or, less frequently, girls-only establishments. Teachers and students were likely to be from different minority religious backgrounds as well as Muslims. They did not usually include separate prayer facilities, and the schools would be closed on key Muslim, Hindu, Christian and Buddhist festivals. The mixed colleges were viewed as having higher academic status, with more likelihood of students progressing to government universities. The girls-only colleges offered a more limited curriculum, but did give girls whose families objected to mixed classes the opportunity of further study. The madrasahs were single-sex (usually boys only), and focused on a religious curriculum.

In Tower Hamlets the demand for a segregated college was argued from different positions: some Bangladeshi parents wanted their daughters who had been in local single-sex girls' state (non-religious) schools to stay in a single-sex environment post-16; while others wanted single-sex education as part of a more central role of Islam in the institution.

When the extension opened, the male prayer room was in its central position on the ground floor, while the chaplaincy next door was converted into an office for senior management. The women's prayer room remained upstairs. Both prayer rooms doubled as office and organising space for the newly created Islamic Society.

During the first years of the new college I began to notice discursive continuities between the student Islamic Society, formed in 1990, and what I had seen and heard in Bangladesh in relation to the Jamaat-e-Islami party and the Chatro Shibir, its student wing. For example, they referred to what is more commonly known as the 1971 Bangladesh 'liberation war' as a 'civil war', and estimated the numbers killed at well below the total given by other organisations. Through their links with the East London Mosque and the Young Muslim Organisation they supported Jamaat-e-Islami leaders who came to speak in London. The prayer rooms had Young Muslim Organisation stickers on the windows and door and a Chatro Shibir calendar. They also repeated the familiar arguments about Bengali Muslim cultural practices being impure, influenced by 'Hindus', and would bring up examples of Bengali customs, clothes, music and art that they described as un-Islamic. It was also becoming clear, through the activities that they set up and their political organisation and literature, that they were linked with other student Islamic Societies, and had strategies for demanding larger prayer spaces and practising more gender segregation.

Because of my experiences in Bangladesh, and participation in WAF, I was not seeing these activities solely in a British context. Several of the Bangladeshi members of staff also spoke about these links between the JI, the discourses of its founder Maulana Maududi and the student organisers, but their voices were not heard: the dominant view in the college interpreted the Islamic Society as the authentic voice of Islam and therefore of all Muslim students. The domination of the prayer spaces by the Islamic Society was an early indication of this.

The attraction of the IS to the college management seemed to be that its organisers were articulate and able to control the predominantly young, male and Bangladeshi section of the student body. In September 1991, at the beginning of the new term, the local press had reported violent clashes between 'Asian gangs' associated with different territories.[2] As a central institution, the college management feared that these perceived rivalries would be brought into the college, and advised staff to be alert to trouble and stay secure. In contrast, the IS appeared to be everything that the 'gangs' appeared not to be – non-territorial, non-violent, clean-living, focused on studying and able to negotiate with authority and to communicate the management's messages to the Bangladeshi students. With their 'offices' next door to each other, the male IS leader and the male assistant principal responsible for student affairs worked closely together, and the IS incorporated the logo of the college into its own logo, thereby adding to its authority.

In November 1991, the IS organised a meeting entitled 'The Ultimate Solution' for two hundred students, with the knowledge of the senior management. It was billed as providing 'reasoned and practical solutions for dealing with … racism, drugs, sexism, morality, justice and oppression'. The speaker was an American, Imam Muradadeen. The segregated audience was told that homosexuality was an 'evil', that 'racism was started by Jews', and that unveiled women were indistinguishable from 'prostitutes'; furthermore, in referring to restaurant workers Muradadeen stated that those who 'sell, drink or transport alcohol are cursed'. In answer to his question of 'what about gay and lesbian Muslims', the out gay president of the student union was told that 'Allah will burn you to a crisp and cut out your bowels', as other students clapped the imam and jeered at the SU president. At this point the senior manager who had welcomed the imam and listened quietly to his earlier abuses of the college's equal opportunities policies took the microphone and asked for respect. The meeting concluded soon after with the leader of the IS saying that 80 to 90 per cent of the students were Muslims, who had every 'right to express our belief'.

The college management were appalled following complaints about the meeting, and its aftermath when gay and female students complained of harassment. They tried to disassociate themselves from a meeting that they had enabled, and attempted to control the IS by vetting future speakers, not allowing them to use the college logo, and reconsidering how the prayer rooms were run.

In the emergency staff meeting that followed the event, the small number of staff who were Bangladeshi tried to make links between political-religious groups in Tower Hamlets and Bangladesh, criticising the space given to and taken by one specific Muslim group in the college and arguing for more teaching about Bangladeshi history and culture, so that students would know more about the complexities surrounding issues of religion and politics. They were concerned about the event as a manifestation of the strengthening relationship between religion and politics and contemporary global struggles. In contrast, many non-Bangladeshi staff members focused on the sexism and homophobia of the speaker and his clash with equal opportunities policies. One member of staff argued for non-intervention, for fear of the College being seen as being involved in 'internal Muslim politics'.

Once the dust had settled, the IS regained their position as trusted transmitters of authentic religious practices, but they were no longer allowed to organise such controversial events. During Ramadan 1992 there was a dispute over the swallowing of saliva by fasting students, many of whom wanted to spit it out. Management informed students that swallowing saliva was not 'in contravention of religious beliefs', and that this would be explained to students who thought it was 'against Islam' by the Islamic Society and in Friday prayers. This seemingly inconsequential announcement served to further legitimise the status of the IS through suggesting that the disruptive practices of less manageable students were un-Islamic.

My involvement in WAF discussions, including of a range of global manifestations of fundamentalism and careful analyses of how multicultural policies worked in British contexts, helped me to understand the politics of the events referred to above. The allocation of diverse students into the homogeneous religious category of 'Muslim', the identification of the leaders of a well-organised English-speaking group as authentic representatives of that category, and the use of those leaders to manage the group, were all common multiculturalist practices that echoed the indirect rule of the British Empire. The IS acted as other groups – associated with Christian, Jewish and Hindu fundamentalisms – have done, in attempting to silence dissent, control women and sexuality, impose an authoritative construction of 'tradition', and derive ideological and economic resources from links with established political organisations.

## WOMEN UNITE AGAINST RACISM

As well as its political analyses and actions, one of the greatest strengths of WAF was the example that it gave of the potential of women from different backgrounds, generations and political perspectives to debate and organise around complex and controversial issues that had been identified by everyone in the group as important. I drew on these experiences during my involvement in an equally diverse women's group that was active during a period of sustained racist conflict in Tower Hamlets in 1993-5.

After the Liberals and Social Democratic Party won control of Tower Hamlets Council in 1986, they divided the borough into seven political and administrative 'neighbourhoods'. Youth workers were instructed to work only with young people from the neighbourhoods in which they were employed. The college therefore became important as a central institution where young people from across the politically and 'racially' divided borough could meet. I was part of a group of female Bangladeshi, African Caribbean, Chinese and white youth workers who organised an annual week that celebrated International Women's Day with artistic, political and cultural activities for young women of all backgrounds and 'neighbourhoods'. In September 1993, after Quddus Ali, a student at the college, was attacked by racists and suffered permanent brain damage, and only a week before a British National Party councillor was elected to Tower Hamlets council, this group of youth workers organised a conference at the college to which experienced women activists, including from SBS and CAPA (Campaign for Police Accountability), were invited. At the conference, 150 women and girls, some of whom had been sexually harassed on anti-racist demonstrations and ignored at meetings, spoke out; they argued for increasing women's involvement in the anti-racist movement through organising childcare, challenging sexism and homophobia and recognising that women also experience racial violence. They identified the most important task as being to get isolated women onto the electoral register and out to vote in time for the full council elections in the following May. The multiracial group chose as its name 'Women Unite Against Racism' (WUAR), and drew on the anti-racist and gender-conscious organising experiences of women who were also involved in SBS, WAF, CAPA and many other women's groups and anti-racist organisations. Along with other campaigning groups and political parties, WUAR succeeded in ensuring that no BNP councillors were elected in May 1994 or in subsequent elections.

## CONCLUDING REMARKS

Throughout the last two decades I have continued to be informed and inspired by WAF's feminist, anti-racist, anti-fundamentalist political analyses, and the cultural and political strategies of friends struggling against modernist fundamentalist movements in the extreme neoliberal economic contexts of Bangladesh and elsewhere. The analyses fed into and were further developed throughout my postgraduate research and writing. At work these issues have influenced me in the development of courses that have offered opportunities to women who have experienced domestic violence, separation and racism to progress on to independent lives and careers. These politics also continue to be important in bringing up our British Bangladeshi children in London, where they have had an impact on our choices of secular, co-educational, multicultural state schools. Meanwhile the unfair restrictions of British immigration policies have ensured that family reunions can only take place in Bangladesh – thereby fortuitously giving our children the opportunity of experiencing Bangladesh in its countless vibrant and contradictory dimensions.

## NOTES

1. Occupation 1984 is discussed by Abdul Momen in *Working with the Bangladeshi Community*: www.bwa-surma.org/files/Abdul%20Momen%20magazine%20version.pdf.
2. See *East London Advertiser*, 20.9.91.

# 10. From Germany to Iraq via WAF: A Political Journey

*Nadje Al-Ali*

My political activism is definitely rooted in the period I spent as a student in Egypt, but the kind of political activism I'm involved with is of course also shaped by the fact that my parents came from two different cultures and two different religious backgrounds, my father being Iraqi and my mother German.

## THE FOUNDING OF MY GERMAN/IRAQI FAMILY

My father left Iraq in 1958 to study in Germany. He was not really interested in politics, but when he was seventeen he had been shot in a pro-Arab nationalism demonstration. When he first went to Germany he planned to go back to Iraq, but then a couple of years later he met my mother. They met at a ballroom dancing school, and went out together secretly for five years before they eventually married.

My mother came from a conservative working-class Catholic background, and the idea of having a relationship with a foreigner, a Muslim, was a big deal at the time. Her stepfather, a car mechanic, was quite strict, and when he eventually found out about my father he didn't speak to my mother for six months. When my father proposed to my mother, in 1965, he wanted to return to Iraq: it was a package deal, marrying this man and going to Iraq.

My mother was in her late twenties. She had wanted to study art but had not been allowed to by her family, and had ended up working as a GP's assistant. Up till then she had never travelled outside Germany beyond the Netherlands, but she decided to take all her savings, sell her bicycle, and buy herself a plane ticket to Baghdad, to see for herself where my father was proposing to take her to live.

The journey was not straightforward. Baghdad airport was closed down and she eventually had to disembark in Beirut. My father came to pick her up from there, and they then had to cross the desert to reach Baghdad by taxi. It was during July, and the temperature was 55 degrees centigrade, with no air conditioning. However, my grandfather, although not happy with the situation, was very hospitable, and he even allowed her to live in their house during the visit.

My parents became engaged in Baghdad, and when my mother returned to Germany she resolutely informed her parents, 'whether you like it or not, I am going to marry this man'. In the end they lived in Germany, and when my father returned my grandparents invited him for Sunday lunch – and the first question my grandfather asked my father was 'are you a Communist?'. At that time it wasn't a question of 'are you a Muslim fundamentalist?' but 'are you a Communist?' It was Germany, and the Cold War was still in full swing. It took some time, but my grandparents eventually grew fond of my father – unlike some other members of the family. There are some members of the family that my parents ceased to have contact with.

My father was born as a Muslim, but doesn't even know how to pray. When he left Baghdad in 1958 he had never prayed, and he had never fasted during Ramadan. He was not active politically, but he did become involved in humanitarian work, especially from the 1990s onwards, when many Iraqis arrived as refugees and asylum seekers. My father spent a lot of time taking them around, finding them housing, dealing with lawyers and immigration laws, and trying to sort out any other problems. During the period of sanctions against Iraq, he was also involved in sending medications and clothes there. People would give him donations and he would send them on to Iraq.

## GROWING UP IN GERMANY

Much of my energy while growing up in Germany (something I only later came to recognise) went into constructing myself as German, trying to be more German than Germans. I never felt racism or experienced being discriminated against, but, retrospectively, I do feel that I was under a kind of pressure to fit in. There were certain points when I felt really embarrassed. For instance, when I was eight or nine years old and some friends were in my house, I denied that I knew the identity of a woman in a framed photograph – my Iraqi grandmother, who was wearing an *abaya*, traditional Iraqi clothes. Then, when I was fourteen, there was one particular moment that transformed the situation. My classmates had seen a picture of me riding a camel during a holiday in Egypt, and had mocked me for it. But I managed to turn this into an empowering experience by writing an audio play about a heroine who succeeds in crossing the desert, and becomes a woman camel driver – something which, until then, had been forbidden for women.

## TUCSON, ARIZONA

My original intention had been to study German literature in Bonn when I finished high school. However, having had a very good experience as a 16 year old during a three-month holiday visiting a pen friend in Tucson, Arizona, I decided to spend a gap year there. By coincidence Tucson is where MESA (the Middle East Studies Association of North America) have their office, and there is also a big department for Middle East studies. So I thought, I am here, I know English, why don't I take some introductory classes about Middle Eastern and Islamic history, politics and culture? And I had such a brilliant year that I decided not to go back to Germany and study German literature but instead applied for, and won, a scholarship to study Middle East studies and French in Tucson. And it is there that an important identity shift took place for me.

There were many Arab students in Tucson, and I became interested in learning Arabic – which I didn't speak until then. During this period, living in an international house, we had political discussions and I went to various events, but at that time I was more focused on fun than politics. Nevertheless, there were two things that shocked me in the USA. Firstly, the flags, the nationalism. While I was growing up in Germany, nationalism was considered taboo and I never saw a flag, literally. I never sang the national anthem. Then all of a sudden I saw flags everywhere. And then, religion. Growing up in Germany, it was clear that it was a predominantly Christian society, but other than during religious holidays, church visits and religious education, I did not notice religion playing an important role in social and political lives. In Tucson, people on campus were preaching and giving out leaflets, and in the international house there were several very religious American Christians. When people realised that I was not practising any religion, I became like a project for them. After I left the international house I shared a small house with a German Mormon, and I had the book of Mormon on my bed as my flatmate tried to get me interested. She came from Germany's second largest family – 14 children – and her parents had converted. Then I had a boyfriend who was a Buddhist. So all of a sudden religion had gained a much bigger presence in my life. And it both attracted and repulsed me. Beyond anything else, it fascinated me. I looked at the book of Mormon, I looked at the Bible, I looked at the Qu'ran, and I tried to meditate with my Buddhist friend. What repulsed me, however, was the preachiness of many religious people, and all the rules and the guidelines.

## GETTING POLITICISED IN CAIRO

I wanted to continue studying for my MA in Berkeley, but my Arabic teacher suggested I first go to Cairo for a year to work on my Arabic. So when my three years in Tucson came to an end I went to study Arabic at the American University in Cairo, thinking that I would only be there for one year. But then I realised that all these amazing academics whose books I had read during the 'Women in the Middle East' module in Tucson were actually teaching at AUC in Cairo; and I thought that it would be exciting to take some classes with them. Within a week I had decided to enrol for an MA in Anthropology and Sociology, and it became clear that I would be in Cairo for a much longer period.

It was really at that time that I became politicised, both in general terms and in terms of feminism. Partly it was because I was ready for it – by that time I was in my mid-twenties. But it was also connected to the shifts in my identity. During the first eighteen years of my life I was very much focused on trying to protect my German identity as it had been constructed. The three years in Tucson were kind of a transition period, when I experienced cosmopolitanism and met people from all over the world, just having a good time. Then in Cairo I was went to the other extreme, feeling embarrassed about my western background and trying to be more Arab than the Arabs. Most of my friends were Egyptian, Palestinian and Jordanian, and I was socialising and trying to catch up with them. And it was also in Cairo that I became aware of all the social inequalities, injustices and gender discrimination that exist not only there but also in the UK, Germany and USA.

I was affected by the gap between rich and poor, and the stories I heard about girls and women and the way their parents or partners were treating them, and later on I understood these in a more political context. I think that, unless you lack a basic sense of sensitivity and justice, you couldn't be immune to that in Cairo: it was so in your face. And this was, of course, reinforced by the way the MA in Anthropology and Sociology was taught at the AUC. I learned so much from the amazing feminist and leftist professors I had there, and from the things I read. But equally I learned so much from my friends and classmates, who were very political and who then started to take me to meetings. AUC is in any case a highly political place, especially at the graduate level. The kinds of events and talks that were going on there were amazing. Almost every week there was something or other happening. It was an incredible educational context.

Then I started to go to meetings outside the university context. I started going to the meetings of a very informal group called *Maan* (Together), which was a Marxist-feminist group. It was a women's rights group, although men came along as well, and the person who was running it was Lebanese, a filmmaker and very left-wing. She had very radical position in terms of not taking foreign funding, but she also took the position that first we had to win the class struggle and then women would be liberated. I started making comments and criticisms, and offering a few suggestions, and my friends asked why I didn't get more involved – and that is what I did. For a period of almost a year I gave seminars, presenting different methodological approaches to gender. This involved a really long process. I would write out the lectures in an accessible way, and then they got translated into Arabic. I would then deliver them in English but people had the script in Arabic, and then there was translation, questions and answers. The people attending these lectures were mostly students, but not from the AUC but from Cairo University and other universities. Some were workers, and then there were always a few men leftist political activists. It was really a quite intense and a good experience for an MA student.

This combination of discussions – in the leftist women's group, in the discussions I had in the classroom, which were academic but also very political, and in the various forums within AUC – was really eye-opening. There was a lot of feminism going on, but also a critique in terms of imperialism and class. And then there were the discussions with friends, who were highly politicised, these guys who knew Marx's every single text backwards and forwards, and could quote from it. This often went over my head, to be honest, but I was still able to engage, and it forced me to read a lot. There was this real ethos of intellectual saturation. Most of my friends are people who have been politically active throughout, and were involved in underground opposition politics before, and, now, more overtly, in revolutionary processes.

## GETTING POLITICALLY INVOLVED WITH IRAQ

For my MA dissertation I wanted to study the impact of the Iran-Iraq war on women in Iraq. Through my readings and discussions I thought that this would be a fascinating topic. So in the summer of 1990 I asked my father to accompany me on a mini fieldwork trip to Iraq – although some people said that this was very unrealistic. Indeed, after the second day that we were there I realised that it wasn't a good idea. It wasn't so much that I was worried about myself; it was more that, once I wrote this up, I might endanger people. So I gave up on the idea, there and then. But I then found myself stuck in Iraq during the invasion of Kuwait, on 2 August 1990. It was the day that my father and I were supposed to fly back and we were at the airport – no one knew anything, it was business as usual. We had already checked in our luggage, but fifteen minutes before our flight was scheduled the airport was closed and the borders were closed. And then we started to hear all the rumours about the invasion of Kuwait. My father and I got our cases and went to the German embassy, where we were told: 'there's nothing we can do, just enjoy your extra holiday and make sure that you have plenty of water'. Unbelievable! So we went back to my family's home, and I spent the longest ten days of my life, watching television and seeing Saddam Hussein on a white horse proclaiming 'Iraq and Kuwait: one history, one future', while my mother was freaking out in German on the phone. During that time I didn't speak to anyone who wasn't terribly upset about the invasion. I was very shocked when I arrived in Jordan – after ten days the border to Jordan was opened for just 48 hours, and we managed to get out by bus – to hear people cheering for Saddam Hussein. This was very different from the mood inside Iraq.

I went back to Cairo and decided to write my MA dissertation about the representation of gender in a selection of modern Egyptian literature, and to compare three men and three women writers. I did a kind of discourse analysis of their writing, but I also interviewed the six authors. I received the first prize for an MA dissertation, which won me a book contract with AUC press – this was my first book.[1]

When the Gulf War began in January 1991 I was in Cairo, studying, but I went back to Germany to stay with my family, as we started to be very worried about my family in Baghdad. Every night my father and I were sitting in front of the television, watching the news and being terribly worried. One incident I will never forget – we took my father out shopping in town in an attempt to distract him, and ended up sitting in a café. The television was on with news about the war, and this woman at the table next to us said 'oh, you know, why don't they just kill them all?'.

## MOVING TO LONDON

I wanted to do a PhD, which I couldn't do at AUC. Also, my brother died in 1991, and life changed. From then onwards, I felt responsible for my parents. But I couldn't go back to live in Germany. I talked about it with my parents and they understood. I had gone out into the world and experienced all these cosmopolitan places, and I associated Germany with smallness, a more parochial context. I initially wanted to go to the US for my PhD, but the UK was my compromise, to be closer to my parents.

At the time we are speaking of, the early 1990s, there was a flow of literature coming out that challenged the homogeneous idea of women in Islam, Islamism, women and the veil, and so on. But what really bugged me was that, within the context of being nuanced about Islam there were sweeping generalisations about what constituted 'secularism' and 'secular politics', especially secular feminist politics. Having been involved in secular organisations but also having become aware of secular feminist spaces, I realised that secular feminists were very diverse in approach and politics. I also felt that there was a gap in the literature – hence my proposal to look at secularism in the context of the Egyptian women's movement.[2] Of course this very much corresponded with Deniz Kandiyoti's interests, and she became my PhD supervisor.

I started my PhD at SOAS in 1994, and then there was the amazing coincidence that when I was looking for a place to rent, by fate or good luck I ended up living in Cynthia Cockburn's house. Hers was the first address I picked up from the SOAS notice board. I didn't even know who she was. It was really through Cynthia that I got introduced to Women in Black and Women Against Fundamentalism. She took me along to meetings. It all seemed to be pointing towards the same direction.

I guess from the very beginning of my time in London I was politically active. Partly because we regularly had people in the house drawing placards on the kitchen floor, and people coming for dinner and passing through, so that there was a constant engagement with feminist scholars and activists, Cynthia's friends from around the world. I then became regularly involved in Women in Black. But working on my PhD very much intensified and deepened my interest in secular feminist politics. Obviously it provided me with an in-depth insight into a specific empirical context, but I was also doing a lot of reading and becoming engaged in different contexts, and WAF started feeding into this.

## WAF

Initially my interest in WAF wasn't so much about fundamentalism but was more about the secularism aspect. Of course these are two sides of the same coin. However, rather than being motivated primarily through negative experiences with fundamentalist religion, I had initially an instinctive sense that the secular was sacred, that it was important to have secular spaces. Secular spaces are clearly important in that they are linked to women's rights and feminist politics. But what had already attracted me at that time was that WAF provided a secular space that was not focused only on Islamic fundamentalism. It provided recognition that the 'fundamentalist trend' was something that existed across religions, whether Christianity, Judaism, Islam, etc; that in all of them there were these fascist right-wing fundamentalist strands; that there are common patterns; that there are commonalities in the way women's and gender issues are singled out by these movements, in the way women's sexuality and bodies are controlled, and the way patriarchy is asserted through religious fundamentalism.

In terms of how WAF related to my previous stages of development, what has stuck is the curiosity about religion. While I do find spirituality appealing, and I am curious about religion, I am instinctively suspicious of anyone who claims to know 'the truth'. This is probably very much rooted in having grown up in a context where there were already different 'truths' as part of my life. Not just in terms of having a mother and a father who came from different cultural and religious backgrounds, but also the different 'truths' I encountered when moving out of Germany: to the USA, Egypt and the UK, with visits to Iraq.

This did not make me a cultural relativist, however. Of course I had to work this through, but even when I was not able to articulate my position in this way, I could see that certain things are contextual but that at the same time there are some universals. I understood that people all come from different places, different experiences and have different perspectives, but I also saw that people could arrive at some sort of similar conclusions.

The discussions we had in WAF gave me the tools to take my understanding out of a specific and empirical context to look at religious fundamentalism in more comparative terms. It also helped me to fine-tune my analysis of a particular empirical context by looking at other comparative examples. The readings, the WAF journal and the discussions we had also helped me in writing my PhD dissertation, in terms of providing some analytical insights, and sharpening my analytical and political lens. Of course WAF also helped me to root myself in Britain, in London. Cynthia played a major role in that as well. Through WAF friendships and political networks I learned a lot about British politics, about racism in this country, about black feminism, about anti-racist politics and about leftist politics more broadly.

## CO-FOUNDING 'ACT TOGETHER'

Another life-changing experience for me took place in 1997, when, having not visited Iraq after the invasion of Kuwait for a period of seven years, I eventually went back there with my parents. The sanctions had already been going on for seven years, and I was shocked by the way the country had changed. Of course, I had also changed during those years. I had some different analytical lenses and saw things that maybe I hadn't seen before. Nevertheless, poverty was very visible. Not only were there children begging on the streets (at this time UNICEF reported that 5000 children were dying every month); there were also middle-class people who were starting to sell their furniture and books in order to survive. You could see the disintegration of the city in front of your eyes. There was nobody taking care of rubbish, parks and green areas. People blamed Saddam Hussein, but they were also asking 'why are we being punished?' – and they were very angry. I could see how my own family was suffering, although they were not suffering as much as many other families because my father was supporting them, sending money, medicines and clothes. I felt very humbled. I was trying to imagine how my cousins who were about my age were feeling about this very privileged family member, who had grown up in Germany, and lived in the States, in Cairo and in England, and who could freely come and go. I didn't, however, feel any resentment from anyone; rather, they were very curious about my life and they were happy for me.

Before that visit I wasn't particularly involved in Iraq-related issues. But I now decided that I had to use my privilege and freedom and somehow channel it, and find out what was happening in Iraq. It was then that I got involved in the anti-sanctions movement, through 'Voices in the Wilderness' and also 'Women in Black'. From 1998 onwards I was involved in a group I co-founded, called 'Act Together: Women's Action for Iraq'.

I was feeling very uncomfortable about the many people in the anti-sanctions movement who were almost apologetic for the Iraqi regime, in the context of being critical of their own government and western imperialism. And there were other Iraqi women who felt equally uncomfortable – some of whom who had been imprisoned and tortured under Saddam Hussein. We wanted to have a space in which we could raise consciousness about the human rights violations by the Iraqi regime, while also pointing out that Iraq is not Saddam Hussein, and that the sanctions were not actually weakening the regime but were targeting the most vulnerable. Women were very much affected by the sanctions.

The refusal to let yourself be hijacked by an either/or position, but rather to have a nuanced but still principled position, which does not accept being put in one corner or the other, and thereby glorifying something that is not alright – this is the kind of politics that Act Together did, and it is the same kind of politics as that of WAF and WiB. During the first two to three years, our emphasis was on trying to educate people that Iraq was not Saddam Hussein, and also on raising consciousness (that was our feminist bit) about the specific impact of sanctions on women – including, more broadly, the specific impact of sanctions on gender norms and relations. That was our remit. We did lots of talking and organising of events, but after a few years we had to change our remit to focus not only on sanctions but also against war on Iraq.

From the time we established Act Together, most of my political time and energy went into it. Part of me didn't want to be myopic, but events were such, and I was positioned as such, that this became my political responsibility – and, at some point, not only in the UK. There were years when I would go six or seven times a year to the USA, to political and academic events, and it was very intense.

In 2005 I had a horrible experience, but retrospectively it was also an important one, which made me much stronger. I took part in a panel on the last day of a war tribunal on Iraq in Istanbul. For three days people had been giving evidence about what happened. In one way or another everyone also said 'Let's support the armed resistance in Iraq'. I was supposed to speak about the impact of the occupation on women in Iraq, but started by saying:

> Before I speak about women, I would like to say that I can't stand in front of you and say 'support the armed resistance'. What kind of resistance are you supporting – people blowing up people in market places? Are you supporting people blowing up Iraqi policemen or people queuing up to get jobs? I can't support that and I think that it's one thing to say 'OK, there's a legitimate right for people to defend themselves and I am willing to have a discussion about occupation', but I think we also need to speak about non-violent forms of resistance, and as far as I know many people in Iraq are not happy with the resistance and they call them terrorists and insurgents.

It was terrible – I was hated. 300 people hated me. Except for Ayse Gul Altinay, a Turkish feminist academic who was chairing the panel – but she was outnumbered: none of the audience said anything sympathetic. Afterwards, however, some people came up to me and said 'thank you for making that point'. But nobody had the guts to say it during the public discussion. Afterwards I wrote an article with the title 'The Enemy of my Enemy is not necessarily My Friend', which helped me to articulate my position at the time, and more generally.[3]

## MOVING TO ACADEMIC WORK ON IRAQ

From early 2000 I started to write articles about the impact of sanctions on women in Iraq. After the invasion of Iraq, the intensity changed. For me there was a choice of sitting in front of the television and being depressed or doing research and writing. For a few years I did it frantically and it was all-consuming.[4] It wasn't sustainable, but it was something that in some ways kept me sane. At the same time, I felt that I was doing something a bit useful. But it took a lot out of me. When I decided that I couldn't go on writing yet another depressing article or book about how awful the situation was in Iraq, I had to find other ways of engaging. So then different strands emerged. One of them was a book that has just come out – it took a long time, almost four years: a collection of cultural productions of Iraqi writers, poets, film-makers and visual artists writing about coping strategies.[5] Another was my greater involvement over the last three years with women's organisations inside Iraq, and capacity-building with Iraqi academics and activists.

This particular work began with CARA (Council for Assisting Refugee Academics), an organisation that started during the 1930s, but which, after a long period of low activity, was revived when there were a large number of Iraqi academic refugees coming to the UK in 2004 and 2005 as a result of a wave of assassinations. CARA stepped in to link people to universities through fellowship and mentoring programmes. I got involved and started a pathfinder project for mainly Iraqi female academic refugees at SOAS in 2007. Then CARA realised that the academic refugees who made it to Britain were only the tip of the iceberg, and that most had stayed in the region. So they started some regional programmes as well, and later on also developed programme links to academics inside Iraq. For the past year and a half I have been organising regional round-tables, to facilitate encounters with Iraqi academics from different parts of Iraq with regional academics interested in women and gender studies. For the first meeting I invited women from Birzeit University in Palestine, from Cairo, from Lebanon and from Turkey to exchange views of how Women and Gender studies had developed in the regional context. We are also facilitating encounters between Iraqi women's rights activists and Iraqi academics, because, obviously, women and gender studies don't emerge in a vacuum.

## PRESENT AGENDA

In the next few years I'm going to focus my political work not just on Iraq but also on local issues. For two years I was active in the trade union at my university as the Equality and Diversity Officer, and attended University and College Union (UCU) national women's meetings. I feel that all this fits together. I am working on the specific problems and challenges that female academics are facing in higher education in Iraq, and I am seeing that there are so many parallels with the situation in the UK. Actually, my research on Iraq has really sensitised me to what's happening in this country. I've recently been elected as chair of the SOAS UCU branch, and I'm also planning to get more involved in the national union. I didn't realise how far the UCU executive mirrors senior managers around the country – it's so white, it's so male. Women and BME members are very marginalised within the union. This is something I am planning to spend the next few years on.

Another space where I have found an intellectual and political home is the *Feminist Review* collective. It is a space in which we are challenging boundaries. There are fourteen people in the collective, representing a range of different positionalities, and very diverse, but there is a common ground of intersectionality, embodying in some ways the history of British feminism and Black feminism. It is thus a space in which I can connect my academic work with activism and also with the arts. For me it is also a great way to take myself out of the Middle East work. This does not mean just Iraq, of course, as I have been doing some work trying to follow what's happening in the region, in terms of the various revolutionary and counter-revolutionary processes, and looking at Egypt again. But *Feminist Review* really allows me to make the wider connections.

## BACK TO WAF – A CONCLUDING REMARK

In the last few years I've been mostly outside WAF, as I have focused my political work on Iraq, and more recently on trying to insert feminist politics into union activism. I also started to get a bit worried about WAF's occasional working together with groups and individuals I perceive to be 'secular fundamentalists' – i.e. those who have a righteous, 'I have the only one truth' kind of attitude – and about whether WAF are being careful enough about disentangling religious fundamentalism and religion. I also feel that if you look empirically at women's movements – and I know most about those based in the Middle East – the secular versus religious dichotomy does not hold true: activism tends to be far more complex and nuanced on the ground. However, I want to emphasise that working mainly outside WAF was not a political decision but rather a result of being pulled in different directions. Although I could see some tensions in WAF as people grew into different directions, any time I took part in a meeting I liked the atmosphere, was stimulated by the questions, and felt it was a good political context.

Between the work I do on Iraq and the work I do now with UCU as SOAS branch chair and then *Feminist Review* – I don't think I have time and space for WAF at the moment. Anyway, for me, although for some years my involvement with WAF included going to meetings and meeting people, the importance of WAF has been especially as a form of politics, a method – it's an idea that cuts across so many things and issues I'm involved with.

## NOTES

1. Nadje Al-Ali, *Gender Writing – Writing Gender: The Representation of Women in a Selection of Modern Egyptian Literature*, The American University in Cairo Press, Cairo 1994.
2. Nadje Al-Ali, *Secularism, Gender and the State in the Middle East: The Egyptian Women's Movement*, Cambridge Middle East Studies, Cambridge University Press 2000.
3. Nadje Al-Ali, 'The Enemy of My Enemy is not My Friend', Women Living Under Muslim Law (WLUML), 22.07.05.
4. Nadje Al-Ali, *Iraqi Women: Untold Stories from 1948 to the Present*, Zed, London & New York 2007; Nadje Al-Ali & Nicola Pratt (eds), *Women & War in the Middle East: Transnational Perspectives*, Zed, London & New York 2009; Nadje Al-Ali & Nicola Pratt, *What kind of Liberation? Women and the Occupation in Iraq*, Berkeley, University of California Press 2009.
5. Nadje Al-Ali & Deborah al Najjar (eds), *We are Iraqis: Aesthetics & Politics in a Time of War*, Syracuse University Press, Syracuse 2013.

# 11. MADE IN 'LITTLE INDIA'

*Sukhwant Dhaliwal*

It can be problematic to define oneself so much in relation to two people and one place. Yet my parents and their decision to move to Southall really shaped my life. It was in response to my parents' incessant beckoning to save them from the hardship of their lives that I sought to recover my own sense of self. Their decision to live in Southall had an equally strong impact, as it meant that I lived out the reality of the glocal – that dialectical relationship between parochialism and transnationalism, between staking a claim to being an authentic 'insider' and being de-legitimised as an interfering 'outsider'.

## JOURNEY TO THE LAND OF MILK AND HONEY

My parents share the classic Punjabi immigrant to Southall story but with its own peculiarities. My father is the son of a prominent Sikh preacher and grew up in Kuala Lumpur where my grandfather was an advisor to Sikh police officers working for British colonisers. I believe that my father's experience of living and growing up outside of Punjab marked him out from his siblings; he is a keen traveller and has a far more cosmopolitan sensibility than his brothers. At some point in his twenties he was called back to the village in Punjab and married, literally overnight, to my mother. Soon after the wedding, he moved to England. He was met at Heathrow by some friends from back home, taken to live in a shared house in Southall and introduced to 'pub culture'.

My mother had a very different life. She grew up in a far less ascetic household and in a 'hip' town in the Punjab, yet, in Britain, she has been the more conservative of the two. My mother says she only met my father once, as a teenager, at an aunt's house, several years before he was identified as a potential partner because of his plan to move to England. No one asked my mother what she wanted and in fact she did not expect to be asked. She was instructed to buy a few outfits and get a passport made. She got pregnant straightaway and my father left for England during the pregnancy. After she gave birth to my older brother, she made preparations to move to 'Vilayat' (England). She arrived at Heathrow, filled with both curiosity and fear.

My father was not there to meet her and she was carted off to a detention centre with my older brother who was less than a year old. Immigration officials tracked my father and informed him that if he did not collect his wife he risked having her deported. My mother says that during her first year or so, she spent many months crying – having been plucked out of the warmth of a large extended family, she couldn't believe the days she spent on her own inside one room with one, then three, clinging children. I think we kids became her best friends.

By my teens, I was completely drenched in my parents' sense of loss – my fathers' stymied sense of adventure and my mother's pining for her immediate family back in Punjab. They both oscillated between their overly romanticised visions of what being in Britain *ought* to be and the pragmatic dirt track of manual labouring jobs and meeting non-stop financial demands from family members 'back home'.

## THATCHERISM, 'GOVERNMENT JOBS' AND ENCOUNTERING 'RACE'

In our home there was a huge emphasis on class and public services. My mother started out as a machinist but soon moved to a 'permanent' job at Ealing hospital. My father worked in various manufacturing plants and eventually got a job with British Airways at Heathrow when the airline was still nationalised. But they were often working the 'double shift' by picking up all sorts of extra jobs to top up their income. My parents emphasised the importance of securing 'government jobs', by which they meant that we should strive for employment in the nationalised public sector, which at that time could provide good terms and conditions and long term financial security. Unfortunately, their employers actively undermined that sense of security by outsourcing their 'menial' areas of work and casualising their contracts. They were both forced to fight this creeping privatisation and inevitably became entangled in trade union disputes.

In fact trade unions and the Labour Party were never far from our home. As with other Asian men of his generation, my father joined the

Indian Workers Association (IWA) and then the Transport and General Workers Union (then TGWU, now known as Unite). Members of the IWA and TGWU were channelled into the Ealing Southall Labour party. My father became a trade union branch chair. He was completely immersed in politics. We knew we were Labour Party supporters and we knew all about the miners' strike. We watched the BBC television sitcom *The Rag Trade* and we imitated our dad by blowing a whistle and shouting 'OK, that's it, everybody out!' My mother was not such an inevitable trade unionist but she is very cognisant of class and the value of public services. She has a hatred of Margaret Thatcher, and still automatically recites 'Maggie Thatcher Milk Snatcher' whenever her picture appears in the news.

As Thatcherism emerged, Southall was discovering its anti-racist feet. I was only six when, in 1976, Gurdeep Chaggar was murdered outside the Dominion Centre in old Southall. I knew there were people out there that hated our presence in Britain, but on our small cosy street and within our predominantly Asian social circle, I really didn't feel any of it. Our white neighbours adored my mother. Most of the children on our street were Asian. The only way in which I directly experienced 'difference' was at primary school when I was placed in the outhuts, in a remedial class, for my inadequate grasp of the English language. Teachers instructed my parents to speak English with us at home. Fortunately, my mother refused. Nevertheless, my primary school steered me down a curious road to Anglicisation – Christian hymns, country dancing and Scottish dancing – our teachers beamed with pride as they toured fêtes with this majority Asian and African girls group dressed in angelic white shift dresses and tartan sashes.

All this changed when we moved house and I started at Dormers Wells High School, or 'Dumpy Dormers' as it was known because of its poor levels of academic performance. It was at high school that 'race' and gender came more strongly to the fore. Most of the students were from poor immigrant families or white working class families so class differences were less strongly felt. Dumpy Dormers backed on to the notoriously racist Golf Links Estate and yet I was taken absolutely by surprise when the most beautiful boy, blonde and blue-eyed, took one look at me and shouted 'Paki!' There was quite a lot of segregation within the classrooms; I found my Asian girlfriends and stuck closely with them.

## ON NOT BECOMING A SOUTHALL STEPFORD WIFE

As I entered my teens, the rules that governed my life abruptly changed. I was now seen as a liability, a female that required a close watch. My parents were overly concerned that I should grow into an eligible wife. I was expected to do a large amount of the housework whilst my mother was out at work. I fought this tooth and nail and like to think I domesticated my brothers. I learnt to make chapattis and curries at the age of 12. I knew everything about good housekeeping, femininity and self-presentation.

Cultural reproduction seemed also to flow only through me; I was the only one out of three kids that was pressurised to change out of school uniform and into traditional Punjabi dress as soon as I got home from school and I was the only one sent to Punjabi classes where girls were taught hymns and programmed into piety. I spent a lot of time slamming doors and many evenings holed up in my bedroom as punishment for refusing to perform these obligations. I was encouraged to postpone ambitions and desires to *after* marriage. Apparently, I could cut my hair, study, travel, go out with friends, only *after* marriage. Already unduly tuned in to my mother's suffering, it was at this time that my gender consciousness grew. It certainly didn't make sense to me that my mother should want me to end up with exactly the same life as hers. Both my brothers were important allies; they actively backed my right to transcend these norms.

Into the 1980s, Southall was becoming a strong dynamic and politically active place. I would hear rumours but my world was very restricted so it's fortunate that the politics of that period crept into our school environment and into the books at the local libraries. The English, History and Sociology teachers at 'Dumpy Dormers' encouraged a lot of political debate – about the ethics of public sector strikes, the miners' strike, Thatcherism, gender equality, nuclear arms, South African apartheid, the Israel-Palestine conflict. My closest friends and I were flowing animal rights, Greenpeace and CND politics. This was mid-1980s, the Cold War threat of nuclear obliteration overshadowed much of our teenage years and we watched horrific documentaries and sci-fi dramas about life after nuclear war. I also started to read stories by the Asian Women's Writers' Collective and then, by a stroke of luck, one of my best friend's relatives took us to a Black women's conference at the London Women's Centre in Holborn. That was my first major exposure to Black women organising and it left a lasting impression.

However, the 1980s also saw the public visibility of Khalistani politics. Soon after Operation Bluestar (where Indira Gandhi instructed an assault on Khalistanis holed up at the Golden Temple in Amritsar) Tarsem Singh Toor, a known supporter of Indira Gandhi's Congress Party, was shot at close range at his restaurant, just a few streets from our house. The CID visited us and other local houses. For the first time I noticed a large glaring portrait in the centre of our living room of Jarnail Singh Bhindranwale, the leader of a new political movement demanding the cessation of Punjab from India and the creation of an independent Sikh theocratic state of Khalistan. My father and most of his friends started wearing turbans again; these socialists turned into Sikh nationalists.

Beyond the occasional weekend service in someone's home, religion had played little part in our lives. In the 1980s, there was a distinct shift in identities. Unpopular Khalistani front organisations that had been kept at arms' length by the main gurdwaras during the 1970s started to draw hundreds and moved to the centre of Sikh networks. Khalistani activists fleeing persecution by the Indian state but also Punjabis fleeing persecution by the Khalistanis, arrived in Southall in the early 1980s and created a political minefield that triggered a series of battles for control over Southall's gurdwaras.

Dumpy Dormers had very little ambition for its students; all of the emphasis on educational achievement came from my parents. Personally, I knew that I was never going to leave Southall or have a life beyond marriage unless I got a place at university. Fortunately, I scraped through clearing to enter Goldsmiths College. My mother expected me to commute from home but I managed to make a case for a room in halls of residence. At that time we had the benefit of public funding for undergraduate degrees – I had a smallish student grant and housing benefit – which gave me access to a life that I otherwise would not have had the opportunity to experience. Moving to university was my big legitimate exit. Suddenly my whole world opened out. I had no intention of studying, I wanted to live, really get out there and experience life and live. I co-opted the help of some wonderful women in the halls of residence to lie to my parents when they called whilst I went out to pubs, bars, clubs and cinemas. This was the beginnings of a double life that went on for about two decades! It was 1988 and I was 18, already quite feisty and yet incredibly sheltered and naïve.

**OUT OF STEP AND OUT OF TIME**

University was the first time I had white female friends. We were united by our class politics. My first year at university was absolute bliss. I don't recall any of the seminars or lectures but I certainly do remember the opportunities to wear whatever I wanted. My newfound working class girlfriends helped me get part time jobs and basically taught me how to manage money and life. My older brother's girlfriend also became a close friend and we would drive out of London to various events and Asian Society gigs organised by him and his friends. Those were the best of times.

By the second year of the degree course, I wanted time out to experience the real world of work. I got a job at the Law Department of the University of East London (then a polytechnic) in the heyday of visits from Paul Gilroy and Phil Cohen. I was employed as a research assistant looking at legal redress for victims of racism on council estates. I went to interview Rajiv Menon at the local anti-racist group, Newham Monitoring Project (NMP). He was very inclusive and friendly and he paved the way for me to interview a number of NMP's cases. This year out from university completely changed my life. Within a matter of months I knew I wanted to work on violence against women. NMP introduced me to Ashika Thanki at Newham Asian Women's Project and I started to volunteer with them. By the time I was back at university for my final year, I had chosen 'race and racism' and 'feminism' as my two option courses and decided to produce an end of year dissertation on racist harassment. I read mountains of material on black feminism. But I spent a lot of time caught up with Newham and more so because I'd started seeing my first long term partner who was working there.

'Race' started to divide me and my white working class friends. There was an inevitability about anti-racism slipping into black identity politics, which carried the baggage of all sorts of uncomfortable debates such as why African women straighten their hair. When I requested tickets for a large anti-racist event, I was quietly asked whether the tickets were for black or white guests. The entire scene was pretty hedonistic but there was a regular injection of black-white distinctions, especially amongst some Afro-Caribbean activists that were drawn to Pan-African politics.

Interestingly, it was also through NMP that I was introduced to Southall Black Sisters and Women Against Fundamentalism, noteworthy because the introduction was based on immense mutual respect but not on an alignment of politics. I accompanied them to a meeting at Conway Hall where Sara Hossein and Gita Sahgal were speaking on a platform and SBS women were gathered in the front row. After the meeting, I also overheard Georgie Wemyss talking about Tower Hamlets. It was an inspiring evening, I could see strong articulate women shaking things up and challenging very confident anti-racist men. Before I point to the clear differences, I want to emphasise that this was also a period where the Islamic Right were still *outside* the anti-racist and anti-imperialist circles that I encountered; I saw many anti-racist activists challenging Hizb-ut-Tahrir and others when they pitched stalls outside left meetings at Conway Hall. On reflection, I suspect this was because in the early 1990s there was still a strong sense of secularism and, despite the fall of the Berlin Wall and unsavoury news about communist regimes, a defence of the ideology of communism and these Islamist groups would rage against *both* communism and capitalism, equating the two as corrupt 'man made' systems.

However, I was privy to, though I can't claim to have affected, anti-racist discussions about Rushdie and Khalistan that would not settle in my brain. For me, three aspects of these discussions are particularly memorable. Firstly, there was a defence of Khalistan on the basis that it was a reaction to state repression and a demand for self-determination. Secondly, WAF's decision to hold a public protest against the anti-Rushdie demonstration through central London (not their objection to the fatwa per se) was questioned on the basis that this was a dangerous line that fuelled racism. In both situations, the feminist critique could potentially undermine the 'necessary' focus on state power and racism. A third problem related to Rushdie's integrity i.e. why side with an insufferably arrogant man whose own politics could be considered dubious. Fortunately, the viability of my own political instinct to oppose Khalistan was bolstered by my irreverent Southall peers. Meanwhile, my general orientation on the Rushdie affair was strengthened back at Goldsmiths where one particularly outspoken Muslim student smashed through any illusion of a consensus amongst

Muslims and challenged those that damned Rushdie, refused to read his book and advocated censorship.

In June 1992, as the degree course was coming to an end, I was twenty two years old, and I knew I would either have to head back to Southall to a marriage time bomb, or leave London and try to stop the clock. I managed to get a job at Subah, a young Asian women's refuge in Manchester. There was a great collective spirit amongst the workers but a strengthening Muslim identity politics crept in when management committee members pushed for the appointment of a specific 'Muslim worker'. Her entry to the staff team was, in my eyes, a staggering blow for a secular Asian women's project. The logic of her appointment connected arguments about post-Rushdie and Gulf War Islamophobia with a claim about catering for Muslim women's specific needs though none had actually come to light. For all intents and purposes she saw herself as a 'Muslim advisor'; she made claims about hierarchies of oppression and articulated a strong objection to WAF's support of Rushdie.

At a very personal level I felt incredibly lonely and disconnected in Manchester; surrounded by 'settled' couples I had the sense that I was ageing before my time. I also felt as if there was something inevitably wrong with my sense of timing, like I was a generation late for everything. I had benefited from the political waves caused by the leading anti-racist and feminist activists of the 1980s, but by the time I arrived on the scene(s), NMP had already been on black delegations to Ireland and Palestine, WAF had already had its foundational moment in Parliament Square, and one time activist organisations were increasingly focused on service provision and tied in to the strictures of funding regimes. I found two temporary outlets – northern WAF and Manchester Black Sisters. It was through the latter that I met Hannana and Meena from SBS. They came to speak at our showing of a Channel 4 documentary about the 'djinn murder' in 1991 of Kaushar Bashir. Kaushar's case revealed that in the north of England Pakistani young women transgressing norms were being taken to local Imams, forcibly imprisoned and subjected to beatings. In Kaushar's case, she had been beaten to death.

Subah faced a financial crisis, the early murmurings of new commissioning agendas that sought to extinguish black autonomy and superimpose a neo-liberalised housing association format on all refuge provision. I was not happy in Manchester and managed to get a job to establish an Asian women's centre for Newham Asian Women's Project (NAWP).

## BACK TO LONDON

Back at NAWP in 1993, we had a huge battle on our hands to convince the local authority of the need for a secular Asian women's centre against a growing lobby by Muslim Labour Party councillors for a Muslim women's centre. We won that struggle but the sense that Muslims, and Muslim women in particular, face a very specific persecution and have very specific needs was brought forcefully to the fore.

My return to Newham was a mixed blessing. On one level it felt like a homecoming. Since Newham has always comprised so many young people building a home from home, there were strong friends' networks acting as surrogate families and a vibrant social life. At another level, I instinctively pushed against tight-knit circles, perhaps the consequence of growing up in Southall. I also felt constrained by the NGO-isation of the women's voluntary sector. At the same time, I was moving into a dead end on the relationship front. I applied, and fortuitously received, a Commonwealth and Fellowship Award to study in Delhi.

Before heading out to India, I quit my job at NAWP and moved back to Southall to spend some time with family and save money for my trip. Somehow I started volunteering at SBS on their schools workshops on 'race, religion and the family' and also on their 'no recourse to public funds' campaign. It was during this time that I noticed the emergence of new Sikh processions through Southall annually marking the founding of the Khalsa (a bounded prescriptive notion of Sikh identity). This was also an active overwriting of the cultural celebration of the Punjabi harvest festival Vaisakhi. I started to photograph and film these processions, which at the time were still relatively small but included sizeable Sikh youth groups shouting Khalistani slogans in an intimidating way at obviously Muslim (often hijab or jilbaab wearing) Somali women.

By then I was also already involved with WAF and I attended a couple of discussions about the WAF journal but primarily worked as a part time administrator from the office above the Red Rose Club in Seven Sisters. This was when we had paying subscribers to the journal and a formal management group. The previous administrator, Michelle, moved over to write for Red Pepper. Michelle and I were both keen on WAF being an activist campaigning organisation but we had landed up just as WAF was petering out and a decision was reached to close the organisation. So I went very quickly from hoping to spark a campaign against the forceful mobilisation of Christian anti-abortionists and a new wave of Islamist organisations on campuses across London to helping with the practical arrangements to close the organisation, to physically emptying the WAF office (actually with the assistance of NMP men) and placing its filing cabinets in storage.

## BEING A BRITISHER IN INDIA

In summer 1996 I left to study at Delhi School of Economics (D-school). I chose India because I wanted to learn more about the north Indian context of Sikh and Hindu fundamentalism and whose tentacles stretched out to ethnic minority communities in London. I specifically chose Delhi because I carried this fantastical sense of getting a 'cutting edge' experience away from the 'less authentic' cosmopolitan city of Mumbai. Initially I indulged a latent fantasy for revolution and went in search of Left organisations, of which there were dozens on campus. I started a relationship with a Left activist from the North East of India and learnt a great deal about the most repressive dimensions of Indian nationalism.

It wasn't long before I encountered the incredibly inspiring Pratiksha Baxi and the university's Gender Study Group. A young woman had been stalked and murdered a short while before I moved to Delhi and a group of female students started to lobby the college on sexual harassment. We organised a mass sit-in outside the Vice Chancellor's premises demanding that he institute procedures and policies for action against perpetrators. The vile comments of one particular lecturer – who suggested that if a student were to be raped during fieldwork this would be an incredible insight for social science research – reflected the endemic levels of violence against women in the area.

Having come from a political space where I did not want to subscribe to a British identity (the 'ain't no black in the Union Jack' school of politics) I found Delhi accentuated it. Even though I am of Indian origin, after two and a half years of living in Delhi, I continued to feel like an outsider. More importantly, the continuous experience of sexual harassment around campus, on buses, the institutional and culturally imposed curfew on women's movement which made evening outings unbearable if not impossible, made me acutely aware of the freedom of movement that I had been accustomed to in London. My rose tinted spectacles had also become tainted by my own personal experiences of harassment. All of this ultimately folded in to a growing feeling that I wanted to stop running from and rather actively engage with my own 'back yard' i.e. Southall.

## HEADING HOME TO WORK IN MY OWN BACKYARD

Towards the end of 1998 I returned to Southall and reconnected with SBS where I was employed as a case/youth worker. Being at SBS was more of a home coming than being in Southall, I felt so completely at one with the politics and I had a great deal of energy not just for intensive case work but also for an active young women's group and campaigning.

The political climate in London had changed. The real shape of Blair's New Labour was not yet entirely decipherable but there was a real feeling of possibility. Soon after the Macpherson inquiry into the murder of black teenager Stephen Lawrence, there was an attempt to start a national civil rights body to connect a number of struggles. I was surprised by how little the initiative took account of women's rights in spite of the decades of work fighting domestic violence and abuse. Pragna Patel and I attended the launch of the National Civil Rights Movement and forced the Zoora Shah case on to the agenda. For me these were early insights into what Gita Sahgal later articulated as the indivisibility of human rights.

When New Labour also established the first ever government group on violence against black women – the Forced Marriage Working Group – SBS joined and it opened new questions about our relationship with the state. Thatcherism had been a period of standing clearly outside the state. New Labour's social democratic tendencies meant they seemed to stand for equalities and so people stepped into government spaces to effect change. However, I would go to 'social' events and have to defend SBS' alleged 'co-option' by an inherently racist patriarchal state. Yet I had never before worked with such savvy political players; SBS moved across different state and civil society spaces but stood firmly by their political principles and demands.

Before 9/11, and whilst I was at SBS, some people were of the view that civil liberties, human rights and left activists had to engage with and try to shape an emerging Muslim political identity and faith based organising towards a left and human rights agenda. We argued for a secular agenda and the need to contest this new discourse at every level. When the forced marriage debate was framed in religious terms as a Muslim rather than South Asian issue, I attended a number of exchanges at which I pushed against the religionisation of the issue and also wrote reports to funders about the new way in which statutory services were beginning to emphasise the 'religious' identity of young Asian women seeking support, irrespective of whether they wanted this to be part of the state's response to their situation.

However, by 2003 I was completely burnt out on SBS casework, which meant I knew about domestic violence on almost every Southall street and had worked on some of the most horrific cases of sexual abuse. It certainly impacted on my ability to engage in relationships but my love of Southall also soured. An interest in trade union activism had never left me so when a friend told me about the Working Lives Research Institute (WLRI) at London Metropolitan University I knew that could be a next step. At WLRI, Mary Davis and I worked closely with Wilf Sullivan, the Race Equality Officer at the TUC, to unpick the shifting concerns amongst trade unionists that, post 9/11, anti-racism was being averted to religious identity politics under the guise of concerns about Islamophobia and new European Religion and Belief Regulations. I believe we produced an accessible research report that, until now, has not been matched in its bringing together of a critique of the new multifaithism, workplace issues and trade unionism.[1] Around the same time, I managed to raise funds for a pilot study about how secondary schools were managing competing equality demands. From this, Pragna and I produced some of the earliest insights into the empirical shift from multiculturalism to multifaithism as it was playing out for ethnic minority girls within the secondary school setting.[2]

## WAF AGAIN

For me, WAF represented a space for sharing experiences and the security that I was not a marginalised voice. I also found it valuable to be in an alliance with women from a range of backgrounds not to mention that the insights on Christian, Jewish and Muslim fundamentalism from the incredibly knowledgeable women within the network were very important for my personal learning curve. This was especially so when I started the PhD in 2007.[3] I don't believe I would have made the theoretical leaps in my learning if I had not been exposed to the hard face of political negotiations involved in challenging fundamentalism and defending secularism.

I was particularly involved with three of WAF's concerns. Firstly, with the sphere of education. With Georgie Wemyss, I made a couple of WAF list presentations about religious mobilisations within higher education and the question of how to balance the need to challenge these with the need to protect educational institutions from authoritarian state interventions that could undermine them as spaces of critical thought. I then joined the WAF education sub group.

Secondly, I was particularly concerned with the sphere of left and anti racist activism. I was working closely with Chetan Bhatt on the PhD and learning a great deal about fundamentalist ideologies. It was at a meeting organised by CAMPACC (Campaign against Criminalising Communities) at the London Muslim Centre in 2008 that I understood the strategic way in which that site is used by different but compatible Muslim fundamentalist activists to network with other Islamists but also with civil society organisations in order to expand their base and accrue legitimacy. So when the Cageprisoners-Amnesty episode exploded in 2010, I could easily relate to Gita's concerns. (Gita was suspended by Amnesty from her role as Head of Gender after she publicly criticised the organisation for its association with Moazzam Begg – see her chapter in this book) I too felt stressed by a seeming unwillingness to counter the swathe of Islamist interventions attaching themselves to human rights and civil liberties concerns while activists in these circles seemed unwilling to recognise the nature of these groups. Whilst I could understand the practical issues for some WAF members of not feeling confident enough or informed enough to carry this issue, I felt at the end that some members simply weren't comfortable working on Muslim fundamentalism.

Connected to this was my third concern – homonationalism. In fact homonationalism and its impact on challenging fundamentalism is one area that, for me personally, brought the tension between activism and academia sharply to the fore. Jasbir Puar's book *Terrorist Assemblages* has gained a great deal of attention in the British context in discussions about the racist dimensions of gay mobilisations. Whilst Puar gathered academic supporters by arguing there is a short distance between liberalism and racism, I began losing friends by pointing out the far too short a distance between anti-racism and the legitimisation of fundamentalist projects. The difficulty for me has not been the concern that gay spaces can be racist – this has been demonstrated by the outing of English Defence League supporters among those that were organising a gay pride march through Tower Hamlets in 2011. Rather the problem with cries of homonationalism in Britain is that these dovetail into projections of 'Muslims' and minorities in Britain as always innocent and as perpetually persecuted. Moreover, the term homonationalism is increasingly used to short circuit debates about Muslim fundamentalism and homophobia within minority communities. If anything, this has brought us full circle to the 1980s debate in which those that wanted to talk publicly about domestic violence would be verbally flogged for allegedly fuelling the pathologisation of Black families.

## CONCLUSION

In recent years, as WAF went into decline, I gained political refuge amongst a handful of friends that I met through WAF and SBS. Religion and politics continues to be the mainstay of my work and I'm now entirely pre-occupied with understanding the co-ordinates of new waves of Sikh fundamentalist mobilisations, which I encountered long before any other fundamentalism. Distinctly contrary to the WAF practice of 'speaking in pairs', I believed in my right to comment on any and all religious mobilisations and I had avoided being pigeon-holed as a 'Sikh woman' that writes about Sikhs. However, the PhD drew me back to the fact that my background – as a Sikh woman from Southall – can provide me with privileged access to a number of spaces that have not as yet been written about or explored. So this is what I intend to tackle next.

## NOTES

1. M. Davis and S. Dhaliwal, *The Impact of Religion on Trade Union Relations with Black Workers* (2007): www.workinglives.org/research-themes/discrimination/the-impact-of-religion-on-trade-union-relations-with-black-workers.cfm.
2. S. Dhaliwal and P. Patel, *Multiculturalism in Secondary Schools* 2006): www.workinglives.org/research-themes/discrimination/cre-multiculturalism-in-secondary-schools.cfm.
3. S. Dhaliwal, *Religion, Moral Hegemony and Local Cartographies of Power: Feminist Reflections on Religion and Local Politics*, 2012, PhD submitted at Goldsmiths, University of London: http://eprints.gold.ac.uk/7802/.

# 12. Making myself through difference

*Cassandra Balchin*

## Editorial note

*This chapter is based on an interview conducted by Nira with Cassandra on 21 April 2012 during the short period she stayed at her home between hospital and hospice placements. It took place shortly after Cass was diagnosed with stage four bowel cancer – just three months later, tragically, she died. This chapter is based on a 17,000 word transcript of that interview. It is regrettable that, unlike the other chapters within this book, there was no opportunity for Cass to consider the selective extracts of the interview that form the basis of this chapter.*

### A FOREIGN KIND OF ENGLISHNESS

I was born and brought up in England. My mother is half Yugoslav and my father was English. My mother had come to live in England in 1939. During the war, her father was an ambassador and had first been posted to France and then fled to England. In those days, Yugoslavia was a sort of wild, exotic place. She experienced racism to some extent, though she would not have identified it as such. Her response was to be more English than the English. Also with my father being a fiction writer, there was a very English atmosphere in our house.

In 1969, when I was between the ages of six and seven, I was sent to live with my maternal grandmother and great-grandmother in Belgrade, Yugoslavia. When I came back, my mother's efforts to make everything English were sabotaged because I had realised that there were other ways of being. My family home was a huge contrast with my grandmother's place and the Mediterranean culture I experienced there. My grandmother was a very sociable person and there had been a lot of aunties and uncles coming through her door. As a result of the time I spent with her, I saw different cultural expressions and it made a very strong impression on me.

My mother had not talked in Serbian with me, but at six years old, I came back from my grandmother's home speaking Serbian. Then my grandmother came to live with us so I was able to keep it up. When I went to boarding school for three years aged nine, I always went on holiday to Yugoslavia: I was very tanned, with olive skin, not pink English rose. Plus my name sounds foreign and I always used to big up the whole Yugoslav connection. So I started *making myself* and emphasising the foreignness.

The other formative aspect was that my father died when I was young – just eight years old. I'd had a very idealistic relationship with him. He was twenty two years older than my mother, so I was a very late child in his life and the youngest of five. He wasn't very busy because by then he had largely stopped writing. We had a very close relationship, albeit a very short one. Even if it might not have been the case, I felt as if I was his favourite. He taught me some poems and I felt an intellectual companionship and a strong connection. So when he died I was hit very hard.

Among other things, I was upset that my mother gave an important personal possession of my father's to my brother as the first-born male, rather than to me. My only choice was to analyse that gesture in gender terms. It did not make me into a feminist at the age of eight, but it was something that stuck in my mind, as 'this is unfair, just because I am a girl'.

There were other gender dimensions as well. At the age of fourteen I announced I wanted to be an astrophysicist, and my mother's response was: 'darling, how will you find a husband?' From her perspective, an intelligent girl was a useful cherry on the top of the cake, but really a girl's job was to be beautiful. She was very obsessed with her own appearance and had a lot of body issues – and she transferred these onto me. So for example, I was put on a diet when I was twelve years old- a whole other dimension to the formation of my consciousness and analysis was a set of issues around my body.

## TRANSITIONING THROUGH IDEOLOGIES

Fast-forward many years, somewhere around the age of 15, I started having leftist inclinations. I had quite a progressive History teacher, who promoted the idea of trade unions so it was in my History classes that I learnt about labour rights. This instinct kept building through the influence of my best friend Catherine's family, who were all Labour supporters. Then at 'A' level, I studied Russian, which involved reading wonderfully political Russian literature and I did History including the Russian Revolution. I fell in love with the whole thing. I used to dream about Bolsheviks and Trotsky. Interestingly, the first card-carrying member of the Communist Party that I ever met was at Westminster School!

This was also the Thatcher era, which was horrific in terms of dismantling the NHS and education, as well as being very racist. I wasn't engaged in any organised anti-racist activity but we were living in Brixton when the riots happened and I was hanging out with friends of all backgrounds. I used to cycle through Railton Road to go to Westminster School, so the anti-racist struggle of the mid-1970s was very much part of my childhood and my consciousness.

Then at eighteen, whilst I was at the London School of Economics and Political Science, studying Russian Government History and Language, I ended up joining the Trotskyist Workers' Revolutionary Party (WRP). At some point I went on one of their summer camps and I quickly ran out of patience with them because they were so conspiratorial and the whole focus was on other Trotskyists or other Communists. Dealing with the Right or with racism was not in their sphere of interest. So I dispensed with the WRP very quickly. Nevertheless, it wasn't through feminism at this stage but through left wing politics that I became engaged with life and society.

At the same time, around 1981-82, whilst I was in the second year of the undergraduate degree at LSE, I also met Holly Sametko, an older American PhD student, who drew my attention to feminism. Catherine, my best friend at school, had already introduced me to Susie Orbach's *Fat is a Feminist Issue*, but Holly gave me Marge Piercy's *Woman at the Edge of Time* and then there was no going back. I remember phoning Holly to say 'I love feminism'! However, I think I turned out to be a very bad feminist because my focus was still very much on political economy and left-wing politics, rather than on feminism and gender. I also became quite involved in nuclear disarmament, because it was very much a period of arms treatise negotiations.

As my degree was coming to an end, I became interested in third world issues because of the friends I made at the LSE. This is where I also met Maliya Lodhi when she was a PhD student. She became the first female editor of a Pakistan English language newspaper and also Pakistan's first female ambassador to the US. Maliya introduced me to a magazine called 'South'. There was a potential offer of a job but they first wanted me to go for a year to a country of my choice and experience the global South.

**PAKISTAN**

The countries I was interested in were Soviet and Central Asia, Afghanistan, Pakistan, and Iran. It was 1983 and Iran was in the middle of all the *Mujahedeen* being killed. Afghanistan was in the middle of the Soviet invasion. And I had no intention of going in a romantic Lawrence of Arabia style, in burka on horseback, secretly across the land. Also that was all anti-Soviet and I was still pro-Soviet. Soviet central Asia was a no-go area so that left Pakistan, which did have martial law, but that was manageable. So I found myself a job in Pakistan through various contacts, and the rest is history. I went there for one year and it turned into seventeen! Within a couple of weeks, a month at the most, I met my future (first) husband, who had studied for eleven years in Bulgaria. His father was the president of the Socialist Party, which you could say is the equivalent of the Communist Party. He spoke beautiful Bulgarian. He was a wonderful Communist. So there was my match and I felt very comfortable in that environment and ended up getting married and becoming very involved in the Socialist Party's work in Pakistan. I also started working as a journalist with the only progressive magazine that survived martial law, which was a weekly called *Viewpoint*. It was a refuge for all the senior Leftist journalists in Pakistan. So I was this young English girl working with these gods of the Pakistani left who were all fifty-plus if not seventy-plus: this was an extraordinary experience now that I look back on it.

During the years I was there, from 1983 to 2000, Pakistan was a really exciting place. It was going through the end of martial law, the arrival of Benazir, the transition to democracy, tremendous social movements, and very hopeful moments in the country's history. I remember the wonderful exhilaration of those days. Those were the days before the end of the Cold War. So there was still hope of a Socialist revolution, and of course one flattered oneself that one was at the centre of all this activism.

At this time, gender and religion played absolutely no role in my life. Religion was absolutely despised by everyone on the left. It was seen as irrelevant. My writing was on labour issues, social issues, disarmament, and peace. I did a story with Sohail Warraich (who many years later became my second husband) on the wives of political prisoners, but it wasn't a gender story, it was about the whole family. I wasn't talking about gender issues even if I was living in Pakistan where there are dress codes and all of that. So for example I drove a motorbike in Lahore. There were five to six million people probably in Lahore in those days and there were six women that rode motorbikes. Two of them were police women who used to ride in police uniform so that they didn't get hassled. The other two used to ride dressed as men. I had my pink flowery dupattas and salwar kameez flowing away. That was quite an outrageous thing to do for a woman. When I went into the bazaar for example I felt very comfortable wearing a chador around my shoulders and body. I was very aware that I was able to get away with both riding a motorbike and being judged as a good woman because I was a foreigner. I was aware of that level of gender and cultural analysis, but it wasn't something that shaped what I did.

I had been working as a journalist since 1984. By 1991, I was the editor of a political bi-weekly, called *Horizons*, part of the *Frontier Post*, which was at that time the most progressive English language newspaper in Pakistan. Then we had a conflict over editorial policy and basically the entire staff, myself included, resigned. In a sense there were no more progressive newspapers to work for, so I was slightly at a loose end. I had started writing on women's issues for a couple of features agencies – Depth News Asia, Women's Features Service and Gemini News – when Farida Shaheed offered me a job to edit and collate the quarterly Women Living Under Muslim Laws (WLUML) newsletters and to edit and produce some of Shirkat Gah's publications. My dear boss from a former newspaper, Abbas Shaheed, was married to Farida, the UN expert on culture and gender rights. Farida was part of Shirkat Gah Women's Collective. At that time, Shirkat Gah had six to eight members of staff – today it's closer to a hundred. Also it was already the Asian regional co-ordination office for WLUML.

I hadn't set out to work for women's organisations but very quickly I became interested in Shirkat Gah's work with WLUML. I liked that it had a lot of leftists in it, that it was international, and their approach and analysis of fundamentalisms made a lot of sense to me. Moreover, within a couple of years, Shirkat Gah became one of the first country organisations within the WLUML Network to launch the Women and Law in the Muslim World programme. I ended up doing the legal research and editing the publications for their Pakistan country research programme. That was the beginning of a love affair with the topic of Muslim family laws. By 1996, I was invited to become a member of the coordinating group of WLUML.

## RELIGION AND SPIRITUALITY

After the end of the Cold War it seemed clear to me that communists or socialists didn't have any answers to what was happening. My first husband, whose life had become so centred around the coming socialist revolution in Pakistan, suffered a severe crisis when the Cold War ended (as many communists did), because their future role became uncertain. I watched that from a slight distance because whilst I felt very bad about it, I didn't feel as if I didn't have a future. Probably by being in WLUML, where there was already a strong gender critique of the male dominated Left, one grew beyond communism while retaining a leftist sensibility.

I can't put my finger on where and how I became interested in religion personally. Even around 1990, I wrote an article about science versus religion which was very didactic, about how science is my religion, which I can still uphold but from a different perspective. Then in 1991, Shirkat Gah hosted what I think was the very first gathering of feminist theologians in a Muslim context, called the Koranic Interpretations Meeting, which brought together activists and scholars. They had an intensive four to five day meeting where they discussed Islam and women and progressive interpretations of Islam. The whole thing was taped and then there was the question of what to do with it. By then blasphemy laws were coming, it was getting difficult to assess how safe it would be to publish this. Whilst they did some public speaking, they were very scared to be put into print. Meanwhile we edited and re-edited the material; I ended up reading the transcript of this four to five days conference many times over. Basically I had a crash course in feminist Islamic theology, and there was no going back from that. It was very, very powerful stuff.

By 1998 I had already separated from my first husband. I was living on my own with my two sons in Pakistan, and I read a book by Alice Walker. She wrote the most beautiful essay on spirituality which really spoke to me, because it wasn't an exclusive spirituality, it wasn't organised spirituality. I felt that spirituality was something that was good, not something to just be rubbished. Imagine being at a point you have just begun to explore spirituality and you are offered the most beautiful option. I wasn't offered standard Islam but anti-authoritarian feminist theology. So I started having a great deal of sympathy for alternative progressive interpretations of Islam and I saw that religion could be compatible with progressive ideas but these ideas didn't yet formulate into anything concrete. I only know that if people asked me: 'Are you Muslim?' I started around that time to answer 'yes'.

I also remember that when my eldest – he must have been seven or eight – had to do *Islamiat*, the compulsory study of Islam, I would be the one who would teach all of the *kalma*, all the saints and prayers, and I actually found it rather beautiful, as poetry. My son was getting treated badly because he was presumed to be a *kaffir* (non believer). I wanted to make sure he didn't have problems at school. So I made sure that my sons did all the religious studies whilst we were in Pakistan but once we were all in Britain, that wasn't a compulsion.

## LONDON AGAIN

I decided to leave Pakistan for a couple of years because my ex-husband was making life difficult for myself and the children. This coincided with an offer from WLUML to be part of the team moving the international coordination office from Grabels in France to another place. As it happened, both Anisa Helie and I decided that London would be the most appropriate place for us personally and for the office. So we ended up in London and I really thought it would be for two to three years but then came a sort of turning point. My eldest son in particular, who was very articulate, refused to go back. The reason he gave was that the education system in London was much better. I think he'd had enough instability in his life. After a couple of years, I began to think 'hm, maybe I got out of the habit of living in Pakistan'. I revelled in the physical freedom of being able to walk down the road without being sexually harassed and the freedom of being completely anonymous. This wouldn't have been the case if I lived in a small town or village with two mix-raced kids but in North London I was completely anonymous. And I did analyse that in gender terms, it was clearly my experience as a woman.

I have very hazy memories of being back in London because I was doing so much. Within six months I bought a house with a huge mortgage and I was busy fixing the house, I was also doing a Masters in Gender and Ethnic Studies and running the WLUML office, I was also looking after my children. What was very liberating at that point was the MA course run by Nira Yuval-Davis because it gave me the means to articulate and bring together all of the different strands of my life in a way that was completely comprehensible. It was the fact that the course contextualised gender, it was gender AND ethnicity, nationalism, fundamentalism, racism, identity. I also knew of Nira Yuval-Davis as someone at the front line of thinking in innovative ways, as anti-authoritarian and non-traditional. As a visual expression, I would say that everything was stuck just under my chin, just at the top of my gullet, there was so much that I wanted to say, so much that I had seen and experienced and wanted to articulate. This course gave me the language. It was a joy to force my brain to think again but god knows how I did it. I was so busy that I did all my readings on the bus and on the train. There was a very practical application alongside the learning at a theoretical level; there were things I wouldn't have questioned before but became able to articulate my discomfort.

## WAF, WLUML AND MWN

I had already known about WAF through Gita Sahgal whom I met in 1998 when we were both working at the WLUML office in France. Also Shirkat Gah used to receive the WAF journals. To be part of WAF was so much a natural extension of my work and activism because WLUML had a very strong focus on fundamentalisms.

For me, WAF's critical contribution has been to make sure that fundamentalisms are not identified purely as Muslim fundamentalism. That is so important, particularly in the post-Rushdie, then post-9/11, periods. And I truly appreciate the fact that WAF is not homogeneous. So some of the discussions are what I would call 'lively' and that is very positive. Personally, I felt that the most useful and positive contribution I could make was to bring an international feminist perspective to emerging feminist or women's movements within Muslim communities in Britain. Eventually, I got involved in (and eventually became the Chair of) the Muslim Women's Network (MWN), which needed quite a bit of input, and I made a conscious choice to focus on that instead of on WAF.

In January 2002, the then Minister for Women during the Labour government, Patricia Hewitt, recognised that post-9/11, there were certain issues that were facing Muslim women and the Muslim community. Maxine Molyneux was tasked with bringing together a group of women to dialogue with her. WLUML was included and I went to a lot of those meetings on behalf of WLUML but there was some discomfort at my involvement. I was very interested in continuing to attend these meetings because I saw that Muslim women in Britain or women in Britain's Muslim communities appeared to have no access to any of the very dynamic feminist movements in the Muslim context to which I had been exposed. I really felt that it was important to share that knowledge and continue to input alternative perspectives, so I kept going to the meetings and over a number of years some of us built up quite strong personal relationships. This includes people who I would have said I had nothing in common with politically, who perhaps I might even have labelled as fundamentalist and dismissed because they wore a head scarf or because they were converts.

The group became more permanent and was supported by New Labour. We turned it into a working group of the Women's National Commission. Eventually, through many bumpy courses we parted ways with the Labour government and MWN was born as an autonomous group. I would say it is very feminist and egalitarian but includes women with very different politics and ideologies. Yet when I am with the board of MWN, there is a huge sense of collective solidarity and tremendous respect. We really have gone through bumpy times. It has been an incredible journey to define ourselves, to understand how to incorporate very different people, with very different ideologies, and yet there is some commonality there in a shared commitment to an egalitarian vision of Islam.

My new focus on the British context was not approved of by WLUML. It was a very controversial issue. This was partly because the MWN group was identified as part of 'the Muslim community', which WLUML had always resisted and always framed as Women living in the Muslim community rather than Muslim women. I tried to get MWN to change their name but I lost that battle. I understood why the battle needed to be framed differently but when you think about it, the WLUML organisation in Sri Lanka was Muslim Women's Action and Research Forum. So why was it OK in Sri Lanka but not in Britain? So there were questions that I found difficult to answer.

Also MWN seemed to be an attempt at turning multiculturalism into multifaithism. As with WAF, WLUML didn't like that approach. Other issues included a concern that I was focusing on Britain when I was expected to focus on international issues and that this was a group of conservative scarf-wearing Muslim women. I think there was also a concern that I was profiling myself at the expense of WLUML. That was part of the reason this became the beginning of the end of my work at the WLUML office. Also, around this time I decided to identify as Muslim publicly and I think that added to the discomfort.

## MOVING ON FROM WLUML

I had personal and political reasons for identifying as Muslim. In Britain, post-9/11, whilst working with WLUML and starting to engage in activism in the Muslim community in Britain, the first question I would be asked was 'are you Muslim?'. For several years I used to give an angry response and question the relevance, but I began to see that this wasn't a satisfactory response, and, increasingly, it didn't reflect what I felt. Internally I identified as a Muslim, but it wasn't that I had a moment of conversion: it was more of a declaration than a conversion. Since I was eighteen or nineteen, years before travelling to Pakistan, I had been hanging around with Muslims, I had had an Iranian boyfriend when I was at the LSE and picked up good street Farsi, I had already been exposed to a lot of issues around Muslim cultures by friends. So I was steeped in Muslim culture, interested in Muslim issues: to all intents and purposes I felt Muslim, it was part of me. And I was also going through a spiritual journey. By that time, I had also become exposed to Sisters in Islam Malaysia, so gained more input on feminist theology and I was also reading widely about other progressive theology.

The crunch moment came one day in the WLUML office. We had an accountant from South Africa and he asked me straight out 'are you Muslim?' And I said 'yes'. And I remember one of my colleagues was passing the room at that time. She was very anti-religion whilst others at WLUML were not and had a more flexible approach to identity and religion, but this colleague literally stopped dead in her tracks and I realised that I had deeply shocked her. Now, whether it is my perception or a reality, things went downhill from there. I felt an element of distrust, an element of distancing. Increasingly I started thinking about branching out, about doing other work. Eventually I went part-time and started freelancing and then in January 2007 I left WLUML and went full time as a freelancer.

Interestingly, on the question of self defining as Muslim, WAF was not monolithic. I found friends in WAF who were completely on the same wavelength as me, who like me might identify as Muslim or as belonging in a similar way to another religion, but it's not my only identity or defining identity. Some were perfectly comfortable with that, because I have a lot of identities as a feminist, as a political activist and as an anti-fundamentalist. But there are other friends in WAF who are definitely uncomfortable with me identifying in any way with any religious identity, because they see religious identity as necessarily being a fundamentalist identity, rather than distinguishing between spirituality and religiosity.

I have a sense of shared identity with progressive Muslim men but not with fundamentalist Muslim men because they don't share my political vision. In terms of religious practice, there has been a huge debate in Islam historically about whether it's just a ritualistic practice or whether we are talking about practice as behaviour? So, I might try to justify some of my behaviour, which perhaps would not follow the letter of the required practice, but I would argue that my behaviour, overall, is of a 'good Muslim'. So I don't say my prayers five times a day, which for my kids is what defines someone as Muslim, but as a Muslim, I would say 'well, it's not for anybody else to judge, it's for God to judge'. At the end of the day I have to judge my practice for myself. Other than that, I haven't gone too deeply into whether I am a religious Muslim or a convert or a cultural Muslim or whatever. Also, I could have become religious from any religion, because as we know there are progressive strands in all religions. Had my life experience been in Uganda, I might have tried progressive Catholicism or something. As it happened, my connection was with Islam. And I reject established religions and the fundamentalist aspects of established religions and organised patriarchal sections of all religions, including Islam.

When I decided to move on from WLUML, I was lucky enough to be offered some freelance work on AWID's 'Resisting and Challenging Religious Fundamentalisms' project.[1] This again led to a tremendous growth in my analysis. It was an extraordinary piece of work and it was not just about Islam, it brought in a broad range of perspectives including an analysis of Evangelical and Pentecostal Fundamentalism, Latin American Fundamentalism, and fundamentalism in Africa. I already had some experience of Africa through WLUML but this was not just Muslim Africa.

## MUSLIM FAMILY LAW

Muslim family law is what makes my heart sing because I feel it's really an area where I can assist individual women and also contribute to global policy.

In 2006, Zeina Anwar proposed to WLUML that a major international project be launched promoting equality and justice in the Muslim family, as a logical follow-on from WLUML's international research 'Women and Law in the Muslim world', which produced some amazing in-country research.[2] For some reason, WLUML were not interested in taking this up. Yet there was continued demand, not least because family laws are one of the main sites for fundamentalist attacks on women's rights; one of the first capitulations of governments whenever there is political pressure from Muslim fundamentalists, as we see now in Egypt, is reflected in family laws. So an independent organisation was set up, called Musawah, which has attempted to be a global movement, even less centralised and directive than WLUML.

At the formal launch of Musawah in February 2009, there were 300 people – 250 delegates and fifty volunteers from nearly fifty countries. There was a tremendous sense of collective solidarity; even though people were very different, they all identified this as something that was important to them. So for this purpose they might identify themselves as Muslims. There were people who very explicitly rejected the identity of 'Muslim' but who were there at the meeting and saw the issue as important and also recognised that it was important to women who identified as Muslim.

One of the things that I was quite pleased with developing was Musawah's project on the concepts of 'guardianship over women' and 'male authority over women'. I produced a one page mapping of how these concepts are reflected in laws. By laws, I utilise the WLUML sense of both codified laws and also practices that are so strong that they have the effect of laws. So these concepts are reflected in: male control over women's body; the husband's right to demand sex; government policies which require a male signature; the requirement for the husband's signature if the wife wants to get reproductive health services; control over the daughter's sexuality in terms of the father's guardianship through who she marries; and economic autonomy as where the wife cannot open a bank account without the husband's signature. These are all patriarchal concepts of male authority deeply rooted within Islam but not necessarily intrinsic to Islam; there are plenty of interpretations of Islam that say this is not Islam. Moreover, whether they personally need it or because they need to be able to convince the family, the society or whatever, some Muslim women are demanding an Islamic justification for the egalitarian sharing of resources in a marriage. So giving them an alternative vision is also important. I was very pleased with this mapping because it brought me back to an awareness of the different strands of politics where you look at the family, Muslim family, and you realise that there is a whole political economy, where government policies compound the problem.

Following on from this, I have been interested in plural legal orders, which in a sense relates back to the AWID analysis of not labelling this as bad per se but rather focusing on the impact. So you could have an interpretation of a religion which is perfectly egalitarian. However, plural legal orders have overwhelmingly played out as highly discriminatory. This analysis of why they do not work to women's advantage is reflected in a chapter that I co-authored for Progress for the World's Women 2011 report.[3]

## CONCLUDING REFLECTIONS: DEBATING SECULARISM AND SHAPING THE LIVES OF OUTSIDERS

WLUML had a very important conference on the warning signs of fundamentalism, which produced an interesting collection of papers.[4] However to some extent I felt that it was an unsatisfactory exercise, because it critiqued fundamentalism, but did not put forward any alternatives. So we ended up hosting a discussion at one of the AWID Forums, I think in 2005, on secularism as an alternative to fundamentalisms, and my hope was to start a discussion that would consider a deeper, more profound, analysis of alternatives. The Centre for Secular Space is a very important initiative in this regard. There is a vital need for feminists to really discuss what we mean by secularism. For me, it's *secularisms* in the plural, because there are so many different varieties. We need to discuss what form would work, in what context and for which women. My understanding of secularism, like my understanding of Islam, is a very personal interpretation. Exploring different forms of secularism is absolutely vital for ensuring not only the rights of women, but also the right to be religious as well as not to be religious.

I find myself in a very odd position that in certain contexts I have to stick up my hand and say 'but what about Muslims, what about believing people'. In other contexts I have to stick up my hand and say 'but what about atheism, what about people who don't identify as religious?' I find myself positioned constantly as an outsider. We've talked about me wanting to be an insider, but my actual experience is as an outsider, because I always remember the people being left outside. If we see religion as a moral code, it's one moral code amongst many that influences people's decisions and practices. If this is so, it's difficult to understand how we can exclude religion from the public sphere. That doesn't mean that I want an established church but I find it very difficult to envisage a structure that would allow for public policies to be shaped and framed by multiple moral codes, whether their source is religion or any other thought process, code, or normative system. But this needs to happen without religion being given an exclusive place that determines and overwhelms all other decision-making. I find that is as yet elusive. There needs to be more thinking about how that would work in practice. Unfortunately I found that so far the discussion about secularism and non-secularism, like the discussion about religion, has tended to fall into polarised positions where secularism means total separation between church and state. But what does that mean? Is that possible? Is the state not made up of people and are people not religious? So I find the debate very polarised. I know there are friends who think a bit like I do, but I find that there is a real need for debate about this within WAF and also beyond WAF.

## NOTES

1. For more about AWID's 'Resisting and Challenging Fundamentalisms' project: www.awid.org/Our-Initiatives/Resisting-and-Challenging-Religious-Fundamentalisms.
2. WLUML, *Knowing Our Rights: Women, Family, Laws and Customs in the Muslim World*, WLUML, 2006: www.wluml.org/node/588.
3. C. Balchin, 'Legal Pluralism and Justice for Women', in *Progress of the World's Women (2011-12): In Pursuit of Justice*, UN Women 2011: http://progress.unwomen.org/pdfs/EN-Report-Progress.pdf
4. See A. Imam, J. Morgan & N. Yuval-Davis (eds), *Warning Signs of Fundamentalism*, WLUML 2004: www.wluml.org/node/224.

# 13. Telling lives

*Rashmi Varma*

As reactionary fundamentalist movements across the world make daily inroads into our everyday lives, into our intimate spheres as well as the public spaces we traverse, the very act of telling lives can be a pointedly political one. It challenges the divisions between the public and the private, and the outer and the inner worlds that we occupy – and transgress – daily as women and more so as feminists. By 'telling' it the way it is, and by making our stories 'tell' us about the worlds which we inhabit differently but nevertheless share, we can perhaps begin to forge a secular feminist project of solidarity.

But embarking on the act of telling triggers a set of questions about *how* to tell the story of my feminist consciousness, which for the most part has been my political unconscious. How do I order and shape my life? Is it amenable to the pressures of narrative? Should I begin with the present and make my way backwards in time? Or should I tell it from the very beginning – but then where do beginnings lie? Do they lie in the fact of my being born, or in my mother's story, or in Lila's story, my daughter whom I adopted but who feels more intimate than my own flesh? Should I begin with the first historical and political 'event' in my memory that triggered an understanding of my place in the world and of others in it? Does that event lie outside the folds of my private life, or is that separation impossible? Is there a way I could string together disparate events to tell a story whose meaning can cohere? The remarkable thing about thinking biographically is that no straight narrative lines emerge. What one has instead is a series of zig-zags and squiggles, parallel lines and curves that never meet, or intersect only in infinity. And then one wonders if the absence of pattern means anything significant – if that is a bearer of meaning in itself.

## HANDCUFFED TO HISTORY

It was a somewhat unusual morning. I was just twenty-six days beyond my tenth birthday and I was blissfully asleep on that hot June morning in 1975 when my grandfather shook us awake in the bed that I shared with my mother and little sister. 'Mrs Gandhi has declared an Emergency!' he shouted, waving a blank newspaper at us. All the news about the mass arrests of people opposed to the prime minister had been censored, but *The Statesman* had decided to publish the blank pages anyway, with the stark headline in bold black announcing the proclamation of the national Emergency. If Saleem Sinai in Salman Rushdie's *Midnight's Children*, born at the very moment of national independence, had found himself 'handcuffed to history', I can say that my turning ten in the year of the Emergency was equally momentous, at least for me!

It was certainly the first moment of the discovery of something like a state that existed outside our daily lives but that nevertheless had an impact on who we were as individuals in our personal affairs. While the Emergency deemed any political talk in public to be out of bounds, politics entered our daily conversations and comings-and-goings with a vengeance. Even as children we could sense the violence that seeped around us everywhere, and when there was the slightest threat of exposure it typically went underground. Aboveground slogans such as *Baatein Kam, Kaam Zyaada* (Talk Less, Work More) were plastered everywhere, as New Delhi was beautified with great efficiency – slums were demolished and slum-dwellers displaced at a rate that was difficult to keep pace with. When the young woman who came daily to clean my grandparents' home in south Delhi stopped showing up for work, we learnt that she had lost her home. I also remember the time we did not go to school, as rumours spread that Sanjay Gandhi, the prime minister's younger son, had let loose a band of goons who were going about sterilising schoolchildren to meet the family planning agenda of the government.

When the Emergency ended two years later, elections were called, and I attended my first political rally. As the radio announced the election results, in which a motley collection of ideologies and opposition leaders had swept Mrs Gandhi out of power, I kept my own tally on school exercise books; each district in each state, each candidate, total number of votes that won each seat, every detail was logged in my books. As a twelve-year-old I was beginning to contemplate a life and career in politics! My grandfather had half-jokingly named me Aruna Asaf Ali, after the firebrand woman who had played an important role in the independence movement. In retrospect, the Emergency laid the foundation for my sense of the importance of activism – the idea that one could act to change the course of politics and history. For the Emergency was being resisted in a million ways, in literature, in underground political opinion, in the collective consciousness of a people that was experiencing the most brutal assault on democracy since independence in 1947. In the immediate years after the Emergency, I devoured the mini-industry of Emergency literature that had sprung up. I read prison memoirs, journalistic exposés and political analyses with a ferocity that seemed quite atypical of an adolescent.

## STANDING UP ON YOUR OWN TWO FEET

If my grandfather opened up the world of politics proper to me with all its chaos and uncertainty, in our daily discussions over the newspaper and the radio broadcasts, my inner world was in a different kind of turmoil. I had a young mother who had been widowed at the age of thirty. She had come to live with her parents with eight-year old me and my baby sister in tow. Having left college soon after she became engaged to my father, she was not adequately qualified for a profession that would have given her and her young daughters any kind of financial independence. So my grandfather encouraged her to sign up for a secretarial course, so that she could work in an office and 'stand up on her own two feet'. My grandfather, with his government job at the Food Corporation of India, suddenly had the 'burden' of feeding three extra mouths. This was something that was uttered like a mantra in the household, even as we knew we were loved and cared for.

It is only with the passing years that I have come to understand how terrifying the future must have looked to my mother. But I already knew then that a lot was riding on my little shoulders – that her future was intertwined with mine, and that I had to 'stand up on my own two feet' as well. This imperative to stand up on my own two feet was, in an important way, my first feminist lesson. For it was widowhood that had plunged my mother and us into a position of what seemed like interminable precarity, albeit one that was leavened for my sister and me with the joys of being children in an extended family of doting grandparents, uncles and aunts. When my uncle, my mother's younger brother, went to university, I would be assigned tasks by him that included copying by hand whole passages from history books about the transition to capitalism in Europe, the French and Russian revolutions, and the Indian nationalist movement. I was reading Marx and Gramsci without being conscious of their world historical importance, but the big words and concepts made an impression, as eventually they came to organise my universe in important ways.

My mother's own inspiration was her paternal grandmother, her beloved *dadi*, who had been widowed at a similarly young age, and who had had three young sons to bring up. My mother remembered her grandmother for her inner courage and her indomitable will. With my mother's widowhood, history was repeating itself, but with a difference. Her paternal grandfather had left a vast and beautiful mansion for his wife and sons in the city of Patna. He had been a well-known and highly successful lawyer, an Anglophile who got his suits tailored in Savile Row, who had ordered a Rolls Royce to be specially delivered to his home in India, and who kept an English cook. He had followed in his father's (my mother's great-grandfather's) footsteps and studied at the Bar in London. They were *zamindars* (landowners and absentee landlords), who had given up life in the village for social and professional attainment in the city. My mother's grandfather was a modern man, one attuned to the times. Although I do not know much about his political beliefs, I know that his father had been in correspondence with the great independence leader Dadabhai Naoroji. I have also heard that Mohandas Gandhi visited the home when my grandfather was a baby. So my educated guess is that this was an affluent liberal and modern family that was part of the elite support for the nationalist movement in Patna.

Before the lure of new money captivated my grandfather in his old age, he too seemed like the perfect product of the Nehruvian times – a staunchly honest government servant who followed the law in both letter and spirit. And, while my grandmother performed her daily *puja* to the *shiva ling* that she had inherited from her mother-in-law, I did not grow up in an overtly religious household: my childhood life was far from the poison of communal feelings that began to take hold among acquaintances, family friends and family members from the 1990s onwards.

I spent many childhood years in the grand house that had been built by my great-grandfather, in states of both blissful delight and later of considerable trauma. Its cool marble staircase, its graceful balconies and long, endless corridors, and its lychee and mango trees in the courtyards, provided an idyllic backdrop to my childhood vacations, before we were forced to live there permanently after my father's death. I did not know then that my mother's ancestral house would later come to stand in for her lack of right to inheritance from her father. And this was not because the laws in postcolonial India had not changed – the new Hindu family laws did allow women the right, however attenuated, to ancestral property: my mother could have challenged her disinheritance in a court of law. But that would have made her a double outcast in her surroundings. She was already seen as a disobedient daughter because she had remarried after widowhood, and had she lacked the decency to accept her disinheritance she would have been regarded as doubly so.

## GROWING UP

When my mother moved with us to my grandfather's house in Patna to take up a job in the housekeeping department in the town's first five-star hotel, it was to 'stand up on her two feet'. My sister and I were enrolled in the town's best school for girls, and my adolescence truly began. But as I went through the usual growing pains and heartaches, my mental and intellectual life also began to flourish. I had always been a good reader, and have vivid childhood memories of books that my father bought for me, or the birthday gifts that were mostly classics of English literature, which I delighted in for hours. And next door, my friend Anshu's house was full of books and literary magazines, so I found another source of nourishment. There I would read short stories by the radical Hindi writer Nirmal Verma, or Shivani's novels, or extracts of novels by Gunther Grass, Milan Kundera and other writers from the then Soviet Union and the eastern bloc countries of Europe. Anshu's mother was a well-known writer in Maithili and Hindi, her father was a top police official in the town, and an uncle who lived with them was underground as a Naxalite (Maoist)! Visitors to the family consisted of writers and academics, theatre personalities and activists. The radical and maverick Maithil/Hindi poet Nagarjuna would be seated daily in their verandah, sipping endless cups of tea. When I look back upon those high school years, I realise that my love and passion for literature took hold of me then, although I did not know then that I would go on to become a teacher of literature myself.

This period came to an abrupt end when my friend, who was barely a few days out of school, was married off to a man much older than she was. Her child-marriage (in a manner of speaking) made a deep impression on me: I was filled with mystery and fear about how such a family could do this to their daughter. At the Notre Dame Academy, the elite Patna convent girls' school that I attended, we had been the recipients of a strange mix of ideas – of Christian virtue, modern femininity and social justice, but all within a largely patriarchal structure. I would say that one of the central lessons, or rather skills, that we were taught was how, as a woman, one could have legitimate ambition to become a doctor, engineer, physicist or teacher, but could manoeuvre, rather than subvert, the spaces of family and society on the way to achieving these goals.

## LEAVING HOME

Leaving Patna to study at a leading Delhi University women's college was a lifeline for me. I knew that if I was to ever stand on my two feet, I needed to get away and to seize the opportunities afforded by education in the nation's capital.

From the confines of the repressive hostel (hall of residence) in which I lived I saw windows opening up to a world of intellectual discovery. But life here was lived as a series of paradoxes. It was a deeply conservative place for young women, and already in the 1980s the city was beginning to be considered unsafe. On the one hand there was a series of restrictions and prohibitions regarding movement and behaviour (no staying out of the hostel 'after dark' or alone, no smoking or drinking on campus or outside, no entertaining of male friends), while, on the other, there was a sense of inner freedom as I experienced the collective force of young, intelligent women who wanted to change the world. These were contradictions that I became quite adept at living with.

For my Master's degree in English I moved to the university campus in north Delhi. This was a far cry from the sheltered, and often claustrophobic, world of the women's college hostel in which I had spent the three previous years. I moved into another women's hostel, but it was one with more relaxed rules. I could now stay out for longer hours, and could venture out alone. However it was also a world of unknown dangers that lurked outside the gates, threatening to trample our young minds and bodies. It was here that on a cold winter night I was called out to meet a visitor, a middle-aged man, a family friend of my relatives back in Patna. He wanted to take me out for dinner and then to a hotel room that he had rented. I ran in to save my life. This man had daughters my age, and the only time I recall meeting him was at a family wedding back Patna. He must have made a mental note then. Girls who lived on their own in Delhi, the nation's capital, must be 'available'. That must have been his assumption.

At the same time, the move to the larger world of the university campus marked the first time that I felt free to break through the physical and personal confines of my social reality, and to think of myself as an activist. Sexual harassment, victimisation and assault were rife, both on campus and in the city, and the university seemed to be in the grip of what were euphemistically known as 'anti-social' elements. When I think back about the sociology of the times, it is hard to analyse who the perpetrators of sexual violence were who were groping us in buses and campus corridors, and on pavements outside our colleges and hostels. For instance, a friend had a man ejaculate on her dress in the bus! In a university where one's class often determined where one could get admission, as middle-class young women we certainly feared the male students from the non-elite colleges, and our class and academic position made us figures of a revanchist lust. But then there were the more dangerous rich men from the city, who made cruising for girls at university into a well-honed hobby. And of course less affluent, non-urbanised women (disparagingly called *behenjis* in the lingo of my times) were equally subjected to harassment. So gender seemed to unify those of us at the receiving end of harassment and sexual violence more than class. In this context the December 2012 gang-rape of Jyoti Kumar Pandey on a Delhi bus had a particularly eerie resonance for me. It reminded me of the time in college when I too had boarded the wrong bus, and was greeted by a horde of whistling, lusting young men. I was lucky that the conductor saw the look of death on my face and let me off. Jyoti had no such luck.

So, in those days of a pervasive sense of unease about being a woman at university, I joined the movement called the *Goonda Virodhi Abhiyan*, a movement against the criminalisation of life in the university, initiated by a group of leftist students and faculty members.

*Goonda* is not a term that is easily translated from Hindi to English. Popular etymology suggests that it is derived from the English word goon. But goon does not exactly capture the multifariousness of the word, which stands for a complex mix of roguery and lumpen proletarianism. Being a part of this movement, and campaigning against the casual and spectacular misogyny that had enveloped all aspects of life on campus, felt empowering. As well as being very much a feminist issue, in the days before legislation against sexual harassment had been dreamt of, criminality was also a broad left issue. Progressive and left-wing professors were everywhere being harassed and beaten up for challenging corruption and criminalisation within colleges and hostels. In retaliation for his resistance and challenge to the power of *goondas* in his college, my friend and mentor Dilip Simeon, historian, ex-Naxalite and radical activist for a democratic and secular university, was beaten black and blue, his bones were crushed, and his teeth were pulled out.

## FLYING AWAY

When I decided to marry Subir, an old schoolfriend, I had already made a somewhat unusual choice. Ever since I had finished school, my mother had been routinely pestered by sundry aunts and relatives with marriage proposals for me. But she was a brave woman and had experienced life's vicissitudes, and the last thing she wanted for me was that I would get married and to give up ambition of a profession. Out of all the marriage proposals that I received, from bureaucrats and doctors to – as Subir jokes – the owner of the biggest plastic cap manufacturing company in India, I chose the one person with whom I shared politics with a passion, and a deep, empathetic friendship.

Soon after our marriage, I followed Subir to the US and enrolled in a PhD programme. I remember landing in Chicago on a cold January evening in 1990, and realising I had no idea what life had in store for me in this alien environment. My sense of elation at being reunited with my husband was tempered by acute homesickness for my family, and a sense of political bereftness, as all the issues of social justice and gender equality that had moved me to be part of larger movements seemed to be receding from view.

But this sense of loss did not last long, for just a fortnight after my arrival I heard about a local human rights group called India Alert.

Desperate for some kind of connection with the life I had left behind, I ended up at a meeting of suburban doctors, university professors and students, discussing fervently a whole range of human rights abuses going on in India.

In the early 1990s, Chicago's inner city and south side neighbourhoods were littered with the unemployed and the mentally challenged, and many houses were windowless and boarded up, or burnt out. Tales of mugging abounded, especially among the foreign students. At the University of Illinois at Chicago, which was still in many ways an inner city university, I was thrown into a sea of challenges. Many, if not most, of my students in the introductory composition classes that I was teaching were working-class whites, inner-city blacks and Hispanics. I embarked on speed self-education about Chicago's immigrant history, and began teaching courses on immigration and exile. Doing so helped me connect the dots of that history to my own as a young foreign student from India.

Things became especially high-wired when the US attacked Iraq and launched its Operation Desert Storm in 1991. I remember that January night vividly – we wandered into the city centre, hoping that there would be others who felt similarly disturbed by America's hubris (Saddam's arrogance had been bad enough). In the darkness of the night, in a city of several million people, I saw my friend Jeff wandering around, like us, not knowing how to respond to this noxious act of war. I then began attending all the anti-war protests and meetings. I covered myself with anti-war buttons – and found myself on the receiving end of open hostility in my working-class campus, where patriotism to the American flag signified the only hope for any kind of social mobility. I began reading Edward Said and listening to Iqbal Ahmed, and taking courses on colonialism and literature. I learnt about the struggle for Palestine and joined solidarity groups. My world as it had existed was getting bigger by the second, and I was hungry to know more. As public space for dissent kept contracting, it became clear that capitalist America was not about to cede its control over the world's oil resources.

Meanwhile in India, the communal forces that had been gathering strength throughout the 1980s were emboldened by the government's craven response to all challenges to secularism. On 6 December 1992, right-wing Hindu fanatics attacked the sixteenth-century mosque the Babri Masjid in the city of Ayodhya, claiming that it had been built by destroying an ancient temple, the birthplace of the Hindu god Ram. For us, as members of India Alert, this was a critical moment. It was no longer enough to sit in living rooms and discuss human rights abuses in India. We began visiting the local temples and homes of suburban community members to open up discussion on the fascist turn that Indian politics was taking, in which Muslims were being targeted as enemies yet again. At the temples we discovered the ways in which the campaign for building the temple in Ayodhya was being carried out through selling bricks for its construction. Each brick was to be sponsored by a devotee, who by paying several hundred – or thousand – dollars could, while still sitting in Chicago, play his or her part in strengthening the Hindutva movement. One wealthy doctor, a 'backward caste' man who lived in a Chicago suburb and had made his millions feeding from the corruption built into the American medicare system, explained his participation in the Hindutva movement as stemming from a fear of deracination, and anxiety that his children would not know what it meant to be a Hindu. But this was also as a response to the pervasive presence of Christian fundamentalism around him. When I asked him why he was so active in the temple's activities, he made this point: 'I started going to the temple when my Christian boss told me: "You know, Doctor, I take my kids to the church every Sunday, and I give copious amounts of money to Christian charities. What do you do to make your kids aware of their traditions?" That day I decided that I would become an active member of the temple community'. And he had gone on to become one of the most vociferous supporters of the temple-building project in Ayodhya.

To help stem the rising division in the South Asian community, we also participated in marches organised by Muslim groups, as riots broke out after the destruction of the mosque. But at those marches we noticed a disturbing trend of Muslim fanaticism, which attempted to match Hindu fanaticism step by step, word for word. Seeing slogans at the marches that asked for Hindus to be slaughtered in retaliation for the destruction of the mosque, a friend and I just simply and totally broke down. We were born into Hindu families by accident, were they willing to kill us? Our disconsolate weeping brought the women in the march to surround us, to protect us, and together they demanded that the men who were carrying those banners take them down. We had succeeded momentarily in stemming the tide of hatred, but for how long? The Indian community remained deeply divided along religious and caste lines. And yet on the surface those differences blended in to make the US seem like a happy, multicultural space.

## GOING SOUTH

My first job took me for the first time to the southern United States, to the state of North Carolina, to teach at its flagship campus in Chapel Hill. The university was already famous for the anti-sweatshop struggle that its students had waged in the mid-1990s, when they had forced the university to divest its multi-million dollar sports apparel industry from factories around the world that engaged in unfair labour practices. Coming out of those campaigns, a group of faculty members formed the Progressive Faculty Network, where we met monthly to discuss issues of social justice in education and work. In a context in which unions were prohibited, it was a unique group, made up of people from different disciplines and political experiences. So when 9/11 happened, we were organised enough to take on the unbearable jingoism and patriotism that gripped the campus and the nation. We organised the first national teach-in, and called it 'Understanding the Attack on America'. Over a 1000 people attended, and we ended the night of 17 September 2001 with hope that the event had, if nothing else, injected a different political analysis to the attacks of 11 September. Little did we know that from the next day onwards there would be a mass campaign – over radio and blogs and right-wing papers – against me and my two co-oganisers (the artist/art historian Elin O'Hara Slavick and the radical anthropologist Catherine Lutz), demanding that we be sacked from the university for carrying out anti-national activities in a public university, or, worse, be shot dead. As a foreigner and a non-tenured faculty member I was perhaps the most vulnerable of the three of us. But although every now and then we looked under our cars or over our shoulders for possible physical threat, we still carried on with our series of teach-ins. It was only later that someone pointed out to me that shooting those seen as anti-national was not an impossibility. Only a few years before, Bob Sheldon, the store manager of the local anarchist bookstore, Internationalist Books, had been shot and killed at point-blank range while he was working the till in the shop – and nothing had been stolen.

Somewhere within the entire discourse of hyper-Americanism unleashed by the right and the discourse of anti-imperialism of the left, I was beginning to sense a deep unease within myself. The question of gender was being increasingly overshadowed, even as we knew that across the globe women would be bearing the brunt both of the increasing tide of religious fanaticism and of US patriotism. Not long before this I had stumbled upon the amazing collection of essays *Refusing Holy Orders*, edited by Nira Yuval-Davis and Gita Sahgal. If I were to list the feminist books that have made the biggest impression on me, this would be right at the top. It enabled me to grasp the complexities of the social and communal construction of women in ideologically charged ways. With my friend Miriam Cooke, a Women's Studies and Arabic Studies professor at Duke University, I organised a joint teach-in on Women Fight Fundamentalism. I had only just about heard of Women Against Fundamentalism then – when researching for a graduate paper on the Salman Rushdie affair I had come across some material on WAF and their work around that time. But I was not entirely aware then about how my own analysis, coming out of my experiences in India and the US, was dovetailing with the work that WAF had done. I invited Gita Sahgal from London, and Miriam invited Nawal el-Sadaawi from Egypt. We also invited Mab Segrest, a radical feminist and writer who was still living in North Carolina. These three women together provided the most astute analysis of how the newly-minted global 'war on terror' and the 9/11 events were going to have a profoundly reactionary impact on women's rights everywhere.

## FINDING WAF

When I moved to London in December 2003, I found that WAF no longer met regularly, and that its status as an existing organisation was ambiguous. But within a couple of years the group was revived, and we began meeting in Nira Yuval-Davis's warm home in what she called her 'soup kitchen'. The discussions in Nira's kitchen brought home to me the fact that Britain's status as a former colonial power meant that it presented a wholly different set of challenges for a feminist analysis of secularism and fundamentalism from those I was used to thinking about. Communal identities, especially as they pertained to South Asians, seemed to be far more entrenched here. With a much longer and more complex history of migration by South Asians, Britain's multiculturalism seemed to have evolved out of a different political logic, which tended to encourage ghettoisation of communities, as a continuation of its old divide and rule politics.

But there was also a rising new trend, whose tail end I had caught in my last year in the US. Much as the right was contracting secular spaces through its rhetoric of patriotic jingoism, the left, too, in the name of anti-imperialism, was stifling criticisms of minority religious fundamentalism. During this time I was also associated with Awaaz-South Asia Watch in London, where I encountered the lingering legacies of the 2002 genocide in Gujarat (in whose wake Awaaz had been formed); but I also found that human rights activists who were involved in defending the rights of victims of extraordinary rendition seemed unable to simultaneously adopt a critical approach to minority fundamentalism. This was most baffling to me, and it was only through a WAF analysis that I could even begin to gain a sense of the terrain. In my own critical work with feminism, the concept of the articulation of race, class and gender has now begun to gain salience as a result of what I learned in WAF.

If what Sartre termed 'force of circumstance' is what leads one to specific social situations that shape the contours of one's life, what one makes of those circumstances can be, and is, a matter of feminist politics. To create a different world requires endless, untiring work, among which is the task of telling our lives. It is in that spirit that I offer this story of mine.

# 14. Change, chance and contradictions

*Sue O'Sullivan*

In 1996 when I re-settled in north London, I was still reeling from the end of an eight-year relationship and four years of living in Australia. Here I was, a fifty-five-year-old lesbian whose relationships always seemed to end in failure. Although I quickly rediscovered how much I liked living alone, it took a couple of years to get rid of the blues. After more than a decade's work around AIDS both here and in Australia, I got a job at the International Community of Women Living with HIV/AIDS (ICW). I started editing their newsletter and immersed myself in ICW work and politics. The majority of ICW's members lived in Africa, Asia and Central and South America. Through communications with members around the world and attendance at global AIDS conferences, all the different ways in which fundamentalism seriously affected the lives of HIV positive women became increasingly obvious. Not only did they have to deal with an incurable and devastating condition (most had little or no access to effective treatments); more often than not, they faced stigma and hatred. Women were specifically targeted and blamed for being the vectors of infection, sometimes facing violence and even murder. It's an old story, and one that is always exacerbated by women's inequality and the impact of class, race and poverty.

Yet the women who were members of the ICW network displayed astonishing resilience and courage. Finding strength in numbers, in different ways, in different settings, positive women criticised the strictures forbidding contraception and sexual autonomy and the laws enforcing dependence and subordination to men and oppressive institutions. Most of these women didn't call themselves feminists, and yet, as the cry 'Ladies, Stand Up' resonated in meetings and self-help groups, who could not be moved by their growing self-awareness?

Fundamentalism had long been making itself felt when I started working at ICW in 1996. And I had also been part of a group of London feminists that in 1991 organised a workshop to look critically at the Gulf War. Ten years on, and after the attack in New York, I longed to be part of a wider political response – one which would engage simultaneously with fundamentalism and any racist and reactionary developments in the west. WAF was tough on fundamentalism within all the major religions, be they Christian twisted weirdoes in the USA, Hindu reactionaries in India, or Jewish extremists in Israel. A WAF statement declared that, 'We hope you will join us in trying to build a secular movement against racism, state-sponsored terror and religious fundamentalism.' I was ready.

## MY FAMILY

I grew up from the age of four in rural Connecticut in the USA. My family were liberal, Quaker and white. My father taught at the state university of Connecticut. In many ways, my childhood was blissful. Forget the clichés of the totalising rigidity and conformity of the American 1950s. I was a tomboy, as were most of my girlfriends. Our favourite outfits included jeans and boys' sneakers. I can't think of a single time when any of our mothers voiced disapproval. Many of the mothers themselves wore slacks or even 'ladies' side-zipped jeans. From the age of six, I could set off on my own on the half-mile walk over wooded roads to my friends. On weekends and holidays as we grew older, we took off on our bikes and roamed, foraging and exploring deeper into the woods and undergrowth, hidden from adult eyes.

My parents had both attended Swarthmore, a Quaker college. My dad's family were 'birthright' Quakers and he had grown up in a small town on the Delaware River in New Jersey, surrounded by his extended family. My mother was born in Illinois and left there after high school for college in the East. Her parents were politically conservative, but once she had met my father, my mother was forever a liberal and a Quaker.

My parents were not radicals. But being pacifists (my father was a conscientious objector during the Second World War) almost automatically put them in a semi-radical place. My dad had spent his war years in alternative service with the American Friends Service Committee in Spain and Portugal. There he was part of a mainly

European team who assisted people fleeing down through Europe into Spain and Portugal, joining the queues for boats sailing somewhere safer. I was proud and a bit boastful about this.

As a child I liked my parents' difference from other parents, even though it was a safe 'difference': we were privileged and mainstream in spite of it. In our town of Storrs I had a small sense of being an outsider while still surrounded by the security of my family, race and class. I had a keen sense of what was fair and unfair and was grimly aware of the unfairness of family life, no matter how mundane. Why didn't my brothers have to iron the family's shirts and blouses as I did? Why was my mother able to smack me when I had no right to retaliate – and she a pacifist? What a self-righteous pain I must have been.

Then, driving the forty-five minutes to Hartford, our nearest big city, we would pass wooden tenement buildings. I could see that poor people lived here, both white and black. Who were they? Whatever explanation I got, it was clearly unfair that those kids didn't have what I had. As I grew older, the poverty and the racial prejudice I knew so little about in my own life but saw at a distance felt 'unfair' and therefore wrong. I didn't have a clue how racism or class informed so much about my own life.

My parents hosted a number of liberal visitors to the University of Connecticut. We children were welcomed (and expected) to take part in conversations, especially at mealtimes. I remember one person in particular who stayed with us in the mid-1950s, Bayard Rustin, a black activist committed to non-violence who later worked with Martin Luther King. Did my parents know he was gay? I don't know, but they never spoke of this, even later when Rustin organised the 1963 March on Washington and we recalled his visit with pride.

Quakerism gave me a moral outlook on life but it didn't answer my questions of why things were the way they were or – beyond moralising – what to do about them. As I grew older this became more and more frustrating.

## TANTRUMS AND CHANGE

Relations with my mother grew increasingly combative the older I got. We fought regularly over many things. I was an upstart, quick to bristle at her authority, and she was driven crazy by me. What a combination – one growing girl, one mother, both screaming, both in tears – but of course she held the power, and I would be sent yelling and furious to my room. I'm sure this situation contributed to me being sent at age fourteen to a Quaker boarding school in Pennsylvania in 1955.

I was up for it. I loved my four years at George School. I ran around with kids who thought they were wild but probably weren't. I encountered new ideas and academic challenges. I called myself a pacifist. Although the school was considered liberal, at that time there were few black students. One of my friends there was Julian Bond, who went on to become a well-known Democratic Party and black activist. But when he started dating a white girl the school wrote to her parents telling them she was dating a Negro. The gentle Quaker religion I grew up in showed some cracks.

I assumed I would go to college and I chose Sarah Lawrence College in New York because of its strength around the arts, particularly fine arts, dancing and theatre – and because at that time it was a women's college. Then there was the proximity and lure of New York City and the boys and men one might meet there. Once I got to Sarah Lawrence I made a sudden switch to dance instead of pursuing my high school passion for drama. My choice of dance was rash: eighteen was too old to start. But I loved it.

I entered college in 1959 age 18, just as the civil rights movement and college protests were beginning. Sarah Lawrence had a strong liberal slant and early protests included a 1960 demo in solidarity with sit-ins protesting segregated lunch counters in South Carolina. By 1962 a college Civil Rights Committee had formed. Later, in 1965, one beautiful dancer, a black girl in the dance department, choreographed a suite of four dances inspired by the civil rights movement. It was evident that politics and art were mutually sustainable.

## LOVE IS COMPLICATED

During the years 1961 to 1963 I spent a year abroad in London. During that time I managed to get arrested on an Aldermaston March. More importantly, I fell in love with J, a young PhD student at the LSE, where one of my roommates was studying. In early summer 1962 I was back in the USA, puzzling over what this relationship might mean for the future. Sure, I'd had a few high school romances and a variety of sexual liaisons since turning eighteen, but I hadn't seriously fallen in love before. Airmail letters winged back and forth across the Atlantic. We wanted to be together. But despite that major decision, I managed to get pregnant during our year apart and had to get an illegal abortion.

I got pregnant by sleeping with someone I'd known, but not well, since I was six years old. I regretted it even as the brief, empty sex was happening. No way would I tell my parents – or the boy concerned. But abortion was illegal and I had no idea where to get advice or practical help. With support from friends, I eventually ended up in Puerto Rico with ten and twenty dollar bills stuffed in my shoes and hidden in my case. The place itself was surreal, the tropical setting lending the illegality of the act a nightmarish quality. The abortion turned out to be skilled, and, thankfully, I suffered no damaging side effects. Luckily for me J, with whom I was deeply in love, dealt with the hurt and we stayed together. I moved back to London in 1963 and we got married that autumn in Egypt, where my father was temporarily teaching at the American University in Cairo.

After a crazy Cairo wedding we settled back into a more ordinary life in London. J's family was different from any I had known in the USA; we may have talked about racism in my family and school, but never, at least overtly, class. Not only were J's family working-class, they were also politically radical, one in the Communist Party, the other in the Labour Party. J had grown up during the war, while his father was away, not coming home from Palestine until 1947. Meanwhile J, his mother and his older sister had been bombed out of South London, ended up in an asbestos shed on the Hampshire coast, dangerously near to German bombing raids.

In London J and I had a dilapidated two-room basement flat in Camden Town, for which we paid about a pound a week in rent. Our bath was in the house next door and was shared by all the tenants. I was back at Audrey de Vos's ballet studio, where I'd spent so much time during my year away from New York, and I was busily typing J's PhD.

In 1965 we sailed for New York City, where we stayed for two years, while I finished my undergraduate degree and then got a job teaching at a nursery school. I also started taking dance classes at the studio of my favourite choreographer, Merce Cunningham. J got his first teaching job at the New School for Social Research in Greenwich Village near where we lived in an old tenement building. His classes on Marxism were particularly popular with a group of graduate students who were all involved in Students for A Democratic Society

(SDS). We regularly took part in increasingly large and militant anti-Vietnam war demonstrations. On one of these I first saw placards saying 'No Vietnamese ever called me nigger' (a saying widely attributed to Mohammed Ali) – being carried by the increasing number of Black Americans taking part in the protests. The slogan 'up against the wall, motherfuckers', a counterculture slogan with strong resonances in the Black Power movement, was much in evidence in those years, and its effect was to jolt white people out of their liberal comfort zones. The impact of these symbolic iterations forced me and many others to problematise 'whiteness', both personally and politically. On the lighter side of protesting, in the spring of 1967 there was a massive Human 'Be-In' in Central Park, where with friends, mainly New School students, we hung out, smoked pot and celebrated the diversity of the crowd brought together in such creative forms of protest.[1]

## BACK TO LONDON

I was pregnant when J and I left New York and returned to London in the summer of 1967. I came back with only a partial sense of what it would mean to live in the UK, though I was looking forward to having a baby. I also came back with a stronger knowledge of socialism, explored through discussions with politicised Americans of my age – the American New Left was in its heyday at that time. But I returned without any close women friends, leaving my many old American ones behind. I assumed I would dance through my pregnancy and continue as before after the baby was born. I had little idea of where I might fit in in London.

By autumn 1967 I was living in a flat in the then distinctly non-gentrified area of Stoke Newington. I was asked to leave my dance class because my leotard-clad bulk scared the other students. J and I went on intensifying anti-war demonstrations, the last of which was in Grosvenor Square, where mounted police charged and hot heads threw steel marble under the horse's hooves.

By the time T was born, J was teaching at the City University, and I was at home with the baby. It was 1968 and the students were revolting. That summer we took T to visit friends and family in the States. While staying in the East Village in NYC, I met up with some old SDS and women friends who were full of excitement about the new women's liberation movement. I wondered how the hell this could include me, baby in tow?

Having a baby changed everything – but that in itself was not an insurmountable shock. What was shocking, though, was an incredibly difficult labour and birth (two days' labour and then a deep forceps delivery). It was as if I went to sleep and woke up in another land, stunned. I felt a blank numbness when I looked at my almost ten-pound baby. Where was the love? What was I to do with this creature that sucked contentedly on my breasts? T slept like a dream and I stared at him, at my stretch-marked stomach, at my husband who was floating in waves of never-ending baby love, and thought: this is a nightmare. The thing was, I didn't have postnatal depression – at least not as it was described in the baby books I'd read religiously (even underlining long passages from Spock).

After I had a second son two years later, I assumed the mantle of 'bad mother' for myself. What else could I be with the feelings I had – and didn't have? I was competent if exhausted, did the laundry, dabbed off baby poo and vomit without a problem and breastfed each baby for almost a year. And the boys were sweet things, wide-eyed and calm. But even by the time I could truly say I loved them, it seemed too little, too late. And I was the girl everyone said would be a fabulous mother.

## WOMEN'S LIBERATION

By 1969 I had decided this 'women's thing' might have something to do with me after all. I heard about a women's 'small group' meeting in Tufnell Park, went along one night and never looked back. Here was a place in which I could describe the realities of my day-to-day life and conflicting emotions and not feel like an over-the-top whiner. Although J was always supportive and consistently did more than his fair share of childcare, something was out of kilter. In that small women's liberation meeting it all became obvious. We were collectively sharing stories about our lives and identifying the oppressive social relations we lived in. In the Tufnell Park group most of us were middle-class, and we were all white. The early Women's Liberation Movement was widely and rightly criticised for its exclusions, initially by black feminists. However, it's important to remember that some black and working class women were part of the movement no matter how critical they were of it. Both realities should be acknowledged.

Most of us had small children and were ostensibly heterosexual. We were all non-aligned socialists and anti-Vietnam war activists. We read about the Chinese revolution. We gobbled up Frantz Fanon and Emma Goldman. We discussed childcare, orgasms, birth control, abortion, how women were being targeted by advertising, what our ideal society would look like, what needed to be done about men, about violence, sharing house work, getting equal pay, ending sexism. Working-class women carried double burdens; poor black women carried triple ones. We insisted that the tangibility of inequality and oppression be addressed. We dreamed of transformation and liberation. We said, 'Who wants to be equal to unfree men?' Revolution might be necessary for all of this to happen, but we had no intention of waiting until 'after the revolution' to change our lives and challenge all the stubbornly deep-seated resistance to our dreams and demands. We were questioning not only class, race and gender oppression – we were puzzling out the way in which these huge divisions and areas of complexity played themselves out in our daily lives. The personal was political but only by breaking free of the myth of individualistic solutions could we explore collective solutions.

## *SPARE RIB*

I moved out into the world more and more as my children started school. In the 1970s I was actively involved in London's Women's Liberation Workshop in Covent Garden, where I exercised political muscles and experienced differences and difficulties between feminists. However, I was more and more convinced that the acknowledgement of these differences and power differentials between women also presented creative possibilities to join together. I cut my writing teeth on the publications being produced by local London consciousness-raising groups, and loved planning and producing these eagerly devoured home-made newsletters – like *Bitch* and *Harpies Bizarre* – as well as the more formally structured Marxist Feminist Journal, *Red Rag*.

In 1979, after teaching part-time in Holloway Prison for much of the decade, I got a job on *Spare Rib* (*SR*) magazine, after completing a Health Education diploma at Southbank Polytechnic. During my time on *SR*, the collective swung back and forth from excitement to misery, all contained by the ongoing necessity to plan and create an issue every month. *SR* set itself a nearly impossible task, trying to be all things to all women – and to sell the magazine in WH Smiths. We had many loyal readers, but we also displeased other women in equal measure, whether they read it regularly or not. I was obsessed with the magazine and the possibilities it presented.

Increasingly the collective tore at itself. In the late 1970s and early 1980s, difficult issues were becoming increasingly obvious in the women's liberation movement – *and* the rest of society too. At *SR* we came to grief over lesbianism – in the first instance over the supposed anti-lesbianism of some of our readers. Dissonance was soon on display again in the rifts and upheavals over the collective's struggle with racism. And the same ragged responses appeared when *Spare Rib* was accused of anti-semitism after we carried a critique of the Israeli invasion of Lebanon. We disagreed on how to grapple with these issues. I believed that blanket denunciations were the easy way out and preferred attempts at actively engaging with the women I disagreed with, the majority of whom I didn't consider to be consciously racist, anti-semitic or anti-lesbian. If we couldn't engage in arguments and struggles around these issues in our own movement, how could we hope to challenge and change them in the larger world?

All of these accusations and disputes – largely focused on identity – ran and ran, both within our office in Clerkenwell and in the wider women's movement. Identity had always played a central role in early feminist politics as a radicalising force, an initial urge to join together around the commonalities discovered in consciousness-raising groups. But when identity became a totalising and organising principle for women's movement politics, it raised a suffocating moralism in which hierarchies of oppression proliferated, often taking over any critical analyses of class, race and sexuality, and the way in which these intertwined and interacted. Anger is always more dramatic than the ordinary business of getting on with day-to-day work and friendship. Thankfully there were also many days on the collective when laughter and kindness, calm and cooperation reigned.

## UPHEAVALS AND POSITIVE WORK

In 1981 I left my family, unable to successfully combine the lesbianism I had embraced enthusiastically in the late 1970s and being in a heterosexual marriage. Bisexuality at the time was considered a denial of one's authentic sexual orientation. I never subscribed to that point of view, but bisexuality just wasn't an option I was interested in. I was convinced the kids were better off staying in their home with J, who was always a committed and loving father. For years I would go back for three or four days a week to re-assume the practicalities of motherhood. But for the rest of time I was living as a lesbian. By the second half of the 1980s, alongside on-going commitments to feminist campaigns and projects, I was caught up in all the denunciations and arguments about what constituted allowable lesbian sexual practices for feminists. My old *SR* friend Susan Ardill and I wrote about this period for *Feminist Review*.[2] Although we defended lesbian sadomasochistic sexual practices from accusations of intrinsic anti-feminism (or even fascism as some feminists suggested), we also maintained that sexuality wasn't above feminist criticism. Today most of the antagonists of that time have mellowed, but there are some who still won't meet my eyes.

I joined the Sheba Feminist Publishing collective in 1986. Sheba was where everything came together after the exhausting discord and exhilaration of *Spare Rib*. The collective was small – there were never more than five or six women working there at any one time, and often as few as four. Nevertheless we were a significant force in the then lively feminist publishing world, and in the large circles of women who responded so positively to our books. The decision to create and maintain what we called a mixed race collective had been made by the majority grouping of black women on the collective. This was a subversive process, more radical than the more usual course of action (for instance at *Spare Rib*) whereby an all-white group of women invited black women to join them at a table they had already set, and with a pre-ordained menu to boot. Sheba specialised in publishing the writing of black and working-class women, first-time women writers and lesbian authors. Audre Lorde was one of our prestigious American authors, along with Joan Nestle and Sarah Schulman. Our bestselling *Serious Pleasure* collections of lesbian erotica stirred up many sorts of feelings and sold many copies. Although we opposed crude identity politics, or notions of essentialism, we also celebrated the way in which identity could galvanise solidarity and collectivism. Sheba went under in 1992. Its unique titles were becoming more mainstream, and it never fully achieved financial stability.

## MEMORIES

Today I remember much more going on than the seriousness of a flawed but meaningful radical movement for women's liberation. Yes, we were deeply serious and proud of it. But when I hear women describing 1970s and 1980s feminists as dour and dull, I snort. There's a received wisdom all these years later that feminists back then were all po-faced and lacking in humour. How untrue – the pleasures, the hilarity and, let's not forget, the sex, matched and were often sparked off by, the intensity of the work.

## AFTER AUSTRALIA

In 1988 I fell for an Australian woman. We were together for four years in London until deciding it was my turn to move with her around the world. So from 1992 I spent four years in Melbourne, working mostly on HIV and AIDS, and in the process I discovered how challenging and thoughtful sexual politics were 'down under'. But in 1996, I was on my own, shocked by the sudden unravelling of my relationship, and desperate to get back to London. I never wanted to see another gum tree again.

Not that everything was idyllic back home. When I left in 1992 I still felt as if I were part of the women's movement, no matter how battered and worn it was. By the end of the 1990s, although there were plenty of on-going projects and campaigns, the landscape had changed. The high waves of feminism, which had provided political meaning to my life from the 1960s through the 1980s, had disappeared.

Where could I find a holistic activist and politically sympathetic home? I was putting all my energies into ICW, where we increasingly drew on a human rights perspective. At first I was uneasy about this and clung to what I thought of as a more radical analysis; for it seemed as if only selected aspects of a human rights discourse were being used by major global players in the AIDS world to address the pandemic. Organisations like the World Bank and UNAIDS had appropriated the language for their own purposes. But the more I saw HIV positive women themselves take up that language, the more its radical possibilities became clear. When a dispossessed HIV positive woman stood up and demanded her human rights she was courageous. When she joined with others to make the same demand, the words were politically transformed into something more powerful and radically intentional. As I watched, I saw that for many positive women, demanding human rights as a woman was akin (in a different time and settings) to the demands of women's liberation.

## ARRIVING AT WAF

I knew about WAF from its beginnings in the late 1980s. A close friend, Sue Katz, was part of the group and told me tales of the bold founders and their defiant demos. So when Helen Lowe and I attended several London meetings dealing with women and the rise of fundamentalism in the middle of the first decade of the twenty-first century, we were both united in our desire to belong to a reactivated WAF. Until her untimely death in 2011 Helen remained my dear WAF friend, one whom I admired hugely for her tenacity, determination and sense of humour.

But no matter how much I respected WAF, once on board it was not all plain sailing. How do you find your feet, your place, and your confidence, as a newcomer? How do the older members relate to new ones and vice versa? What were my expectations? I admired the WAF women I'd heard speak and agreed with their analyses. WAF women's political insights and practices were sharp and sophisticated. They stood up fearlessly and spoke out in the face of attacks from fundamentalists, and countered the troubling inability of so many on the left to criticise them for fear of being accused of racism. They were committed feminists, who were prepared to look at the complexities of culture, class, race and gender when exploring the impact of fundamentalism on women. I felt I had much to learn, both about struggles against fundamentalism around the world and about what was going on in the UK, with our own home-grown reactionary groupings.

But I wonder if I made WAF into more than it could be, more than any one organisation, no matter how admired, could be? In all my years of belonging to a movement, of activism, I'd always felt most at home in feminist small groups, community organising and grassroots projects – with regular participation in local and national conferences. I valued connecting with black and white women, trying to forge a politics which recognised the ingrained nature of racism but also the complex and often difficult ways we might work together creatively, not only as anti-racists but also as radicals and women.

Without realising, did I bestow on WAF the impossible task of standing in for lost movements? Not only was such a task impossible, hoping for it also skewed the way I engaged. I put WAF up on a pedestal and wanted it to 'fast track' me to new knowledge and ways of organising. I never fully gained confidence, and that meant I never fully participated in the way I wanted. More than once I was anxious about saying the wrong thing, nervous that I hadn't grasped something which others seemed sure of, even though no WAF member, old or new, ever suggested any such thing. Sometimes I felt disappointed in myself. Where had my political acumen, confidence and flair gone?

Helen's WAF path was different from mine. I would have been happy enough to go to WAF organised meetings in which knowledgeable women spoke, and where I and growing numbers of women learned more. Helen was also a learner, but she wanted action more keenly. One time I sent her an emailed saying 'I'm so admiring of how you have really made a leap into WAF activism. I am still lurking on the outskirts.' Helen replied: 'Obviously different women have different interests, different levels of commitment, and political thought/action plays a different role in their lives. I think we should be as open as possible to everyone following their inclinations. My own inclination is to do the active type of thing – demonstrations, pickets, etc. I don't want to be endlessly meeting with WAF women to raise our consciousnesses on different issues – I want to be out there letting the bastards know we're on their tails.' Her energy and drive became a focus for renewed WAF spirit. She revitalised the WAF website, and she took part in demonstrations and meetings. She found her WAF voice. Then, when her 'voice' was silenced so suddenly, it was almost as if we lost our drive.

I won't end on a note of loss. WAF-informed work continues in many organisations, workplaces and campaigns across the country. Late in the game I realise that I *have* changed through being in WAF. I was a radical and activist over many decades, and I still am, even though today my feet aren't so happy on big demonstrations. Being in WAF added to and sometimes challenged older ways of thinking, but only in a creative way, and I still want to be moved by those challenges. Now I am connected to an expanding network of projects and events where I find WAF women as organisers and participants. Former WAF women work in and with Southall Black Sisters; others are engaged in running symposiums focusing on fundamentalism and the defence of secular spaces in their universities; still others are continuing their participation in community-based projects. A WAF perspective influences the newly energised networks of younger feminists, and ex-WAF women often speak publicly on different platforms. I wear my 'Save the NHS' badge and am amazed at how many people take the trouble to tell me they agree, whether I'm in the checkout line or on the bus. In my political study group (three former WAF members included) we ponder the state of the world, and what will finally make the streets echo with people bent on transformative change: enough is enough!

There is no neat trajectory in my life, with stepping stones clearly demarcating a path from one year to the next, a journey free from personal and political contradictions. No matter how liberal my upbringing, nothing guaranteed that I would be pulled into radical politics or collective action. But I was – and for that I am grateful.

## NOTES

1. Human Be-Ins were a creative manifestation of the 1960s counter culture, with a growing emphasis on anti-Vietnam War content, anti-racism and civil rights commitment. A number of 'be-ins' were held in New York's Central Park, including two in the spring of 1967. These events brought together increasingly diverse groupings of people. The Be-Ins had a strong initial element of hippy counter culture, with an increasing left or left leaning participation.
2. 'Upsetting an Applecart: Difference, Desire and Lesbian Sadomasochism', in *Feminist Review* 23, Summer 1986.

# 15. One of My CVs

*Eva Turner*

A life story and a CV contain both a certain amount of factual information and material interpreted through experience and hindsight. This is one of my CVs. Much has been left out.

I was a lively, rebellious and yet an unpretentious child, often in trouble without knowing why. My teens were marked by large breasts and wide bottom, which left me with no end of hang-ups and much unwanted male attention. I had lots of growing up to do before I could call myself a feminist and an activist.

## MY FAMILY

I was born in 1948 in Prague, Czechoslovakia, first of two children. Both my parents came from bilingual Czech/German lower middle class backgrounds. Their families were Jewish; both were secular and assimilated into the mainstream society. Both my grandfathers were travelling salesmen and my grandmothers were housewives. My father completed his education at the age of eighteen, my mother never completed hers because the family was expelled from the 'Sudetenland' after 1938 Munich Agreement.

To save them from the Holocaust, both families decided to send their children abroad. This became possible with the help of the Zionist Betar based in Vienna whose aim was to populate Palestine with strong young Jews. The journey from Prague in November 1939 began as a transport of young people, but the refugee numbers swelled to 2000. The organisers in Prague all died in concentration camps. In most cases of pre-war emigration many families only had the financial means to send children and young people, using all possible ways of escape. By chance my parents travelled together on a metal coal hull called *Sakaria* from the Romanian port of Sulina. After months of a very difficult journey they arrived in Haifa in 1940.

There all men, including my father and his younger brother, were detained for six months in a British concentration camp in Sarafand. My mother, who was still a minor, was sent to a residential agricultural school for girls. Expelled for misbehaving, she travelled to Tel Aviv and worked as a domestic servant until she was eighteen. She then joined the British Army and served in Palestine and in Egypt until 1945. On being released from Sarafand my father worked at a sand brick plant in the desert and later in Tel Aviv in domestic service. When Sarafand was returned to British military use, he was employed there as a civilian responsible for front supplies. By chance my parents met again in 1943, married in 1944, were demobbed in 1945 and repatriated to Czechoslovakia in 1946. They were not Zionists and never doubted their Czech nationality; their Judaism was cultural. My father joined the communist party during the war, my mother after repatriation.

Both my parents had extended families, very few of whom survived the Holocaust. On returning to Prague in 1946 they were given a small sum of money and a room. They learned about the Holocaust at the end of the war in Palestine, but only realised the extent of it on their return to Prague. In 1960s they found few relatives who survived in various parts of the world.

My father returned to work for Shell from where he was sacked again for being a Jew in 1950 (worked there until being sacked in 1939 for the same reason) and sent to work as a labourer in an aeroplane factory where he contracted tuberculosis. He returned to work in 1952 as a clerk for a newspaper distributor. There he remained until 1969, when he was again expelled from the job and from the communist party for disagreeing with the 1968 invasion of Czechoslovakia by the Warsaw Pact armies. He had a heart attack and was prematurely retired. He spent the following thirty- five years translating books from and into German and English and when he was eighty nine years old he completed a university degree. He is still alive and is now 101 years old.

Since her repatriation my mother worked continually in a variety of clerical posts until early 1969 when she too was expelled from the party. She later found employment in a publishing house as a German book editor. After retiring at fifty five, she freelanced as a German-Czech interpreter until her decline into dementia at the age of seventy four. She died three years later.

**MY CHILDHOOD**

My brother and I were born in a one-room flat, within sixteen months of each other. My parents then managed to get a tiny two-room flat on the outskirts of Prague, where we grew up. My childhood was marked by playing on the streets, local fields and the next door building site, spending summers in school or factory organised summer camps and by being at school six days a week. Just like all the others, we were latch key children. Sundays were spent polishing everyone's shoes, vacuuming, running outside or walking with mum or dad. Occasionally, for a treat, we went to the local cinema.

My father spent many Sundays at political meetings or working on building public projects. When he had time for us, he made kites and baked potatoes in the fields. He made a wooden dolls house for me and a stable with animals for my brother for Christmas and allowed us to watch him shave on Sunday mornings. Very rarely he sat at the piano and played. He killed the carp that was allowed to float in the bath for days leading to Christmas Eve. He turned every corner in the flat into a storage space and made mum an electric washing machine out of electrical bits he brought from the factory. I don't remember him ever actively involving me in any of these activities, but I must have absorbed some of it. When we were very small he took us to the obligatory May Day demonstrations and military parades. Later these became compulsory school activities.

My mother was always busy, suffered terrible migraines, and was probably often depressed. While caring for us and holding down a full time job, she also did all the housework. She read us books and cited poems, sang songs and baked the occasional cakes. She tried very hard to assimilate with the Czech population and insisted on celebrating the traditional Czech Christmas. We baked the special Christmas cookies and plaited bread and she took us to hear the Midnight mass. She showed us Prague architecture, including the historical Jewish quarter and picture galleries. She hated the flat, felt claustrophobic and trapped in it and regularly shifted the furniture around in a vain hope to make it look bigger. Both my parents loved classical music and took us to hear it and to see operas.

Mum was never able to recover from the traumas and losses of the war. She regularly, over her whole post-war life, carefully guarded and then in fits of sorrow destroyed the few family and childhood memorabilia she possessed. She collected Jewish writers and the holocaust literature and gave them to us to read. She was very emotional and suffered badly from dad's 'rationality' – his way of coping.

My parents made a decision to save us from their past by not explaining anything. It was a general phenomenon for many secular Jews. It was difficult and dangerous to talk about it during the Stalinist era and possibly too painful to discuss it with us. They believed that by not explaining, they would make us 'Czech'. We had no idea what Jewish meant, but despite their best efforts they ensured that we were very aware that we were different. We ate differently, my parents' spoken Czech was full of German expressions, we had no grandparents and relatives and only had family friends 'the same' as us. Both of them reacted fiercely to any anti-Semitic incidences which came from children and from adults – a child was told not to play with me because I was a Jew, a caretaker swore at us using 'Jewish bastards'. Again there was no explanation. When family or politics were discussed, they spoke German or English to prevent us from understanding. Thus asking questions became an unspoken forbidden. Only funny or happy stories from the past were volunteered.

I did not like school, never got good marks and did not develop any academic confidence. I was good at mathematics, but not much else. School itself was regimented and gave little opportunity for inquiry or discussion, which suited me fine. I joined the Young Pioneers and later the Communist Youth Organisation because everybody else did. I had a few friends whom I made mainly through attempts to become one of them. I liked reading, but never really managed to develop any specific interests or hobbies. For health reasons I was not allowed to do sports even at school, so mum found a swimming club where I competed for a few years.

I remember being taken to Lidice Museum and to Terezin Concentration Camp where I saw my father cry for the first time, but, as before, nothing was explained.

## MY GROWING UP – POLITICALLY AND OTHERWISE

The political atmosphere of Communist Czechoslovakia only left shadowy impressions on me personally. The regime professed equality and practiced strict gender differentiation. While women worked full time they also carried out the child rearing and full domestic duties.

While my father was undoubtedly a caring man who provided for us, household duties were never his. I only ever remember mum queuing for food and carrying home the daily shopping after work. Most women worked and most queued for food and other goods in short supply. Dad liked an order in life; things had to be done in the way he wanted them to be done. Mum often protested but always succumbed to it. And then it was mum who enforced it with us. However, after his heart attack at the age of fifty- six and premature retirement, Dad learned how to cook and bake and actually became the 'house-husband'. I think it gave him a project, rather than him realising that mum needed help.

Gendered expectations prevailed in the behaviour of the girls around me. I knew I was not interested in fashion and clothes, and hated what my mother wanted me to wear. But I always succumbed to her wishes as in my mind, not to do so would have hurt her. I left school at 16 and went to sixth form college. I had an excellent young female physics teacher for whom I chose physics 'A' level. Unfortunately, she was replaced by an older man, who did not see me as a potential candidate. Though I passed my 'A' levels, I got 'the worst marks in the whole school'. I know that because the head announced in the school assembly her 'huge disappointment'. In 1966 I was eighteen, very immature and politically and sexually unaware. For my mother sex, and even menstruation, were taboo subjects and sex education at schools did not exist. 'Christian morality' was embraced by the official communist ideology and was enforced by the society.

It was mum who, despite my results, managed, through personal contacts (corruption was rife) to secure a place for me at the Faculty of Electrical Engineering at Prague Technical University. I lasted less than one semester because I did not fit and I was not particularly interested in anything. Instead, I got a job, without my parents' knowledge, at the main Prague mental hospital as a ward orderly. The conditions were terrible.

As part of my training I had to be present at two post mortems. I did fourteen hour night shifts and was given full nursing duties. I was present when women with post natal depression were given insulin shocks. It was a hard school of life but still did not lead to any more than observational memory (I did not have any analytical tools at that stage). In 1967 my mother dispatched me to Nottingham to work as an au-pair for a large family; Mum understood the value of languages and was desperate for me to 'get an education'. I knew nothing about children and had no knowledge of English so this was a nightmare arrangement for both sides.

Knowing that I was Jewish, the family found a group of Zionist students at Nottingham University for me to join. The 1967 Israel war was just over and many of them wanted to fight for the 'mother country'. I had no clue what they were talking about. When it was my turn to bring food to the meeting, all I could manage on my pocket money was a homemade pig trotter brawn and I was expelled from the group. After all, my mother made it at home, so I could not see the problem.

When the Warsaw Pact armies came to Czechoslovakia on 21 August 1968, I was hitchhiking round Britain. I did not follow the 1968 Prague Spring and again the political enormity of this act was mostly lost on me (the easing of the regime from January 1968 to the invasion of the Warsaw Pact armies of Czechoslovakia on 21 August 1968 was called Prague Spring. Some called it 'socialism with a human face'). My mother had a letter smuggled out in which she pleaded with me never to return home. This was the second invasion of her life. She wanted to protect me, again without any explanation. I was homesick, could not quite understand a regime in which I was supposed to rely on myself for every decision about my life (unlike the regime I came from) and after a string of manual jobs, I returned to Prague in 1969.

With my good English I got a job at the Prague University Library in a small international department, which was responsible for organising international conferences, library contacts, exhibitions and concerts. My Jewish boss was the first person who taught me to see the world in a different way. The library was then a haven for people of many different persuasions. There were a variety of intellectuals, artists, active dissidents and religious people. It was also the first place where I met active and educated physically disabled people. It was an environment of intensive learning and a complete surprise about most things in life. When I decided to study librarianship with the support of my boss, 'the Party' refused the permission because of my 'A' level results. I worked at the library for nine years.

I married an English man working and living in Prague and moved away from my parents. I continued to observe and admire artistic and political dissent in particular, hovering on the edges. It was their ability to think freely, to express opinions I could never verbalise, but also to organise, meet and act without fear. My marriage was failing and we decided to move to the UK to 'start again'. Many of the dissidents were forced to emigrate or were in prison and the political situation culminated in the political and human rights movement called The Charter 77. While I was in no personal danger, there were pressures from the library management for me to disassociate myself from these 'influences'. I applied for a so called 'emigration passport', an elaborate and costly process of being allowed to move with my husband to the west. During that process my husband left me and I had to choose between moving to the UK without him or moving into my parents' living room and trying to find another job. I chose the former and came to London in 1978.

## ENGLAND AGAIN

Shortly after my arrival, my ex-husband's first wife introduced me to the East End, to people who were left wing and alternative, who were practicing artists and politically active. Through them I began to understand political issues such as class, poverty and international politics. In some way gender issues were present too, even if unspoken and unrealised. I was thirty years old and I had to learn how to think for myself and how to make the smallest of decisions about my everyday life. In 1979 I had a bad miscarriage. This scary experience was not the first and had, in the behaviour of an arrogant male consultant gynaecologist, very similar features to my experiences of Communist Czechoslovakia. But I also heard of Wendy Savage; it was a revelation to move beyond perceptions of sex, pregnancies, abortions and miscarriages in terms of 'fault' and 'guilt' to understanding 'choice'.

A friend introduced me to the modular DipHE at Middlesex Polytechnic. I managed to share a council flat and cycled everywhere. I had no money. I studied maths, computing and economics. I worked very hard to prove to everyone that I was not stupid. The DipHE collected all sorts of non-traditional students, mostly mature people with life experience. I was not the oldest and certainly not the odd one out. Some were gay and some had mental illness and all treated me as one of them. It was the most exciting part of my life, my most free and most exhilarating. I travelled to Canada, Africa, Israel and Europe mostly on my own and I began to see myself and be myself (I knew nothing about safety and was very lucky on all my travels). I was also beginning to be politically active. I attended Greenham Common and other political demonstrations. But it took me years before I was able to say 'I am Jewish' (though I did know that I did not want to live in a Jewish state), even longer to say 'I am a feminist'.

I completed a BSc at City of London Polytechnic and got a first in Computing and Statistics. I then continued to take an MSc in Computing at Imperial College in 1984. That was a completely different experience. Out of the forty young computer 'techies' and 'anoraks' of that time, there were three women. I was old and a woman and thus again the odd one out. On the basis of my educational success I then got a job as a programmer at a large company of city stockbrokers, where again I was the only woman sharing an office with rich and privately educated young 'techie boys'. The environment was sexist and I once more felt alone. I met my current husband who, incidentally, is Jewish, a fact which my parents embraced with tangible relief.

After I gave birth to my first daughter in 1985, I was not allowed to go back to work on a part time basis so I decided to quit. In January 1986 I got an hourly-paid lecturing job back at Middlesex Polytechnic. In 1987 my second daughter was born and we managed a small mortgage and bought a house. With all this, I fulfilled all my mother's dreams for me. She lived to see me get a university education (the first in the family), have two children, an academic career, financial security, and a husband. My parents visited me often and I took the children to Prague regularly. I joined a local Co-op nursery, a very progressive local establishment where parents looked after other people's children. While this was a difficult learning curve, it gave my children and me the opportunity to make friends for life. With these friends I lost the fear of being seen to be politically active.

In 1989 I was approached by a colleague to construct, organise and deliver a women 'returners' course in computing. This was a one year women only programme, which was equivalent to the first year of a degree and enabled a large number of mature women to get to university education or a job. I learned a lot through organising this course. I was able to verbalise discrimination, women's rights, role models and gender stereotyping. Five years and 200 women down the road I was not able to persuade the university to continue the funding. I got a full-time position in the male-dominated School of Computing and taught a variety of computer science subjects. In 1994 I attended my first academic conference and published my first academic paper on my experiences as a woman in computing. There I met Women into

Computing (WiC), a group of mostly academic women, who were fighting the misogynistic and discriminatory nature of the computer industry and education.

Polytechnics became universities and the Research Assessment Exercise began to rule academic life. I enrolled on a postgraduate diploma in Social Science Research Methods. This programme included a module on women and law and one on feminism, which further broadened and formalised my understanding. Unfortunately research in gender and technology was not 'valid' in the Computing RAE (a point which WiC later challenged and won), and my research was not acceptable to the department. However, I continued to research and publish on gender and computing, attended conferences and was invited to Germany as a guest lecturer. I became active in WiC, organised conferences, published and organised public events. WiC ended its activities in 2005 after its last conference.

My understanding of feminism came from observation, listening, life experiences and contacts. Reading sociology texts and classical feminist texts was difficult; I lacked the courage to get into it as an academic discipline. I became interested in the newly developing discipline of computer ethics within which I could position my interest in gender. I went to the US and Europe on courses and conferences in this discipline and struggled hard to change the predominantly male 'Computer Science establishment' to accept ethics and gender within it as a valid discipline.

I eventually managed to construct a Computer Ethics module, which in time became compulsory for some students. In 2000 I obtained the post of Principal Lecturer at the University of East London. There was a group of women researchers specifically interested in Gender and Technology, and Innovation Studies were taught as a discipline within Social Sciences. The Information Technology programme there was unlike any other IT degree taught in computer science faculties. It gave students a unique understanding of issues of IT and society and was located in Innovation Theory. I taught, amongst other things, ethical, cultural and professional issues of computing but sadly not to the UEL Computer Science students, for whom, as future computer professionals, such an education is crucial.

During my academic career I joined the trade union NATFHE, later UCU, and became active (this was new for me because under Czech Communism, trade unions were controlled by the Communist

Party so for many years of being in London I had refused to join any organisation). I continued to take part in national and local political activities and demonstrations.

On the more personal level, I took myself and my little girls to see my Muslim neighbour who, after the first Iraq war, stopped talking to us because we were Jews. We have been friendly neighbours ever since. I had a real battle at my daughters' local state secondary school, when a deputy head (a Catholic), sent home a letter warning girls to 'dress modestly' and in effect blamed them for the attempted abduction of a school girl. I never managed to get the school to discuss sexuality, dress or women's bodies with the pupils. My daughters also reported that the same deputy had told them that abortion means pulling live babies out of women's bodies.

I became interested in Green politics and issues, attended Climate Camps and some direct actions. I began to see the issues of the planet's resources, consumerism, climate change, capitalist expansionism, labour issues and gender politics as being closely linked. And of course racist issues which I recognised very clearly in the UK and in other parts of the world. I remember a visit to my parents, when my brother and his son were proudly telling racist anti- Roma jokes. To my surprise it was my mother who said to my brother: 'You need to be careful, because if it were not for the Roma, it would be you'. This was the first political statement that I knowingly heard my mother make.

I attended the Stop the War meetings and the subsequent demonstrations, and the first Respect meeting, aimed at joining a variety of anti-war elements into a political party. However, the SWP rhetoric reminded me so much of the reasons for which I never wanted to be politically organised, that I never joined.

## WOMEN AGAINST FUNDAMENTALISM

I joined WAF in 2006 after attending a WAF public meeting on the 'war on terror' and fundamentalism. The meeting was big and all the women there seemed to have a long history of political and feminist struggles. I joined because I liked what I heard and wanted to learn more. I wanted to understand why my mother hated orthodox Jews. I knew about Salman Rushdie and was astonished when the fatwa was issued against him, but knew too little in 1989 to be able to evaluate it further. I realised that, years before joining, I had heard Pragna Patel speak at a seminar where she had talked about the role of SBS in protecting women.

As I became more engaged, I understood the term 'secularism', which enabled me to see my (predominantly Muslim) neighbourhood in a new way. I was able to form my own opinions on the veil and recognise my own intolerances and discriminations and those of others. I began to understand the politics of WAF and its anti-sexist and anti-racist struggle. I learned about the influence of fundamentalist religions on UK schools and the education of girls, on government's gender and political decisions and on the rights of women in domestic law. I improved my understanding of the lives and plight of women abroad.

As a personal tutor at the university, I discussed arranged and forced marriages with students as well as their trips to Mecca during term time.[1] With the university I discussed the way religious groups were given uncritical access to secular public university spaces. For example, the university atrium was being used by fundamentalist Muslim students to separate men and women to discuss religious issues; a lecture room was being used as a prayer room for men during Ramadan; and a public right of way at the university grounds was used to hold an Easter prayer meeting by a Christian group. I argued that secular public spaces should remain secular and not be used for proselytising and aggressive preaching as it disempowered secular members of the UEL community.

All these discussions were informed by my new understanding of religious fundamentalism. I understood why some of my trade union colleagues and some Student Union representatives, particularly those engaged in Marxist politics, reacted to fundamentalist Muslim elements at UEL (UEL has a very large proportion of Muslim students), and also how fear of being accused of racism influenced the UEL management responses to fundamentalist requests. I also took part in a postgraduate student project discussing 'the head scarf' as a gender and cultural issue.

Despite this I felt like an observer within WAF. I joined the Organising Committee where I hoped to be able to help with practical organisational tasks. I met wonderful women at WAF, who accepted me without judgement. I found quiet support and encouragement in Helen Lowe, with whom I could talk with about my WAF insecurities and about my Jewishness. While I understood why WAF had to come to an end, I was sorry to lose the regular contact and the education I was getting through it.

The politics of WAF is as important as ever and hopefully will continue through other feminist groups. However, as with WiC, WAF as an organisation had ceased to exist mainly because the political environment, in which the younger generation of women grew up, had not allowed for the political debate needed to create a movement. A small group of old women can only educate small groups and individuals and thus new structures and more localised approaches are needed to carry on WAF's feminist politics. I also believe that non-violent direct action is now the best form of activism.

I am still active in local campaigns such as 'Save our local cinema', which was bought by the Universal Church of the Kingdom of God (UCKG) to turn it into a church. I took part in public meetings and demonstrations and stood as a witness at one of the local council's planning meetings. I see UCKG as an exploitative organisation and a ruthless business, with no interest in working with the local community. I also joined the fight to stop the English Defence League (EDL) marching twice through the streets of Walthamstow. They chose this borough precisely for its ethnic make-up and it was a joy to see all local religious, ethnic and political groups joining a campaign called We are Waltham Forest. I take part in the local activities of Keep Our NHS Public and support a local homeless person.

At the time of writing this chapter I am still the main carer of my 100-year-old father. Thus while retired I have not quite had the time to think about my next move in the political arena. I would like to remain active in the women's movement and also take an active role in the environmental movement. I would like to find a way to combine the two as they truly are connected. I am sure that my years in WAF will be very instrumental in the process of developing my future activism.

## NOTES

1. At the time, when absence from lectures was used to inform immigration authorities, and students were threatened with expulsion, I lost the argument against the university that trips to Mecca did not need to happen during term time.

# 16. No clear pathway, just a lifelong zigzag

*Jane Lane*

Our society is deeply institutionally unequal. This is the quagmire into which each of us is born and from which we are now trying to disentangle ourselves in order to identify the influences that led us to become members of Women Against Fundamentalism. The influences are not just our families but everything that surrounds us and impinges on our lives – how, where, and when we, whatever our individual identities, learnt to formulate, understand and interpret our concepts of gender, age, ethnicity, ability/disability, sexuality, religion and belief, social class and their various institutionalised realities. This contrasts with how many people innocently approach the process of living in our society, with a certain sanguinity about the inevitability of it all, unaware of the reality of how the society is constructed in practice.

## EARLY DAYS

I was six when I first realised that a girl could be subjected to a man's power; when I realised that my gender was significant. My younger brother and I were walking home from school when a car came alongside us and the driver demanded that I masturbate him. Although I had no words to describe this, we must have told our mum something, because we never went back to that school again. I do not remember the incident being discussed with me and, interestingly in view of more recent and no doubt valid interpretations of such abuses, it just blended into my history with little apparent effect. Importantly, I never had the impression from my family that I was in any way to blame – for being female, for attracting male attention, for being weak or for not resisting.

The school itself, however, was a problem for my family. The Second World War had started and the head teacher openly questioned my dad's patriotism because he was a pacifist. I was very aware that our teacher herself saw us as different, as pariahs.

My mother left school aged thirteen during the First World War, trained as a shorthand typist and initially earned more than my father. She was sharp-witted and artistically creative but her enforced lack of much formal education and knowledge about social and political issues limited her engagement in family discussions. I loved my mother dearly, but now reproach myself for not having been more understanding and am ashamed of possibly belittling her obvious qualities. My husband later described her as 'grandma who makes mince pies with love in them', an apposite tribute.

My father's father forbade him to take up a secondary school scholarship because he saw little value in education. My father, therefore, left school at fourteen, worked as a railway clerk and attended evening classes in management and office skills, eventually working as a manager in the nationalised and denationalised road services. His obvious skills were never adequately rewarded because he refused to become a Freemason on principle, the covert and only way that promotion could be achieved. He seriously missed out on the opportunities provided by a university education, for debating with others, sharing ideas, reflecting on different concepts and socialising with a range of people from a variety of backgrounds and experiences. Instead he had to make do with debating issues with himself, not a satisfactory method of challenging and considering differing viewpoints. When I compare his life with the opportunities I have had, I grieve for that lack in his life and how stoically he bore it, ensuring that his children were never denied what he was denied.

During the Second World War we lived in Coventry, a heavily bombed city, and war conditions dominated our lives. Every night for several years was spent in the communal air-raid shelter with noisy and frightened families, while bombers raged overhead and fires seemed to be all around us. We struggled to unheated school classrooms filled with a hundred children huddled in overcoats, rushing to the shelters when there was a daytime air raid. There were consequently few learning opportunities. I was too young to understand war and just thought it was life, but the impact was terrifying and, as I grew older, made me determined to oppose war and its destructive consequences for so many people. The sound of sirens haunts me still.

My parents were initially Anglicans. My father was involved in the 1930s peace ballot and Toc H (an international interdenominational association for Christian social service, which worked to bring disparate sections of society together) and was moving away from traditional church orthodoxy. My parents became Quakers, visiting conscientious objectors in prison, having open house on Sundays for pacifists to be temporarily free of the hostility directed towards them elsewhere, and, after the war, we had German prisoners of war to visit. Most prisoners became friends for life, offering me visits to Germany. Our Home Guard neighbour monitored my father's activities to assess if he was a 'German spy'.

Neither of my parents was active in political parties but both had basic beliefs in equality for everyone, born out in the Quakers' belief of 'that of God in every man', although my dad challenged the latter term. I asked him once what he meant by 'God' and he replied that he just put another 'O' in it. My parents' values were largely socialist, although not explicitly so, derived from their pacifism and their Quaker faith – no hierarchies, icons or rituals and equality as a central principle, a contrast with many other religions. Although I am not a practising Quaker I recognise that I am deeply imbued with its values and it is without doubt the source of my involvement with Women Against Fundamentalism – I see the values of equality, socialism, and pacifism as integral to concepts of justice. I am also aware, however, of how these values and beliefs may be perceived as impossibly utopian unreality and, significantly, of institutional inequality being latent in the reality of some of its practices. I realise how different Quakerism is from the fundamentalism of many religions and how anti-feminism and racism may impact on them.

I grew up in a very loving family where education was seen as not only essential for future success but as a liberating force to be enjoyed for its own sake, for my brother and me equally. Shakespeare and poetry were valued and 'recited'. And above all my mum and dad lived their lives as basic equals, respectful and sensitive to each other's needs.

I was acutely aware of how my dad fearlessly stood up for what he believed. He wrote to the editor of *Sunny Stories*, Enid Blyton, which we children read, complaining about her eulogising war in a children's magazine, and he frequently challenged MPs and others on their policies. He always sought liaisons with like-minded people and gathered around him a wide and diverse group of people who recognised his worth, his vulnerability, and inner strength. When there was an arson attack on the local Hindu temple he proposed that the Free Church Federal Council support its refurbishment. One Baptist member objected saying 'we went over there to convert the heathen and now they're here among us'. This led to Dad finding out in detail, as he always did, the arguments against this position and challenging the Baptist member. Of course there was a price to pay, as there inevitably is, in sometimes being ostracised, having to harden his heart to face it all and thus perhaps making him appear less tolerant than he really was. He certainly often appeared to have a very black or white view of things. He has had a powerful and enduring influence on my life.

## ADOLESCENCE AND EDUCATION

I won a county scholarship to grammar school. But the war had so upset my education and peace of mind that it was decided, very reluctantly, and much against the personal wishes of my parents, that I should go to a Quaker co-educational boarding school to get away from it all, funded by the county and a grant. I learnt to cope, but I was desperately homesick, and I now bitterly regret not growing up within my own family and regret the scars that this severing of relationships left on us all.

Although many aspects of the school were egalitarian and reflected Quaker values, the ethos, probably unwittingly, did not challenge, debate, or address many ethical, political, and social issues, including the underlying causes and reality of inequality and privilege. It might have been expected that any bullying of pupils would be seriously addressed but this was not so. I was aged twelve when I first witnessed overt racist bullying, of an Indian boy, the only black child in the school, who was pushed down some stairs. I can still see those stairs in my mind and feel the guilt that I did nothing to support him and to challenge his tormentors.

Unbelievably, when my parents complained to the headmaster about the appalling bullying to which my brother, also at the school, was subjected (although I suspect they knew little of its reality), the Head responded by saying that he was bullied and it did him no harm – a comment that was clearly untrue. All my school life I felt acutely responsible for my brother and his treatment but at that time I felt powerless, as with the Indian boy, to do anything about it. I castigate myself perpetually for not taking action, which is perhaps the spur for being intrepid in standing up for justice for most of my life. It has left me angry that someone should be subjected to such abuse with no alleviating intervention by anyone, not even me.

There was no careers advice at school. I decided to be a doctor and got into medical school. Later, surprisingly on reflection, I thought that five years was too long to study so applied to study natural sciences. At that time, the early fifties, several universities did not accept women and some reserved a few places only – at University College London, for example, only 6 per cent of zoology places were kept for women.

At the end of my schooling I see myself, with hindsight, as beginning to 'own' an emotional response to distressing issues and as engaging with them as an antidote to perceived indifference, often masquerading as objectivity. I was very aware of and emotional about incidents of injustice and was in many ways isolated from my friends by feeling as I did. I believed strongly in justice and our individual responsibility to challenge inequality but had little idea of its realities. I see my Quaker schooling as having blessed me with some strong women friends for life but as having done little to prepare me for its vicissitudes and the realities of injustice.

## HIGHER EDUCATION AND REALISATION OF SELF

University opened my eyes to another world with people from many backgrounds, experiences and study subjects. For the first time I became friends with students who had grown up in working class communities. It was an exciting, liberating and challenging time where I felt free of some, but not all, of the influences that had previously constrained me.

I was a serious student and took advantage of any activities that I had not previously experienced. Specifically I met a few key people with whom I discussed a range of social, political and cultural issues and who I still know today. One of these was a sculpture student who I later married.

I took part in a contrived fund-raising stunt – I was dressed 'suitably' with others more overtly flamboyant – to raise funds for charity by taking a petition to Downing Street about valuing British university women. University staff considered this to be shameful and I was 'gated' for three weeks.[1] It attracted huge publicity and our photos were on the front of the Daily Express, causing my mother considerable embarrassment in her local community.

Looking back, I was someone on the brink of independence, not well informed or politically literate, but active and intellectually curious. I was not a scientist at heart and if I had been aware of more opportunities in life when I left school I would not have taken the route that I did.

Although I always believed that women were equal to men, it is sobering to realise the mostly unarticulated, unrecognised, and institutionalised inequality of society in the 1950s and 1960s, including rampant, overt, and deeply embedded sexism, racism, classism, and homophobia. This is perhaps not intrinsically culturally different from within many communities who migrated to Britain. It was only later that I understood the particular inter-relatedness of race and class. It is difficult to appreciate now – particularly for those who are too young to have experienced them – the gigantic and positive structural shifts in society, its attitudes and behaviour, which have taken place since then.

## THE BEGINNINGS OF ADULT LIFE

In the mid-1950s I started work as a geologist with BP; most other organisations did not employ women geologists. I saw advertisements for bus conductors, with conductresses being paid about 20 per cent less for the same work. I was aware of this inequity but thought of it just as 'how things were'. I was not involved in trade unions or party politics and had not yet learned the importance of workforce solidarity and campaigning for change.

My first two children were born while their father was a postgraduate art student. I loved my first-born to distraction and imagined that I could never love my second one as much. So it came as a complete revelation and relief to me when my second child was born and I realised that love is infinite.

The 'art world' was not constrained by the limiting cultural norms of wider society. In that world, it was not only possible to be different, it was expected that those of us who lived in it should be unconventional – dress, conversation, living styles, and attitudes to most things were just accepted. Parenting wherever possible was shared and this gave me the freedom to think and to develop my own interests. I started a sociology degree in evening classes and met many other like-minded people. I marked examination papers and later did a postgraduate course in educational research and methods.

We were living in the late-1950s and 1960s and beginning to open up a world where many existing attitudes and practices were identified and challenged. Women were beginning to join together in feminist groups and write about their ideas.

At the same time, it was a world of overt racism – race riots, campaigns against black immigration, control of entry of British citizens, rooms to rent ('No Irish, no coloureds, no dogs'), and, in contrast, the enactment of the first (limited) Race Relations Act. The concept of religion was almost exclusively Christian, with its history of colonial oppression, and few other religions to counter this. In the context of increasing national political activity against war and nuclear weapons, the challenges to overt sexism, and the rise in overt racism, it is unsurprising that I have been active in these fields for most of my life, taking part in demonstrations, forming alliances, and trying to prioritise the issues on which to work. These activities made clear to me how vital trade union movements are, both historically and in the present. Their support and involvement were, and remain, crucial to maintaining momentum, solidarity, and focus.

In my local community, my activities became more specifically focussed on racial equality. Under the 1965 Race Relations Act I was involved, against considerable odds, in setting up the local race equality council – my local authority refused parallel funding.

In 1967, during a period of some racial tension internationally, a large meeting, allegedly about Black Power, was called to discuss the situation in Reading – I was one of four white people present. Stokely Carmichael had been invited but was banned from entering the country so Michael X (Michael Abdul Malik/de Freitas) attended in his place. At one point he said 'let's kill all the white people!' I thought this was going to be 'it', until a Barbadian friend defused the situation. Michael X was charged with inciting racial hatred and spent time in prison.

## ADULT LIFE AND REALITY

In the late 1960s my husband and I parted, resulting in my having no money, no property (or share of one), and losing custody of my children – due to 1870 legislation, repealed a few years later. I felt powerless. My parents stopped communication with me for a few years. The whole situation was exceedingly painful for everyone and, for me, remains so.

I lectured in general studies at my local college but when I became pregnant the offer of a full time appointment was withdrawn – just prior to the 1975 Sex Discrimination Act. I taught day release craft, technical, and building students for ten years. Most of my students saw books as reading and school; they had left school so did not see the relevance of books. They were mostly white, male, often overtly racist and sexist, ill-educated and without the skills to negotiate their ways through the system that largely engulfed them. Most of their other lecturers constantly shouted at them. I tried to interest them in fields that they perhaps knew little about and provide opportunities for open discussions. Sanctions against South Africa were being enacted and I decided to talk about the reality of apartheid with a class of motor vehicle mechanics. They were shocked at the laws banning inter-racial marriages, at segregation, the removal of black people to the Bantustans, and the privileges of white people. When I tried to transfer the principles they had espoused about South Africa to a discussion about Britain, they could not make the links. So I showed them *Last Grave at Dimbaza*, a film of life in the Ciskei, a Bantustan. They were totally stunned by what it portrayed and one young man who had been one of the most virulent racists came up to me and said 'I have to admit it, I was wrong about the wogs' – regardless of the terminology, his heart had been touched. But the overall experience was so depressing, not only for me, but also for many of the students who had an unfulfilling future to look forward to with so very little respect accorded to them.

Campaigning in the 1970s and 1980s together with committed people, including from a wide range of minority ethnic communities, was a relatively new experience for everyone. It opened doors to the reality of many people's lives and the personal consequences of the combination of migration, racism, and the variety of traditional cultural practices on their housing, education, employment, the practice of their faiths and cultures, and their life chances. The joint action was empowering, leading to actions after the expulsion of Asians from Uganda, anti-deportation campaigns, setting up a refuge for Asian women, and the race equality council taking up many examples of discrimination. One anti-deportation campaign in support of a Muslim woman was 'won' after large local demonstrations and a night vigil in black bin liners outside the Royal Courts of Justice (to depict the deportee as 'rubbish').

The campaign for an Asian women's refuge in the eighties paralleled many national campaigns to set up refuges for local women, as domestic violence became officially recognised. It was clear that the issues facing Asian women were significantly different from those of white women; traditional religious ties and cultural practices meant that leaving their husbands detached them from their usual support networks and exposed them to the harsh realities of an uncaring, ill-informed, often prejudiced, and unfamiliar world. We had a strong steering group but faced enormous opposition from many Asian men and most councillors, and apathy from nearly everyone else, except the other existing seven refuges in the country. Their workers joined with us and gave us solid support, advice and encouragement – the solidarity of women in adversity. We applied for central government Urban Aid funding and were refused on the grounds that Asian women should join the main refuge and learn about British ways of life. Eventually we got minimal funding for a worker and set up a small drop-in centre which later developed into a fully-fledged refuge with consistent local authority support and funding.

I was beginning to see the early years of a child's life as significant in terms of their experiences, opportunities, and particularly in learning racial attitudes. I was involved in a national 'dawn watch' monitoring the number of children cared for by individual childminders. Some were responsible for more children than they were registered for and many of those children were black. Their parents were working long hours on shift work with few other options for childcare.

In the late 1970s I started work at the newly established Commission for Racial Equality (CRE) as an education officer, identifying unlawful racial discrimination in the education system generally. I was immediately taken to task by one of the directors for my activities in my local community, which were seen as being in conflict with the role of the CRE. I refuted the charge and it was eventually withdrawn. I saw working in my local community as integral to my national work, personally enriching, and enhancing for my understanding of how the various guises of racism were manifested. Later, four members of our education team were seriously disciplined for challenging the bullying behaviour of a senior officer. Despite eventually being vindicated and supported by our unions, I knew that I would never fit into the CRE hierarchy.

In my education work I suggested that the CRE should liaise with the Equal Opportunities Commission (EOC) in their overlapping interests of black and other minority ethnic women. This was not taken up. I did, however, work with the EOC on issues of sex and race discrimination in the early years of children's lives but their remit did not address institutional sexism so my work came to little. I also suggested that the CRE should take action about the early age that children learnt their attitudes to racial differences – unless the cycle of learning racial prejudice was broken, CRE work would never end. This was refuted at higher levels as being a non-issue compared with employment. Despite this rebuff, I coordinated a group of about twenty black and white people, nearly all from outside the CRE, and we met regularly to identify and make recommendations on the key concerns about young children and racism – language, child development theories, resources, adoption, training, employment, qualifications, assessment, the law (Race Relations and Children Acts), access, policies, and early childhood services. This work resulted in a CRE publication that proved to be a bestseller.[2] Subsequently several of us wrote articles about the issues, including in journals, which led to a form of samizdat national unofficial circulation, sharing of ideas widely across those working with and responsible for young children.

The discussions that we held, although often uncomfortable, had a lasting impact on us all – raising awareness and deepening our understanding. Raising potentially difficult issues, some of which many of us had never thought about before, and considering different ways of viewing them, meant that much of our previous thinking was fundamentally challenged. For me it was liberating, and was an opportunity to reflect on my assumptions and judgements about the people and organisations I encountered. Talking about racism openly and honestly, within a no-blame culture, is a powerful strategy to counter its institutional and personal manifestations.

I was aware that some Catholic and Church of England schools applied discriminatory admission criteria, on grounds of religion, but this was permitted by the existing laws at the time. In 1989 I was a member of the Children's Daycare Law Reform group contributing to the new Children Bill. At a meeting with the civil servant drafting the Bill, I suggested including a section about cancelling the registration of a childminder or daycare provider whose care of a child was seriously inadequate with regard to their needs – their religious persuasion, racial origin, and cultural and linguistic background. To my amazement this was included in the Act (S.74), and meant that, in some cases, there was a framework to ensure that young children were not 'indoctrinated' with particular religious beliefs, and that the religious and cultural needs of a child were not flouted.

While raising issues of racial equality with national early years organisations and working on formal investigations into discrimination, I helped set up national antiracist organisations in teacher education, early years training, and practice and children's resources.[3] By the time I left the Commission in the mid-1990s the importance of racial equality and the early years was well on the national agenda – and the enthusiasm of many of us contributed to making this possible.

After leaving the Commission I worked as the coordinator of Early Years Equality, a national charity acting to remove racism from national and local early years policies, guidance, training, practices, and procedures. By this time, the New Labour government had begun to prioritise the importance of young children and their families, setting up Sure Start as an innovative, well-funded, and well-supported project. This provided significant opportunities for some of us to influence, advise on and contribute to new legislation, guidance, the Early Years Foundation Stage, inspections, assessment and training programmes. Although terms such as sexism and racism, let alone their institutional varieties, were anathema to the government, equality issues were taken very seriously and, despite some lapses, overall, real progress was made to ensure a comprehensive, equality-based early years system was implemented.

I am now an advocate worker for racial equality in the early years, writing, editing and continuing to respond to government consultation documents, and I campaign on discrimination and race equality in the education system generally. I updated an earlier book, which most represents my thinking. On publication, not for the first time, the publishers and I were subjected to a worldwide barrage of media obscenities, distortions and ridicule although only one journalist (Daily Mail) had seen the book.[4] Much of the media remain a real barrier to truth and are obsessive in denying fifty years of research evidence showing that children notice skin colour differences well by the age of three, and, unless countervailed, this may result in the development of prejudiced attitudes and behaviour.

Since 2010 the combination of the recession and the objectives of the coalition government have severely curtailed progress toward equality – in legislation, the enforcement body (the Equality and Human Rights Commission), and education.

## MY INVOLVEMENT IN WAF

My specific path to WAF is somewhat belated, perhaps due to my own background and innate assumptions that principles of equality would, and certainly should, apply to all religions. But my antiracist politics have always incorporated feminism, religion and working with people of a variety of faiths and beliefs. I recognised the way certain religions are demonised, Judaism and Islam in particular. More recently, as a result of publicity and activities by organisations, including Southall Black Sisters, opposing forced marriages, opposing particular religious laws denying equal rights to women in divorce, and supporting freedom of choice about abortion, I have become more acutely aware of the reality of some women's lives.

In the late 1990s a work colleague, Clara, a founder member of WAF, suggested that I might like to join the organisation. I already knew about it through its campaign against Khomeini's fatwa against Salman Rushdie but, largely through lack of time, childcare responsibilities, and because I did not live in London, I had not become involved. I was aware of the hostility that WAF activists sometimes engendered and admired their bravery and tenacity in standing up publicly against fundamentalist practices in all religions. WAF's objectives fully accorded with my own beliefs about the injustice of fundamentalism so, tentatively, I joined. I came to see it as a group of passionate (but never aggressive), dauntingly erudite, strong, and welcoming women determinedly reflecting on and seeking ways of resolving the positions of subjectivity and inferiority ascribed to some women through fundamentalism, both nationally and internationally, and across many religions. Although I was familiar with many of the issues and had indeed been involved personally in some, my own experiences had only partly included the specific and current realities facing some Jewish, Sikh, Hindu, Christian and Muslim women and girls. WAF discussions inspired me and increased my awareness of how religious 'laws' and cultural traditions permeated the lives of these women.

There is often a balance to be considered when apparently conflicting analyses of human rights occur. While the left has historically so often torn itself apart through ideological differences, thus giving ammunition to the right, it is vital that the principles of the universality of human rights are identified, if the specific rights of everyone are to be assured in practice. This inevitably leads to conflict with others who are prepared to brush over some rights in order to pursue their own main agenda.

I see myself as agnostic, neither believing nor denying the beliefs of others, but permanently ambivalent about those who I revere, some of whom believe and others who have no beliefs. Furthermore, being white British and acknowledging its historical (and continuing) oppression of others, often through 'traditional' Christian beliefs, I must always question my 'right' to comment on the religious practices of others, including those with which I might disagree. The basic principles that WAF identify and espouse in determining what is my right and my responsibility are empowering in answering this question.

At the same time I have tried to understand more sensitively how and why religious differences arise and are perpetuated and why, compared with my relative religious agnosticism, religion plays such a significant part in the lives of some of my closest friends and in the lives of those people I often admire. I have African Caribbean friends and colleagues who say that if it were not for the black churches they would not have survived the racism they experienced when they came to Britain. I have Muslim friends who say that abuse of Islam is like what I would feel if my own father was abused. I have Sikh, Hindu, and Christian friends who say there is no way they could upset their families by not agreeing to their proposal for a religious marriage. Culture and religion are so entwined. But over and above this is the fact that fundamentalist thinking runs counter to my acceptance of religion. That is where the challenge lies and where WAF comes in for me – as an organisation that accepts everyone's right to pursue a religion, but one that opposes the unequal treatment and denial of the basic rights of women in whatever religion they belong.

It is in an unfamiliar role as a relative bystander, listening and learning from others, that I find myself involved in the values of WAF. I value the teasing out of principles and identifying ways to oppose fundamentalist practices and have contributed to an unpublished paper on the role of faith schools and religious education, in which WAF sought the allegiance of others working for a secular education system.

For WAF, like any pioneering group, strong consistent action, support, and solidarity have been important in facing down heavy opposition and forming effective alliances. People claiming unlawful discrimination need support; black and other minority ethnic groups trying to get their voices heard need support; people fighting unjust deportations need support; isolated women subjected to fundamentalist actions need support. They can rarely beat the 'system' alone. Antiracist, anti-fundamentalist feminists, whether they see themselves as these or not, have played a vital part in so many of these struggles for equality and justice.

## POSTSCRIPT

Writing this chapter has been a sobering and disturbing experience, bringing back memories and feelings ranging through regret, sadness, gratitude, frustration, and anger.

## NOTES

1. By 'gated' I mean confined to a hall of residence.
2. Commission for Racial Equality, *From Cradle to School: Practical Guide to Race Equality and Childcare*, Commission for Racial Equality, London 1989.
3. The Anti-Racist Teacher Education Network (ARTEN), the Early Years Trainers Anti-Racist Network (EYTARN, subsequently Early Years Equality (EYE) and the Working Group Against Racism in Children's Resources (WGARCR).
4. J. Lane, *Young children and racial justice – taking action for racial equality in the early years – understanding the past, thinking about the present, planning for the future*, National Children's Bureau, London 2008. The media reaction is described in J. Bourne, *Media hysteria around new book*, Institute of Race Relations, London 2008.

# 17. Sexual and gender-based violence against women

*Ritu Mahendru*

This chapter traces the dominant stories that shaped my feminist thinking and led me to take a feminist path. This feminist path involved partnering with organisations such as WAF and involved membership of various projects of belonging, each of which presented challenges and intersectional power relations through which I constructed and reconstructed my identity as a young female, Indian, migrant, secular, human rights worker. By contextualising my experiences, this chapter explores how the personal became political. I have organised my chapter according to the different stages of my life: first to India where I grew up; then moving to the UK, where I first came as a student; and more recently in the international contexts of my international development work. The common thread throughout, relates to my questioning of patriarchal discourses and particularly the way that patriarchy and religious discourse facilitated the sexual abuse of girls by their male relatives. Unsurprisingly, issues around sex and sexuality became the mainstay of both my work and political activity. While all the events described in this chapter actually happened to me and people around me, I have anonymised references to particular people.

## THE CULTURAL AND RELIGIOUS SUBJUGATION OF WOMEN'S BODIES AND SEXUALITY

I was born in Ludhiana, Punjab and was seven years old when my family migrated to Karnal, Haryana. I do not have many memories of the Punjab or of Haryana. However, as part of the complex role of religion in my life, I grew up learning about both Hinduism and Sikhism. While growing up, I observed dozens of older men, so called religious agents of morality, gathering outside my house to rebuke women who broke the societal codes of conduct, such as dress codes for women, and access to public spaces. In the men's discussions, women's identities were reduced to their body parts, which were described in pejorative terms. Women who took charge of their bodies sexually, and challenged the status quo, would be labelled as '*Badmash*' (which literally means 'scoundrel', but when applied to women it connotes 'slut').

These conservative discussions made me question and re-examine my identity as a female. The customs, traditions and attitudes that were being invoked in a desire for domination over women, deeply affected me. This was when I first began to observe gender inequality and to problematise gender. I could not resist protesting the injustices that I came across.

## A QUESTION OF COLOUR

Another element of my feminist radicalisation is related to skin colour. Up until age ten or eleven, my family lived a nomadic life. My early experience of moving to Delhi was of a traditional and controlling neighbourhood where dominant values privileged lighter skin colour and in which I often felt socially excluded. The political impact of skin tone was always direct and personal and also linked with views of female sexuality. People around me were convinced that lighter skin tone indicated a higher status and better marriage prospects. But in my case, they did not have any hope. I was dark skinned, and therefore deemed to be ugly. I was also rebellious. This is where the seed for my first (personal) political engagement with feminism began – at the age of ten or eleven – when I started to resist gender stereotypes, refused to assist my mother in the kitchen and decided to play with the boys in the park.

## SEXUAL HARASSMENT AND SEXUAL ABUSE

Up until we moved to Delhi, my family often moved locations, but I found that patriarchal gender relations were everywhere and dominated every woman's life, irrespective of whether they were young or old. Two stories about friends in Delhi aptly illustrate the gravity of all this.

Puja confided in me, that at the age of thirteen, her father was sexually abusing her and she had also seen him harassing her older sister, other girls and women. Her father used both emotional pressure and his position as the head of the family to perpetrate this abuse. He threatened that if she revealed anything to anyone, he would divorce her mother and they would not have social or financial support. Her mother was dark skinned, she stammered and was bullied by her husband and neighbours. Puja's father was a well connected drug dealer (an open secret to many in the community). His wealth and frequent religious advice had gained him a revered status. Like many other men in the area, his views resonated with a hyper-masculine, anti-Islamic heroic Hindutva movement. He had enormous wealth and social capital. However, at the age of twenty, Puja courageously married against her parents' wishes, though she is now going through a divorce.

Another friend, Seema, narrated a similar experience. She told me how she was subjected to sexual abuse at the hands of her guardian uncle. He had entered her room with a Hindu prayer bell in one hand, pretentiously chanting 'OM' and producing long strains of sounds, while he fondled her genitals with the other hand. Seema had her first period the next day. A couple of years after this incident her father could sense that something was amiss. He confronted Seema and discovered the secret. He instructed Seema not to disclose this information for fear that it would bring shame on the family. A couple of years later, under the same guise of secrecy, Seema's father started to abuse her whilst he forbade her from wearing dresses that might undermine conservative notions of femininity. Seema concealed these experiences from her mother. She did not want to cause her mother pain or to be the cause of violence in the house. But she also remained silent because it would have been almost impossible to convince the community that these acts had occurred. Years later, Seema's mother learnt about the sexual abuse by her uncle. She confronted him but the entire family and community accused Seema of provoking the abuse on the basis that she was 'too pretty and talkative'.

I began questioning the social position and stereotypical images of women as home makers and sexual objects of desire. I started challenging the revered men in my family. At one point there was a complete chaos throughout the extended family when I had discussed sex and sexuality matters in public and the oppressed status of women within these discourses. I fell into the category of *Badmash* women at the age of fifteen. I was becoming acutely aware of gender inequalities and voiced my opinions fearlessly. Community criticism only made me more defiant. I started to decipher the ways in which fundamentalist values undermine women and their rights and also how fundamentalism feeds male supremacy and further exacerbates gender inequality. My distrust in community and religion grew. I was profoundly affected by all this and I felt that I had to respond to these experiences in order to show that I did not collude.

## WORK LIFE

At the age of sixteen, I started providing private tuition from home. I would teach primary level school children, who were often from slums. After finishing school, I took a part time job as a Marketing Officer in East Delhi and started selling wrist watches in an industrial area, a male-dominated environment. Alongside work, I undertook an undergraduate degree in Commerce at Delhi University. The job meant travelling to the outskirts of Delhi to unsafe industrial locations where I discovered new male-dominated spaces. But it was here that I realised the power of female sexuality; I was the only female amongst male colleagues who would insist on accompanying me because they believed that they could make more sales.

At the age of twenty, I started working for an International NGO in Delhi, which was established to fight HIV/AIDS in India. The charity mainly focused on children's rights, women's empowerment, and condom promotion programmes. This was the time when I became officially engaged with social politics but also came across structural misogyny in terms of the exclusion of women from the workplace. The dominance of religion created additional dynamics. The manager of the organisation explicitly promoted masculine normativity and treated women as sexually, physically, morally, and intellectually inferior.

While the office environment made me aware of gender discrimination, in the field I worked with women in slums, the majority of whom were Dalits and migrants from the Indian states of Uttar Pradesh, Haryana and Bihar. These women worked long hours in hazardous conditions, they headed their families and also survived violence. During this time, I also worked for a few months in Rajasthan where girls and women reported unintended pregnancies, Sexually Transmitted Infections (STIs) and Human Immunodeficiency Virus (HIV) because they did not have enough power to negotiate safe sex with their husbands. The NGO uncritically worked alongside religious institutions to encourage condom use. The organisation did not challenge right-wing masculine attitudes that placed women in powerless positions.

## MOVING TO ENGLAND – IDENTITY, FEMALE BODIES AND BELONGING

I moved to England in 2002 and soon discovered that sexual harassment and abuse is not a national phenomenon limited to India. In the UK, I became familiar with additional axes of power and difference that exacerbated gender inequalities. In particular, migration, representation, identity and belonging became central issues for me.

I moved to Canterbury in 2002 to study an MSc in Public Health at Canterbury Christ Church University. My dissertation looked at the reasons young people engage in unprotected sex. I conducted a comparative analysis of white British young people from Kent and Indian young people in Delhi. My study revealed some similarities across these two countries. In both countries young women felt concerned about their reputation if they suggested condom use in heterosexual encounters. In both countries, men thought contraception was women's responsibility. However, in the UK men suggested that they may not establish a relationship with a woman after a one night stand whereas Indian men reported establishing relationships with women that they had engaged with sexually. It was during my MSc that I became familiar with feminist theory and conscious of my feminist self.

Alongside my MSc, I started working at a restaurant as a waitress and also volunteered at the Naz Project in London (NPL), a group that works with South Asian communities on sex and sexuality issues. NPL staff and community groups are formed of individuals with diverse sexual orientations and identities. Some of the users told me that their families were unaware of their sexualities. Part of the work of the organisation was to deconstruct the challenges faced by sexual minorities and the impact of those challenges on Black communities.

After the MSc, I was offered a scholarship to do a PhD in Sociology at the University of Kent. My doctoral research focused on the sexual and social lives of young British Indians. I was intrigued by several issues that emerged during my conversations with individuals at NPL, which led me to explore British-Indian lives, histories, identities and surroundings, and the associations between sex, risk, 'race' and culture. I began deciphering the experiences that shape British-Indian society and continue to preserve cultural and religious identities. At the same time I considered British Indians' engagement with British identities and challenges to being stereotyped as the 'other' by mainstream British society. In British society, through cultural and religious frameworks, South Asian women are often essentialised as oppressed figures of victimhood and despair but are also sexualised and fetishised 'others' (Brah, 1996).[1]

During my PhD I immersed myself in identity politics and the literature associated with Black feminism. I moved to London in 2006 to gather data for my research and this move provided a completely different social lens. I noticed huge social divisions between neighbourhoods within London; white people, South Asians, Africans, Caribbeans, Turkish, etc, seemed to form their own community groups and these groups tended to be located in rundown neighbourhoods. For me, the only time exclusive neighbourhoods appeared inclusive and acceptable were when white, middle-class young people started to inhabit them and became the majority.

The British-Indian women that participated in my doctoral research constantly demonstrated an internal power struggle with their religious and cultural identities, which operated as cultural preservation tools. The young women asserted that the only reason they visited temples and gurdwaras was to preserve their Indian identity and for social support that they may not receive in the context of racism. Women expressed enormous loathing towards religious leaders and faith based organisations who they believed caused the gender divide that treats them as inferior.

Additionally, as a single woman and a migrant myself who does not place herself in either traditional/modern or eastern/western categories, I found myself dislocated and culturally displaced. I do not fit into essentialised Indian-British binaries, nor do I have a legitimate claim on these two identities, although socially I belong to both societies. At times when I do feel nostalgic, religious places and faith-based organisations are not the places that I would visit, as they would not ever afford me any legitimacy.

My research revealed that gender discriminatory practices were also prevalent amongst parents. The women I interviewed spoke of the risk of violent repercussions from their parents if they engaged in premarital sex, whereas men were given a pack of condoms and/or taken for sexual health screening. Families and communities promoted myths related to sexual health. For example, young women were told that having menstrual cycles is a curse from God. Through these communications and experiences, my female participants grappled with their identities; they contested, constructed and reconstructed a sense of belonging. Young people in my research evaluated school sex education as far from satisfactory. Sex education brings in to focus not only the tensions around gender but also around ethnicity and religion, especially when official guidance on Sex and Relationship Education allows parents to withdraw their children from sex education classes and gives faith schools the power to deliver sex and sexuality related sessions.

Moreover, the combination of fundamentalist and racist attitudes that I encountered in the UK led me to respond to stereotypes associated with South Asian Indian women. My real sense and understanding of marginalisation as the 'other' in the UK began when I had to contest even more in the UK than while living in India. In India, the social relations and exchange between me and other women was somewhat equal. The social hierarchies and power relations I experienced in England were both similar and different. Although I had directly experienced skin tone discrimination (a form of racism) and gender inequality in India, I was part of the dominant religious and caste sections of society there. In the UK, the combination of race and being a female in a white majority context, presented new challenges; I confronted racism and sexism, including vehement anti-immigration sentiment and policies. As a migrant, I have always been at the receiving end of immigration reform and control.[2] I have been compelled to prove that I am part of the British social integration agenda, investing emotionally and economically in order to continue my stay in the UK. I am continually subjected to government reminders of the differences between 'us' and 'them'. I see UK migration policies as violence against migrants – a form of everyday mental torture. A number of people approached me during a campaign that I organised to challenge the Home Office's unjust migration policies. They highlighted how religious organisations and places of worship have now become more useful spaces where they could while away their worries, gain community support and welfare assistance in the context of anti-immigration policies, which are increasingly pushing fundamentalist and racist agendas, further exacerbating gender inequalities and discriminations.

## SOUTH ASIAN SEXUAL HEALTH FORUM

Alongside my PhD, I worked as a researcher at the Bromley by Bow Community Centre to increase sexual health knowledge and confidence among Bangladeshi women living in Tower Hamlets. The need for the project stemmed from research evidence that the Bangladeshi community were less likely than others to access sexual health services, despite having a similar pattern of sexual health problems to the wider population. Evidence suggested that confidentiality concerns, cultural and religious taboos were preventing them from seeking help, leading to undiagnosed and untreated health problems. The female respondents in this piece of research reported difficulties in discussing sexual health matters, a lack of understanding of the relevance of sexual health services, and difficulties in discussing sex openly because it is perceived as culturally inappropriate. Sexual health promotion tools and sexual health services were perceived to be culturally insensitive and in conflict with community values. The women that participated in this research felt that provision needed to move away from a multi-faith approach in order to provide young people and/or children with appropriate sex education. The respondents preferred schools to take responsibility and saw working with religious groups as a challenge to educating young people on sex. The research findings contradicted the sex and relationship education good practice guidance published by the Muslim Council of Britain (The Muslim Council of Britain, 2007),[3] who expressed ethical and religious concerns around sexual health and Muslim communities and recommended educating young people about sex and sexuality matters through morality frameworks.

During the same time, I founded the South Asian Sexual Health (SASH) charity in the UK. SASH is a secular organisation and an online forum. It addresses and makes visible the sexual health needs of South Asians through an intersectional approach using Social Determinants of Health model.[4] I collate and collect sexual health related news and policy updates and publish a weekly digital paper. We find it a challenge to collate information related to South Asians and sexual health due to the lack of gender and racial disaggregated evidence. In 2012, I attended the Tower Hamlets Sex Education Strategy Consultation meeting. Worryingly, this Strategy uncritically embraces faith based organisations as important providers of sex education to ethnic minority groups. While there is no uniform model of sex education in the UK, sexual health activists are advocating that sex education should be delivered within a human rights and equality framework not a religious framework.

## JOINING WAF

In 2008 I attended a talk by Southall Black Sisters (SBS) on defending secular spaces. The talk resonated with one of the PhD chapters I was writing at the time on religion and feminism. This was how I became part of feminist networks such as WAF and SBS in the UK. Following that, I started attending WAF meetings wherein I was part of discussions that challenged fundamentalist values in all religions and their impact on women's rights across the world. SBS and WAF gave me the language to percolate ideas and themes that were emerging from the experiences that I have described above. While I had always been critical of religion, WAF provided me with an anti-oppressive, intersectional framework to critically challenge and analyse fundamentalist values. Their views resonated with mine. We could collectively find ways to extend our financial and social support to women and feminists in other parts of the world. International feminist issues were our issues. I felt that we were part of feminist struggles across the world, which gave us a common agenda to fight against fundamentalism.

## INTERNATIONAL DEVELOPMENT WORK

After finishing my PhD in 2010, I was given the opportunity to teach Gender and Health Equity (as part of the Master's in Public Health) at a University in Rajasthan – a predominantly Hindu state with one of the highest levels of caste and gender discrimination in India. I taught 180 Afghan medical doctors, only 10 of whom were women. While gender disparities were clear in the classroom, I tried minimising them by giving special attention to female voices even though at times male voices became louder and rougher. I used my power as a female lecturer to make additional efforts with my female students who felt powerless amongst their male colleagues. The men would set codes of morality and conduct by raising their eyebrows in response to the interventions of female students and I tried my best to break these acts of intimidation. However, the male students were persistent and used their physical presence to control female bodies and dismiss their voices.

I often went to classes in my traditional outfits, with my dupatta (scarf) draped around my neck. Since my Indian male colleagues, especially the ones who were in power, instructed the administrative staff not to provide me any support so as to undermine me, I was engaged in a lot of operational and hands-on work. This involved, for example, fixing projectors and serving tea to my students. I decided, therefore, to ditch my dupatta as it interfered with my work activities. While my students blushed painfully, the main protests came from the male staff at the university and female dress codes became a matter of discussion.

In July 2011, I went to Kabul for the first time. I was invited by the World Health Organisation to write Afghanistan's first National Health and Human Rights strategy. I found that Kabul and Jodhpur share many aspects of their cultures. This came as no surprise, since the geographical proximity of the two cities is less than 1000km. In both societies, women were required to cover their heads in certain spaces, especially around men and the elderly. In both Afghanistan and Rajasthan, women only ate after the men finished eating, regardless of the woman's professional status. In Afghanistan, I had an opportunity to interact with the Afghan feminists who expressed discontent both with the international community and with the Afghan government for not giving them enough space to address issues pertaining to women's rights. If there are gender units at ministerial levels, these have simply been put in place to gain international funding and do not carry real significance on the ground.

After this, I travelled to several other conflict zones to continue working on gender, health and development issues. Gender inequities persisted in every country. What made these travels more interesting was my own identity as a young Indian female born in India but residing in London. The international development sector is mainly dominated by white men and some white women, but hardly involves Black women and quite possibly no people with disabilities. There is a very limited perception of young Asian women as international development consultants. Men often feel threatened by them and resent women who outperform them. Women are either subjected to sexual harassment or their views are completely dismissed. Working as a Black woman is so challenging within the International Development sector that enhancing women's status becomes even more difficult; there are not that many of us in powerful positions within the sector. This was one of the many reasons I protected my Afghan female students and went out of my way to try and build their capacity and arrange scholarships so that they might continue their education to Master's level.

## THE DELHI GANG RAPE AND PROTEST AGAINST VIOLENCE AGAINST WOMEN

I returned to London in July 2012 and took a temporary lecturing job at the University of East London to teach Health Policy. On 16 December 2012, I read about the brutal gang rape of a young female paramedic student in Delhi.[5] This case opened discussions around the rape culture in India. I was involved with SBS who decided to do something to show solidarity for an emergent Indian uprising against violence against women. SBS organised a protest outside the Indian High Commission. At that time, we did not realise that this case would provoke such uproar and gain such huge international momentum. As the protest day approached, people grew angry at the Indian government's poor response and incompetence and also with the general discourse, which sought to blame women for dressing 'inappropriately', drinking alcohol, staying out late and breaking with social codes of conduct. Many young men on social media sites claimed that it was their *right* to rape women that they considered to be dressed inappropriately or behaving in an unfeminine manner. The Hindu Right Bhartiya Janata Party blamed 'the west' for supposedly corrupting India's pristine heritage and culture. Additional concerns arose from demands from some quarters to invoke the death penalty as punishment for those guilty of the assault and murder of this young woman. In Delhi, police used heavy wooden sticks and water cannons to disperse protesters. On 7 March 2013, an unseasonably cold wintery day for London, over 1000 people came out to voice their disgust and demand justice for the paramedic student who had been raped. Most of the demonstrators were Asian women but there were also women and men of other backgrounds. There was a lot of anger as the international community searched for an outlet and some analysis.

## CONCLUSION

In this chapter, I highlighted the relationship between culture, religion and sexuality. In my personal political journey I have been keen to understand how female bodies are experienced in private and public spheres. It is clear to me that while gender and culture are two main forms of oppression threatening women's existence and rights to freedom, fundamentalist values have also been instrumental in underscoring anti-feminist agendas. Throughout different stages of my life, I have attempted to negotiate a secular and an independent space as young, Black, female, migrant. Each stage presented new themes that shaped the development of my understanding of feminism and my political activism. I came across self-proclaimed religious believers who also perpetrated sexual abuses on women. These intimate and proximate incidents made me question religion, and the hypocrisy of that which surrounds the concepts of 'community' and 'honour'. I confronted and challenged hyper-masculinity intertwined with fundamentalist values from a very early age. However, joining WAF helped me to develop a complex consciousness of the issues that threaten feminist struggles and spaces. WAF was a mechanism for me to reflect upon some of the connections between the dilemmas I faced at a personal level and their political significance.

## NOTES

1. A. Brah, *Cartographies of Diaspora: Contesting Identities*, Routledge, London 1996.
2. You can read more about my experience of being a migrant in the UK at www.agimag.co.uk/migrant-in-mourning-and-fury-a-narrative/.
3. The Muslim Council of Britain, *Towards Greater Understanding: Meeting the needs of Muslim pupils in state schools, Information & Guidance for Schools*, The Muslim Council of Britain: London 2007.
4. Social Determinants of Health is a model that makes visible the social and economic conditions in which individuals live and distribution of health based on an individual's identity and social status (class, caste, gender, race, income, wealth, power, etc).
5. You can read more about this incident in my article in *Asian Global Impact*: www.agimag.co.uk/when-the-indian-womans-independence-day-will-come/.

# 18. Anti-fundamentalist feminism and green politics

*Natalie Bennett*

## A FIVE-YEAR-OLD 'FEMINIST'

My first politics was feminism. At age five, I was told that I was not allowed to have a bicycle because it wasn't 'ladylike', but if I had had a little brother he could have a bicycle. I remember feeling passionately that that was not fair or right, although it would be at least another decade before I'd encounter the word 'feminism'. But I didn't get that childhood wish; I was an only child. I was well into my teens when I won the bicycle argument. It is a lot harder to learn to ride at that age. I remember hopping around with one foot on the ground. I am very pleased to say that I now cycle all around London as my main means of transport.

I was born in Sydney, Australia. I was the cause of a classic 1960s more-or-less shotgun wedding. Mum was just eighteen when she had me and dad was just nineteen. My mother's father was a radiator mechanic and her mother, unusually for that era, was a legal secretary – she was very much aspirational working class. My father's father was an accountant working for the tax department and his mother worked at home. They were frugal to the point of meanness – everything was patched, repaired, recycled. She was absolutely wonderful at growing vegetables and fruit, and home baking and preserves. One of the things that I regard as a real loss in my upbringing is that my parents were of the generation that regarded anything that didn't come from the shop in a packet, preferably heavily processed, as not proper food, so I didn't learn my grandmother's skills.

My father was an apprentice carpenter when I was born, and he worked in the building trade as a foreman and site manager. My mum had a series of part-time admin roles. When I was about eleven, mum was keen to get into selling residential property, which would have been her first professional job. But it came down to her and a man – this was before equality legislation – and the employer told her 'you've got a child and she might get sick, so I am going to give it to the man'. It really disheartened her. She never really tried to get a professional job again. She never had much personal confidence, and it was a real blow.

I liked primary school in that I loved learning things, I was a voracious reader, but I was very poor on the social side, in mixing with other children. I was an only child, both my parents were also only children, and through the influence of my grandmother on my mother's side I wasn't allowed to mix with the children in the street, so I never really learned to deal with my peers as a child. I was a five year old who behaved a lot like a thirty year old.

In the late seventies, I got a scholarship and attended a private school, what had been the Methodist Ladies College (renamed MLC School). It hadn't decided whether it was educating us to be the wives of solicitors, or solicitors ourselves. So we wasted vast amounts of time learning how to curtsey. I really hope that's stopped now! There was absolutely no political education or political engagement among the students. I read my way through the library, which was quite varied – I remember raising eyebrows by borrowing a book on witchcraft – but I didn't come across a single political text.

MLC was theoretically a religious school, although few of the teachers or pupils were religious. Most of the teachers were female but the head was a male minister of the Uniting Church. In sixth form he especially took a 'personal development' class. He drew on a blackboard a graph that showed us that men's sexual arousal was a steep curve and women's arousal was a flat one and said 'that's why women shouldn't wear low-cut blouses'. I went back to the sixth form common room, which was near the staff room, and raged very loudly, making sure the teachers would hear. But I didn't have any tools to take action.

Some fellow pupils 'discovered' religion in about year eight or nine, which had more than a little to do with attractive male Christian youth group leaders. Being contrary, I immediately declared myself an atheist – but as they argued with me, that conviction became a true one.

My grandmother on my father's side was genuinely religious and it sustained her, rightly or wrongly, through some fifty four years of a horrible marriage. He was the kind of husband who would drop his dirty clothes at the end of the bed and she would pick them up. And he demanded a cooked breakfast every morning. But it was my other grandmother who was very influential in my upbringing. She wanted me to go to Sunday school only because she thought that was the proper, polite thing to do. My parents exclusively went to weddings, funerals and christenings. Church wasn't on their radar, and when I said I was bored with Sunday school, they didn't try to make me continue.

In high school we had quite a few girls from Greek and Italian communities, whose parents had come to Australia after the war. There was a big influx of Vietnamese refugees into Australia about that time, which I was aware of because of the racism in my own family and across society. The primary source of racism in my family was my mother's mother. She would say things that were absolutely horrible. Challenging her – which led to rows – helped to reinforce my own anti-racist views.

## FIRST IN MY FAMILY AT UNIVERSITY

At MLC the normal thing was to go to university, even if you were going just to find a husband (which some said they were going to do, and did). I began agricultural science in 1984 because I had a romantic idea of becoming a farm manager. When I was a child we went on a few family farm holidays. They were quite often big farm families with a lot of kids who lived the kind of life that I had only read about in books. In retrospect it was definitely not what I should have done – it should have been humanities, but no one in my family or their circle had been to university before, so there were no sensible sources of advice, and it was the era of pushing girls to do science.

I only lived at home for the first year. After that I bought a bedsit. I had a very weird teenage period; I wasn't doing the usual social stuff, so I did a vast amount of work for our neighbour who had a hardware business. I did things like pack sheets of sandpaper, ten sheets in a plastic bag with card on top, so it hangs in supermarkets. That, and a small legacy, helped me get a mortgage, and it was cheaper than renting.

I didn't enjoy my studies. Agricultural science was an intellectually limited course. But I really liked animal physiology, and I also developed a passion for soil science. And I liked doing hard physical work on farms as part of my degree – including learning to shear a sheep, a fact about me that the media has rather enjoyed since I became Green Party leader! I also started – fairly ineptly – to socialise with my peers. That was accompanied by large amounts of alcohol; it was traditional in the agricultural science faculty. We were rivals with the engineers for alcohol consumption, which was extremely unhealthy. I wouldn't recommend it. However, I basically was single right up until about four years ago. Now I live with my partner, Jim. I'd decided at age five that I didn't want to get married and have children; I looked at the life of my mother and her friends and thought 'I don't want that'.

## FINDING THE MOVEMENT

I can date my discovery of feminism as a movement precisely. From age sixteen I used to babysit for the couple across the road, very badly because I had no idea about children at all. I used to ring my mother to rescue me when it got out of control. But they had books and in the bookcase, and, hidden at the back, was a copy of *The Women's Room*.[1] As I read it in snatches while babysitting I thought 'wow, there are other people out there who think the way I do'. And then, once I moved out from home, I lived in Glebe, an arty student area of inner Sydney, and the second-hand bookshop had a feminist section. I bought every feminist book I could afford, and that was my feminist education.

I tried to meet other feminists but feminism at the University of Sydney, at least as I found it, was lesbian-separatist feminism. I wasn't prepared to accept that. And I really had no idea at all how to fit in – I was an eighteen to nineteen year old studying science, who had none of the necessary language, none of the academic background. I didn't dress right and I didn't speak right. I played lots of sport – cricket, football (soccer) and later rugby union – often with and against men; I enjoyed challenging gender stereotypes through sport.

In the third year of university I did philosophy, as a non-degree course, one element of which was a section on feminism taken by Elizabeth Grosz, the most brilliant course I have ever taken. But that was my final year on the main Sydney campus – had I been able to continue with that, I might well have found a way into organised feminism in Sydney.

When I graduated, I recognised that I wanted to be a generalist – to rediscover my joy of learning about new and different things, which high school and university had just about beaten out of me. What they taught me was to be very good at doing exams, and that that was the whole purpose of school. I consider that a lost intellectual decade, my high school and first university years.

## A GENERALIST PATH: JOURNALISM

I got my first job as a journalist on a country paper in Henty, population 1000, mid-way between Sydney and Melbourne. I was the editor, writer, photographer – and it was a lot of fun filling twenty four pages, with virtually no adverts, every week. It was mostly local news – from the new Brownies making their promise to the agricultural field days. I did introduce an editorial and occasionally I wrote probably not very sophisticated stuff on the Middle East. I was trying to branch out and be a 'proper journalist' – it was heavily reliant on what I'd read in the *Guardian Weekly*, to which I had a subscription, even though at that time lots of it must have gone straight over my head. I was there for two years, which was traditional for that job; the third year of covering the agricultural show, Mrs Brown winning the sponge-baking again, would be too much.

After that, in 1990, the year after my mother, to whom I was very close, had been killed in a car crash, I spent a year travelling in Europe – the traditional Australian thing. I flew to Turkey and then travelled overland to Britain. It taught me an enormous amount. I was very callow in a lot of ways and it exposed me to facts about life that were new to me.

But I went back to Australia. Had it not been for Mum's death I think I might have moved on then, but I wasn't ready for that big a step, and ended up doing two years on the *Northern Daily Leader*, my first daily newspaper (very roughly comparable to the Yorkshire Evening Post). It was broadly right-wing, reflecting the communities it served, but not in a very 'political' kind of way – defending state funding in the region was a bread-and-butter issue. But when I got to be news editor I did manage to get some radical stories published, particularly on indigenous issues. For instance, I was proud that I was able to shape our coverage on the 'Terra nullius' Mabo ruling, acknowledging Aboriginal peoples' prior ownership of the land.[2] I included a lot of stories debunking misinformation: 'no, it doesn't mean that the Aboriginal people are going to take your back garden'.

When I went to Henty, I started an arts degree, studying as an external student, and managed to complete a degree in Asian Studies, broadly history and politics. It was very disparate, from Indian history to Byzantine history to postmodernism, but the strand that ran through it was women's history and feminism. Byzantine history was a very traditional course – all emperors, generals and battles – so I made up my own question and wrote a big essay on why Byzantine elite women were relatively prominent, while Arab women of the time weren't. My supervisor went on to write a book on Byzantine empresses – I do wonder if I had an influence there. My honours thesis was on the female prime ministers of South Asia.

It was only as I completed the degree that I really felt I'd had something of an education, that I had the tools to start to understand the world, to throw away a lot of the casual certainties that I'd been brought up with. I had a framework for my instinctive feminism and my instinctive concern with fairness. This concern continues to shape my politics on issues of inequalities of all kinds, and how they fit together and often multiply impact on people, particularly women.

## AN INTERNATIONAL FRAMEWORK

Building on my degree, in 1994, at the age of thirty-three, I moved to Thailand. I applied to Australian Volunteers Abroad, and they offered me a role at the National Commission of Women's Affairs in Thailand. They were behind on CEDAW reports, so we did a combined second and third report to CEDAW which I put together and edited. It felt worthwhile, although often very frustrating – I experienced a dual culture shock, both of being involved in a very different national culture, but also of going from newspapers into a very rigid bureaucratic framework.

I wrote the Thai minister's speech for the Beijing women's conference, built around a poem translated from Thai about a woman reaching the sunny side of the mountain after being trapped on the dark side – which I believe the poet intended as a metaphor for women's emancipation from traditional repressions. I was rather proud of it, but it was delivered by a minister who didn't speak English, so he had it phonetically written out in Thai. Nobody understood a word, I was told.

After two years at the NCWA, I worked for two years as a sub-editor at the Bangkok Post. At the same time, I did consulting work for the World Health Organisation on women's health, and for the International Labour Organisation on child labour. I enjoyed the chance to get around Thailand doing the research, talking to a wide range of women and girls. I particularly think of an eleven-year-old flower seller in Chiang Mai market, who obviously shouldn't have been there, but would have been home alone if she wasn't. This was clearly not an ideal situation either way, a reminder that there are no simple solutions to many problems. I wrote a little for various publications – one article I particularly remember was a profile of feminist activist Khunying Supatra Masdit – 'Will she be Thailand's first female Prime Minister?' – To which the answer was sadly, if unsurprisingly, 'no'.

There's a lot I could say about Thailand. It's a place where democratic development never really got going, despite regular – when I was there very regular – elections. In terms of women's rights, everyone is aware of the sex industry in Thailand but there is a religious underpinning to this, which is less understood. In Thailand there's a phrase 'paying back the breast milk'. In many communities, children, as soon as they are able, are expected to support their parents. Boys can become monks, which are believed by many to ensure their parents' spiritual future. But in the Thai Buddhist tradition there are no formally recognised female monks. So the girls have to make money for their parents, and the way they often do that – frequently the most lucrative way – is in the sex industry. [3]

A very senior bureaucrat once asked me: 'how can we make ordinary Thai women sympathise with the hill tribe (ethnic minority) girls, who at age twelve or thirteen have been forced into prostitution?' For some of those who believe in reincarnation, having a miserable time in this life is an indication that you behaved badly in your last life. This view very much colours some attitudes towards people who are having a miserable life now. There have been many campaigns and laws about the minimum age of sex workers. Progress had been made, but the rule of law doesn't really exist in Thailand. Corruption makes many things possible.

I had started writing a book about the economic crash but chronic bronchitis forced me to leave Thailand; the doctor said I'd have it until I left Bangkok and its air pollution. I came to the UK, in mid-1999, because I really liked the feel, the history, and the culture (theatre, museums, galleries – the kind of wealth that Australia is poor in). As a newspaper journalist, this is the most competitive, interesting newspaper market, but I must be one of the few people to have ever come to London for the fresh(er) air!

## SETTLING DOWN IN LONDON

I started off, as you do, as a sub-editor with casual shifts all over the place, on *The Telegraph*, *The Guardian* and *The Times*. *The Times* offered me a contract, so I took it. I started living in Walthamstow in East London and then I moved to Camden. I've stayed in Camden ever since. I always lived on my own. Having been an only child, I never really lived in a shared house. I think I would find it difficult.

I was with *The Times* for about three years then I went to *The Independent* for about eighteen months. At that time it was very male-dominated, a very locker room type of environment. So for about eight to ten months, I tried to make money out of blogging; among the things I did was start the blog *Carnival of Feminists*. It was a way in which people who blogged about similar subjects could find each other. This was before Twitter, and it put me in touch with lots of feminist groups.

I was working at this time on a book, which has turned into a four volume series, a history of the women of London. (I will finish it one day!) I have written about a third of the first one, on Tudor and Stuart London, which starts with Isabella Whitney. She should be known as the first professional poet in Britain, an Elizabethan. She is the woman who inspired me to start the project – although I'm also a great fan of Moll Cutpurse, who you might call the Jordan of Charles I's London – she basically traded her celebrity and notoriety for cash.

## NEW YEAR'S RESOLUTION: JOINING THE GREENS

When I stopped working nights, I was able to get involved in political organisations. Looking at the state of the world, not just climate change, but also soil degradation, fresh water shortages, damage to the oceans, biodiversity loss, I thought 'this is getting really serious and I feel a responsibility to do something'. So, on 1 January 2006 – a New Year's Resolution – I joined the Green Party. I had no inkling of where that action would lead me!

The Green Party had all the right instincts and all the right intentions but there had not been anyone within the Green Party who had focused on feminism for quite some time. So I did a lot of work in the first couple of years, with others, on updating the Green Party policies on abortion rights, equal pay, parental leave, and maternity services. It surprises some people when I say that but the Green Party is definitely democratic! If four members sign a motion, that motion goes through an open democratic process, with possibility for amendments, but then conference decides whether to accept it. When I suggested that Green Party policy on abortion should be to abolish the two-doctor rule, I had only been in the party for about eighteen months and I didn't quite know how it was going to go. But the vote was at least ninety per cent in favour.

We didn't have an organised women's group. There was Women by Name, acting primarily as a support group to encourage women to stand for election, but it didn't meet outside conferences. It didn't have a constitution or an elected structure. So, with others, I set up Green Party Women, which was designed to be outward facing, to work with NGOs, to ensure we had spokespeople at all major feminist events, and to work within the party around policies, etc. I was the founding chair. This was after Sian Berry, then the Green Party London mayoral candidate, got me on to the National Executive body. I had been a member for about six months and she said to me 'there is this little national job, it just involves writing a few newsletters and emails'. I had no idea what I was taking on! I did four years as an internal communications co-ordinator on the executive body. In the Green Party, 'co-ordinator' is a bit of a misnomer – you do most of the work – but I learnt a lot about the party.

## ENCOUNTERING WAF

In January 2007 I attended my first WAF meeting. I wrote immediately to Sian Berry, highlighting WAF's stance on faith schools and its resistance to the government's 'war on terror', and pointing out the 'collusion of elements on the left with fundamentalist religious leaders who are attempting to undermine rights and freedoms, including in their own communities'.

I found involvement in WAF valuable as I learnt from the experience of veteran, high-profile activists; I'd always done politics, but had little experience of organised groups – or even the basics of organising events, activities, lobbying etc. Also I appreciated the subtle political perspective of working against fundamentalism from a feminist perspective, while not being anti-religion. It helped me to grasp the need to build alliances, to not alienate those basically onside with your views but with whom you might also have quite large disagreements. It was also encouraging to hear through WAF about victories – such as the Southall Black Sisters legal victory over Ealing Council's funding cut in 2008.

I felt that I was adding something to WAF. I was aware of the issues around Buddhism, and I was becoming aware of attempts by fundamentalist Christians to influence British politics. I was getting involved with Abortion Rights, and as a journalist I'd seen a great deal about the American religious right. That was always one of my main concerns in WAF partly because, although I am not and have never been in my adult life, a Christian, that is the community, the culture that I come from. It feels more comfortable to be critiquing and expressing concern around something that is in my own cultural background and I think this is an important thing to do.

I see Christian fundamentalism in Britain primarily as a product of American evangelism. And that's also its weakness, because it clashes with British cultural mores – that wonderful British anarchism, and that sense of the ridiculous. Transplanting American fundamentalist literature and ideas here will not work. Christian Action Research and Education, have placed a lot of interns with MPs, and have one MP who was a former intern, but they recently got into trouble because they believe in re-educating homosexual people to be 'ex-gays', as they call it. A lot of people withdrew from them over that. I hope they are not well-equipped to do well in Britain in the long term, but we need to keep a close watch – Britain influences American culture, so it is in their interest to try to influence British culture.

I didn't know anyone from WAF before attending the meetings. I knew of Gita Sahgal and Pragna Patel, had seen them at other meetings, but didn't know them personally. I was just copied into an email and went along. It struck me that people in the room all knew each other very well and they were surprised that someone had just walked in without knowing anybody. For me it wasn't unusual.

I do recall the Rushdie affair that in part inspired WAF, but I very much belong to the organisation's second phase. I would have read about it in the *Guardian Weekly*. There were large parts of the Guardian Weekly I didn't quite understand or really appreciate when I started reading it – that was probably one of them.

## A SURPRISE MOVE INTO FULL-TIME POLITICS

It was during those years (2007-2012) that I was also appointed editor of the *Guardian Weekly* – which was my dream job. If you had told that twenty-three year old in Henty reading the *Guardian Weekly* that twenty years later she'd be editing it, she wouldn't have believed you. It draws on the editorial work of *The Guardian* and the *Observer*, plus the *Washington Post* and *Le Monde*; it is basically a digest of serious world news and culture, something like a left-wing *Economist*. I spent five years editing that, while also getting more and more involved with the Green Party – and I loved both.

For me, five years of doing the same thing is a long time, so I took voluntary redundancy in April 2012, with the aim of writing a book with the working title 'Our economic and environmental mess and how we get out of it'. But first I had to fight the London Assembly elections, and then shortly after that, Caroline Lucas announced she wasn't going to restand as leader, which came as a total surprise. Becoming Green Party leader certainly wasn't the plan – but I have loved my first few months of it. After many years of reporting the news, it's great to be working full time trying to change it.

Feminists are prominent in the party, and there's no sense in which saying 'I am a feminist' is controversial. I think I am the first person who has been elected as leader of a British political party who also explicitly identified as a feminist while standing – it was a very clear part of my platform. I am also very proud of the fact that this is the first time that one woman, Caroline Lucas (who definitely is a feminist!), has handed on the leadership of a political party to another woman.

## WAF AND THE GREEN PARTY

I'd group the Green Party's anti-racist work into a couple of areas. We do have a problem, like all parties, with attracting ethnic minorities to be members and candidates. I've worked with others to establish a group for black and ethnic minority members, modelled on our Green Party Women. I think the latter has been a success; seven of the eleven candidates for this year's London Assembly list election were women, for example. Hopefully we can work in similar ways for ethnic minority candidates.

Within the Green Party there is real recognition of racism in British society. Peter Cranie, our lead European candidate in the North West, was very much part of the struggle to try to stop the BNP (British National Party) in the region in the last European elections. Unfortunately, he just lost out to Nick Griffin. Internally we've been expanding our policy, making a very strong statement against the government's immigration cap and introducing rules to strengthen ethnic minority representation in our European election list in London.

Also, Jenny Jones has been a real leader in the London Assembly, speaking out about the misuse of police stop-and-search powers. Jean Lambert has done a lot of work in the European Parliament on the rights of asylum-seekers, on forced marriage, so-called 'honour' killings and FGM (Female Genital Mutilation). The last three are issues that have too often been put in the 'too hard' file by the authorities.

A lot of anti-racism work is actually practical policy work: action against cuts in public services that hit ethnic minority communities hard; campaigns to get everyone paid a living wage, with ethnic minority workers, particularly women, disproportionately represented among the low-paid. I've been working with the cleaners at the University of London, who are primarily from Latin America, and the Camden traffic wardens, many of whom are from ethnic minority communities, who were getting less than the London living wage for these difficult jobs. The cleaners now have the London living wage, so they're going after pensions, holidays, and sick pay, which is great to see!

Rather than things coming under the label of anti-fundamentalist work, what you can see when you look on the ground is Jean Lambert, Jenny Jones, Caroline Lucas, and others, all working in different fields. There are, then, a lot of people and politicians encountering situations in which they try to intervene as best they can – a bit like WAF in a way.

The Green Party is also very strong on removing the financial privileges enjoyed by religious groups in running fee-paying schools. We're in favour of democratically controlled local schools that reflect the mix of their communities. There's an underlying understanding in the party, I think, of intersectionality, although it's not something that is explicitly discussed in those terms.

## NEW ALLIANCES, NEW THREATS

With regard to the current state of Britain, thinking about issues around race, religion and politics, it struck me as disturbing in June

2012 when elements of the Sikh community allied with the EDL (English Defence League) in Luton over an alleged sexual assault. In that, we can see the potential for alliances between fascists or quasi-fascists and fundamentalists of different stripes. There is a general trend towards fundamentalist authoritarianism, which exists in almost all communities and societies. If fascists and fundamentalists become allied then we are looking at a potentially powerful and dangerous force. This is my personal view but it does tie in with the Green Party's strong anti-authoritarianism. Defence of human rights is an important part of our politics, speaking up for people who no one else is going to speak up for and who are suffering under the power of authority, whether those people are the disabled, people from ethnic minorities, asylum-seekers or any other group that no one will speak up for in these times.

## NOTES

1. M. French, *The Women's Room*, Virago, London 1997.
2. *Terra nullis* was the legal doctrine applied to Australia that, before the arrival of European settlers, the 'land belonged to no one'.
3. I personally prefer the term 'sex industry' since it is broader (covering, for example, telephone sex workers). At the time I was studying these issues, it was the preferred term of workers' advocates. I know some have now reverted to the form prostitute or 'prostitute women', sometimes as a form of reclaiming, but I tend to prefer the 'sex industry' formulation as it recognises people's role as workers. Green Party policy backs the New Zealand model of decriminalisation of sex work, which is a position I strongly back as the best way (as shown by evidence) of keeping vulnerable women and men as safe as possible.

# 19. The Spirit of Resistance: Helen Lowe 1944-2011[1]

*Judy Greenway*

## INTRODUCTION BY THE EDITORS

*Very sadly, Helen Lowe died suddenly in 2011 and we were not able to interview her for this book. However, we are very grateful to Helen's life partner, Judy Greenway, who agreed to write this chapter in Helen's memory. The main part of this editorial introduction is drawn from words that formed the basis of WAF tributes at Helen's funeral.*

*Helen joined WAF in 2007 and she was a determined and consistent presence during WAF's second phase. As we have noted in our introduction to the book, the end of WAF's second phase to a great extent coincided with Helen's death, because she had held WAF together at an organisational level, managing its website and its email list. She was a constant reminder of the call to action, and two particular campaigns highlighted her interests. When the United East End coalition joined forces with members of the right-wing East London Mosque to call a demonstration against the English Defence League in Tower Hamlets, Helen raised her concerns about this partnership, and then produced a WAF leaflet 'No to Fascism No to Fundamentalism', which she distributed at the United East End rally. At a subsequent, highly self-congratulatory meeting of the United East End coalition, she criticised the lack of women at the rally, and raised the need to hold meetings at secular venues. She also spoke on the twin pressures of fundamentalism and fascism at a meeting of No One is Illegal.[2] The second moment of WAF history with which she is strongly associated is the British Pakistani Christian Association's (BPCA) demonstrations against the blasphemy law in Pakistan, at which she gained space for WAF speakers. WAF women recall marching with Helen and the BPCA protestors and suddenly finding the BPCA demonstrators had dropped to their knees in the middle of Piccadilly Circus in order to pray. Clara, Helen and Sukhwant were the only ones left standing! All three laughed heartily about this at a post demo /early Christmas lunch at the Crypt, St Martin's in the Field. Helen's wicked sense of humour was tickled by such incongruity. Helen was also a great photographer and took some terrific pictures of WAF activism. The last time that many of us saw Helen was on 7 June 2011 at a WAF e-list discussion about the Arab Spring. We persuaded her to go for a drink afterwards to celebrate her birthday with an exchange of irreverent jokes and stories. Many of us will forever remember the characteristic twinkle in Helen's eye and her smile. She is very much missed.*

*

Months before her death, Helen was leafleting against fascism and religious fundamentalism in the streets of East London, where her grandparents, Jewish immigrants from Russia and Estonia, had once lived. Passionately committed to feminism, anti-racism, secularism and social justice, she was always more interested in campaigning than theorising, in talking to people rather than writing articles. WAF was only one of the many organisations that benefited over the years from her hard work behind the scenes. As she said of activist poet Allen Ginsberg, she was never one for a quiet life.

Helen discovered Ginsberg and the Beat Generation when she was sixteen. They represented a life scarcely imaginable to the young woman growing up in grim post-war Glasgow. 'I fell in love with freedom', she wrote, 'freedom to live the life of my choosing'.[3] That same year she scandalised her parents, themselves Communist Party members and peace campaigners, when she was arrested at a sit-down protest at Scotland's nuclear base. All her life she favoured direct action and resisted authoritarianism.

At twenty, she moved to London, had her daughter Debi, and began a lifelong involvement in housing campaigns. Her experiences then, of how some leftist groups colluded with white working-class racism and anti-semitism, influenced her more recent ideas about creating an effective movement against racism and fascism while confronting misogyny and homophobia:

> 'What seems to be beyond [the Left] is the capacity to understand the dynamics of the intersections of race, ethnicity, class, gender and sexuality.'

But:

> 'it's one thing to criticise [them] for not addressing issues of inclusion ... another thing to build an inclusive movement in which everyone feels welcome and able to play a role.'[4]

In the 1970s and 1980s she threw her energies into the Women's and Lesbian Liberation Movements. She was committed to anti-racism, and though for a time she worked only with women, her community activism continued to connect her with a range of diverse groups. As she noted:

> 'our oppressions are multifaceted, so our responses are too. And if we're going to get on with understanding both the responses and the oppressions then we have to ... open up the discussion'.[5]

Years before joining WAF, she spoke of its appeal as 'a force for uniting women from different cultures to get on and give ourselves some spirit of resistance'.[6] In 2001, she was inspired by a meeting called by WAF and others to discuss feminist responses to 9/11 and the 'War on Terror'. She and Sophie Laws subsequently co-edited a special issue of radical feminist journal *Trouble and Strife* that brought together women's voices from round the world, including Helen's own discussion of religion, gender and politics in Israel.[7]

In the following decade, Helen became increasingly concerned about the political promotion of 'faith agendas' and 'family values' in the UK. And she feared the resurgence of European fascism. She joined WAF in 2007, hoping it would once again become a campaigning organisation, which could re-energise older generations of activists, enthuse younger ones, share ideas and take action. She was only too aware of the dangers of exhaustion and burnout; of how hard it is to sustain democratic structures, learn from past mistakes without discouragement or cynicism, and maintain 'the dignity of fighting even when it feels like the battle can't be won'.[8]

In a discussion towards the end of her life, she concluded that to build 'a secular and inclusive movement, one that affirms the role of women and gay people, people of all religions and no religion, and people of all ages and abilities', we need to 'abandon traditional forms of left versus right and embrace alternative strategies [such as non-violent direct action] developed by ... brave people in their struggles for equality and human rights.'[9] She called for a politics enacted with creativity and courage, and her own creativity, courage and commitment helped to nourish those she worked with. As she once wrote, in a note to herself:

> 'Giving in with no resistance is not what I grew up to be about, and I want to be part of the resistance now. After all it was not just hatred of injustice that started me off, but also inspiration from those who resisted.'[10]

## NOTES

1. All quotations are Helen's own words, taken from unpublished material in my possession.
2. H. Lowe, *No to Fascism, No to Fundamentalism*, a talk given at No One is Illegal on 22 September 2010, and available on the WAF website: www.womenagainstfundamentalism.org.uk/nofascism.html.
3. Notebook, 12 May 1997, reflecting on the news of Ginsberg's death.
4. Notes for talk given as a WAF speaker at a meeting against Racism and Fascism organised by No-one is Illegal, London, 22 September 2010.
5. Notebook, 19 November 1987.
6. Notebook, 12 October 1990.
7. *Trouble and Strife* 43, Summer 2002: www.troubleandstrife.org/articles/issue-43/.
8. Notebook, 2 December 1987.
9. Notes for talk given as a WAF speaker at a meeting against Racism and Fascism organised by No-one is Illegal, London, 22 September 2010.
10. Notebook, 2 October, 1990.

# APPENDIX 1

## *Women defend Salman Rushdie*

On 9 March 1989, nearly 200 women gathered at the Dominion Centre, Southall, to mark International Women's Day and discuss the resurgence of religious fundamentalism across the world. Women talked about the effects of fundamentalist religions in Pakistan, India, Iran, Ireland and in Britain. At the end of the meeting, the organisers, Southall Black Sisters and Southall Labour Party Women's Section, issued the following statement:

As a group of women of many religions and none, we would like to express our solidarity with Salman Rushdie. Women's voices have been largely silent in the debate where battle lines have been drawn between liberalism and fundamentalism. Often it has been assumed that the views of local community leaders are our views, and their demands are our demands. We reject this absolutely.

We have struggled for many years in this country and across the world to express ourselves as we choose within and outside our communities. We will not be dictated to by fundamentalists. Our lives will not be defined by community leaders. We will take up our right to determine our own destinies, not limited by religions, culture, or nationality. We believe that religious worship is an individual matter, and that the state should not foster one religion above any other. We call upon the government to abolish the outdated blasphemy law and to defend, without reservation, freedom of speech.

Reproduced from *WAF Journal No.1*, 1990, p12.

# Appendix 2, WAF Stop the War leaflet

## No to imperialism – No to all religious fundamentalism

**Women Against Fundamentalism condemns the illegal war in Iraq and the destruction wreaked on the country, its people and its resources by the military occupation. We offer our support and solidarity to all Iraqis who are suffering from the occupation, which has fuelled the fragmentation of Iraqi society along ethnic and religious lines.**

WAF condemns the 'War on Terror' which is unleashing state terror on populations and communities that will not succumb to the USA's New World Order. The 'War on Terror' also poses a threat in this country to trade union, socialist, feminist, anti-racist and other progressive movements, in the mainstream as well as in minority, migrant and refugee communities.

While condemning the 'War on Terror', which is fuelling increased anti-Muslim racism and criminalisation of certain Muslims, we oppose the fundamentalists in the USA, in Iraq and across the world, who are using the conflict as an opportunity to promote reactionary, violent, discriminatory and divisive politics under the banner of religion.

**What is fundamentalism?**

By fundamentalism we do not mean religious observance, which we see as a matter or choice. WAF defines 'fundamentalism' as modern political movements which use the imposition of one supposedly 'authentic' version of religion as a basis for their attempt to win or consolidate power and extend social control. Fundamentalism appears in different and changing forms in religions throughout the world, sometimes as a state project, sometimes in opposition to the state. But at the heart of all fundamentalist agendas is the control of women's minds and bodies.

**Women in Iraq**

In Iraq the new constitution has allowed the Family Code to be superseded by the power of the clerics and new religious courts, with the result that it is largely discriminatory against women. At the same time there are attacks, abductions, death threats and assassinations of women's rights campaigners, of women who wear western dress, of lesbians and even of women who simply go out to work. Lesbians and gays are being systematically executed by Shia death squads.

As the *Observer* reported last October: 'Iraq's women live in terror of speaking their opinions; of going out to work; or defying the strict new prohibitions on dress and behaviour applied across Iraq by Islamist militants, both Sunni and Shia. They live in fear of their husbands, too, as women's rights have been undermined by the country's postwar constitution that has taken power from the family courts and given it to clerics.'

**The enemy of my enemy is not my friend**

In contrast to the tabloid press and those waging the 'War on Terror', who use the term 'fundamentalist' as a generalised term of racist abuse against Muslims, we challenge those in all the major world religions who are using political conflicts as an opportunity to build their political and economic power.

This includes

- Evangelical Christians in the US who are promoting an aggressive imperialist agenda
- Jewish fundamentalist settlers occupying Palestinian land in the West Bank
- Islamist militias that are operating as death squads to undermine any prospect of equality and democracy in Iraq, Iran, Afghanistan and elsewhere
- Hindu fundamentalists violently attacking Muslims and their religious institutions in India
- Sikh fundamentalists in Birmingham who frightened a theatre into closing the play Behzti.

Despite commandeering the rhetoric of progressive liberation movements, fundamentalism does not pose a challenge to imperialism, and thrives on the conflicts promoted by the New World Order. WAF is alarmed that elements on the Left are colluding with fundamentalist religious leaders who are attempting to undermine rights and freedoms, including in their own communities.

WAF believes that the anti-war movement has been silent too long on the reactionary and destructive role of Christian and Muslim fundamentalism in the occupation of Iraq and in the 'War on Terror'.

**The anti-war movement here and across the world must uphold the principles of secularism, social justice, democracy and human rights, and oppose any attempts to fragment the struggle on religious grounds.**

# Women Against Fundamentalism

## Who we are

WAF is a feminist organisation which was launched in 1989 to challenge the rise of fundamentalism in all religions, when battle lines were being drawn simplistically between religious fundamentalists on one side and racists and liberals on the other, leaving no space for women's voices. WAF includes women from across the world and from a wide range of backgrounds.

WAF recognises fundamentalism as a worldwide phenomenon in all religions, which mobilises religion for political ends.

WAF believes that resistance to racism and fundamentalism also involves a struggle for secularism, which is one of a number of preconditions for equal rights for those of all religions or none.

## WAF calls for

- The disestablishment of the Church of England
- Repeal of the blasphemy laws
- An end to impositions of Christianity in state schools, including Christian assemblies
- A phasing out of state funding of all religious schools
- The development of a social policy which addresses the genuine needs of women and which does not attempt to deal with them on the basis of racist and sexist assumptions as to how they are expected to behave according to their particular racial or cultural origin.

**We hope you will join us trying to build a secular movement against racism, state sponsored terror and religious fundamentalism.**

## Our tradition – struggle not submission!

**You can contact Women Against Fundamentalism at: waf_m_ail@hotmail.co.uk**

# Notes on contributors

**Nadje Al-Ali**

Nadje is Professor of Gender Studies at the Centre for Gender Studies, at SOAS, University of London. Her main research interests revolve around gender theory; feminist activism; women and gender in the Middle East; transnational migration and diaspora mobilisation; war, conflict and reconstruction. Nadje is a feminist and peace activist academic who co-founded Act Together: Women's Action for Iraq in the late 1990s. During this period she also started to get involved with Women in Black UK. Her feminist activism started in Egypt during the early 1990s. Her involvement in a leftist secular women's organisation triggered her interest to study secularism in the context of the Egyptian women's movement. She joined WAF while working on her PhD at SOAS. Nadje is a member of the *Feminist Review* Collective and is currently President of SOAS UCU.

**Julia Bard**

Julia is a freelance writer and editor. She was a member of WAF for many years, is on the National Committee of the Jewish Socialists' Group, and is a founder and editorial committee member of *Jewish Socialist* magazine. For several years she wrote and edited websites for Channel 4, including one on religious affairs, and she has contributed to a number of publications and books, including *For Generations: Jewish Motherhood*, edited by Mandy Ross and Ronne Randall, and *A Time to Speak Out: Independent Jewish Voices on Israel, Zionism and Jewish Identity*, edited by Anne Karpf, Brian Klug, Jacqueline Rose and Barbara Rosenbaum. She has recently reviewed *Jewish identity in postcommunist Russia and Ukraine* by Zvi Gitelman in *Ethnic and Racial Studies* (Vol. 37, Issue 5, 2014), and she is co-author of *Contemporary Slavery: Teachers' Resource*, published by the International Slavery Museum, Liverpool. She also teaches journalism at London Metropolitan University, and writes, edits and produces materials for educational, cultural, human rights and refugee organisations.

**Natalie Bennett**

Natalie is an Australian-British feminist politician and the leader of the Green Party of England and Wales. She is a journalist by profession, and between 2007 and 2012 she was editor of *The Guardian Weekly*. She blogs regularly for *The Guardian*'s Comment is Free and for *The Huffington Post*. She has two Bachelor's degrees, one in Agricultural Science and one in Asian Studies, and holds a Master's Degree in Mass Communication from the University of Leicester. Natalie has also edited *Thailand Country Study: Best Practice Guide on Sustainable Action Against Child Labour*; and *Women's Health and Development, Country Profile Thailand*.

**Cassandra Balchin**

Cass was a researcher, writer and trainer, specialising in the intersections of gender, law and culture. In addition to a focus on Muslim family laws, her research and advocacy work on religious fundamentalisms and on plural legal systems helped her develop a trans-regional and trans-cultural analysis of the factors obstructing women's rights and of the opportunities for strengthening them. She was a founder member, and later Chair, of the Muslim Women's Network-UK, and was part of the international solidarity network Women Living Under Muslim Laws for many years; she was a coordinator at the WLUML international coordination office from 2000 to 2005. She was also a founding member of the International Advisory Group for Musawah, a global initiative for equality and justice in the Muslim family; and a member of Women Against Fundamentalism. While based in Pakistan, where she lived for seventeen years, she worked as a journalist, and with Shirkat Gah Women's Resource Centre in Lahore. Recent publications include: *When Legal Worlds Overlap: Human Rights, State and Non-State Law*, International Council on Human Rights Policy, Geneva, 2009; and *Towards a Future without Fundamentalisms: Analyzing Religious Fundamentalist Strategies and Feminist Responses*, AWID, Toronto, 2011.

**Clara Connolly**

Clara is a co-founder of WAF and of Voices for Rushdie, and was a member of *Feminist Review* editorial board from 1979 to 1995. She has worked at the Commission for Racial Equality and the University of North London on issues relating to equality and discrimination.

She has been a feminist activist for many years around issues of domestic violence, abortion for Irish women and the effects of Christian fundamentalism. Clara is currently an immigration solicitor, working mainly with victims of gender persecution and trafficking at ATLEU (the Anti Trafficking and Labour Exploitation Unit – www.atleu.org.uk).

**Sukhwant Dhaliwal**

Sukhwant grew up in Southall in the shadow of an emergent anti-racist and Black feminist movement but also during one of the earliest diasporic fundamentalist mobilisations, the Khalistani movement, which called for secession from the Indian state and the establishment of a Sikh theocracy. Sukhwant moved over to academia after ten years of working on violence against women and girls, including for Southall Black Sisters. She joined Women Against Fundamentalism in 1995. Her experience in the voluntary sector complements an academic/research career that has covered projects on five out of six of the equality strands – 'race', gender, disability, age, religion and belief. Sukhwant recently completed a PhD entitled *Religion, Moral Hegemony and Local Cartographies of Power: Feminist Reflections on Local Politics* in the Sociology Department at Goldsmiths, University of London. She is now a Research Fellow at The International Centre: Researching Child Sexual Exploitation, Violence and Trafficking.

**Judy Greenway**

Judy is an independent scholar currently researching and writing feminist, anarchist and queer histories. She shared many happy years of political engagement and debate with her partner in life, Helen Lowe, and the editors of this book invited her to write the chapter in Helen's memory. Her website includes a page dedicated to Helen. http://www.judygreenway.org.uk/wp/helen-lowe/.

**Jane Lane**

Jane is an advocate worker for racial equality in the early years. She works to ensure racial equality is embedded in national and local government early years policies, procedures and practices, and early years settings more generally. She was formerly an Education Officer at the Commission for Racial Equality and the Policy Director of Early Years Equality. She has campaigned, trained, dissented and written widely about racial equality and young children and education generally, and is passionate about the need to remove racism from our society. Although some of the issues that WAF faced (though not all) cannot be resolved by laws, she believes anti-discriminatory legislation is a vital tool in dismantling inequalities and their institutional manifestations, and is seriously dispirited by its present dismantling by the Coalition government. Her work includes *Young children and racial justice – taking action for racial equality in the early years – understanding the past, thinking about the present, planning for the future*, National Children's Bureau 2008.

**Shakila Taranum Maan**

Shakila is an award-winning British director, based in West London. Shakila created the iconic WAF banner used in the Parliament Square demonstration. She has been a member of Southall Black Sisters since 1984. Her first feature film, *The Winter of Love*, was shot on location in Southall, London and opened the Raindance East Film Festival. She won the Best Art Film award at the Asolo Film Festival, for her arts documentary *Alone Together.* Her graduation film *Ferdous* (Paradise) was picked up by Frameline Distributors and is an innovative short film exploring the powerful themes of homosexuality in Islam. Shakila has been at the forefront of creating radical and avant-garde British Asian theatre since the late 1970s. Her work includes ground-breaking film and theatre such as *Rani, A Woman in Southall, The Bride, Not Just An Asian Babe, All Gods Angels, A Thousand Borrowed Eyes, Restless Skies, Calling* and *Zakhme Dil* (A Scarred Heart). She established Southall Asian & African Caribbean Arts Collective in 1982, now known as Heritage Ceramics.

**Ritu Mahendru**

Ritu holds a PhD in sociology specialising in ethnographic research on race, gender and religion. As a feminist and an activist, her research interests lie in gender based violence, sex and sexuality issues, HIV, ethnicity, migration, displacement, health and human rights. She is currently working in Afghanistan on rural development issues at policy level, promoting the rights of girls, women, socially excluded, nomadic and minority communities, and the poor. She has worked in the UK, South Asia, South Africa and Serbia. Ritu is author of *Young people's perceptions of gender, risk and AIDS: a comparative analysis of India and the UK*; and

'Gender Analysis and Use of Intersectionality in Health' in K. Regmi (ed), *Decentralizing Health Services: A Global Perspective* (2013). She was editor of *Population Trends and Policy Options in Selected Developing Countries* (Sub-Saharan Africa and Asia), which had a specific focus on gender inequalities and reproductive health. She also authored the Health and Human Rights Strategy of Afghanistan in 2011, and developed the Policy for Traditionally Nomadic Groups in Afghanistan for the Ministry of Rural Rehabilitation and Development Afghanistan (2014).

**Sue O'Sullivan**

Now 73, Sue O'Sullivan hasn't lived in the USA, where she was born, for almost fifty years. She was part of the new women's liberation movement in the UK from its first angry cry at the end of the 1960s. She has worked in a variety of jobs, most of them to do with publishing, from zines and magazines – including a long stint at *Spare Rib* from the late 1970s – to book publishing, primarily Sheba Feminist Press, a self-defined mixed race collective with a commitment to publishing writing by black women, and by first-time women writers, lesbians and working-class women. Her major areas of interest in the old days were collective work, the women's health movement, class, and the right of women to have babies and refuse abortions – as well as the right to want abortions. She has also been involved in other social movements, primarily in anti-racist groups and in discussions which problematised whiteness, as well as working against racism, institutional and other. After four years in Australia she returned to London in 1996, where she worked, until it closed down in 2009, for the International Community of Women Living with HIV/AIDS. ICW was a network run by and for HIV positive women, along with a few women like Sue who weren't positive. The main membership was in Africa. She joined WAF on seeing that a radical, feminist, position against fundamentalism was needed more than ever, post-2001 especially.

**Pragna Patel**

Pragna Patel is a founding member of the Southall Black Sisters and Women Against Fundamentalism. She worked as a co-ordinator and senior case worker for SBS from 1982 to 1993 when she left to train and practice as a solicitor. In 2009 she returned to SBS as its Director. She has been centrally involved in some of SBS's most important cases and campaigns around domestic violence, immigration and religious fundamentalism. She has also written extensively on race, gender and religion. Among her many publications have been 'The Time Has Come … Asian Women in Struggle', in H.S. Mirza (ed), *Black British Feminism – A Reader*, Taylor & Francis 1997; several essays in R. Gupta (ed), *From homebreakers to jailbreakers*, Zed Books 2003; 'Faith in the State? Asian Women's Struggles for Human Rights in the UK', *Feminist Legal Studies*, spring 2008; 'R v Zoora (Ghulam) Shah', in Rosemary Hunter, Clare McGlynn and Erika Rackley (eds), *Feminist Judgements from Theory to Practice*, September 2010. 'Multifaithism and the Gender Question: Implications of Government Policy on the Struggle for Equality and Rights for Minority Women in the UK', in Y. Rehman et al (eds), *Moving in the Shadows*, Ashgate 2013; and, more recently, '"Moral Panics" and "Social Evils": Forced Marriage and Gender-Related Violence in Immigration Law and Policy in the UK', in F. Anthias and Mojca Pajnik, *Contesting Integration, Engendering Migration*, Palgrave Macmillan 2014.

**Ruth Pearson**

Ruth Pearson is a socialist feminist who has researched and written widely on women, work, migration, development and globalisation. She is Emeritus Professor of International Development at the University of Leeds. She is also an activist and trustee of a number of women's organisations in the UK and internationally. A founder member of WAF when it was established in 1989, she has supported anti-fundamentalist and pro-internationalist initiatives in the UK, Europe and Latin America and South East Asia. She is (co) author and editor of a number of publications including 'Nimble Fingers Make Cheap Workers', *Feminist Review* 1981; *Feminist Visions of Development* (Routledge 1998); '*Globalization, Export-Orientated Employment and Social Policy: Gendered Connections*, Palgrave 2004; *Burmese Factory Workers: Thailand's Hidden Workforce*, Zed 2012. She has also co-produced an interactive website for schools and community groups offering resources on migration, women's work and workers' rights, based on research on South Asian women workers in the UK, from Grunwick to Gate Gourmet (www.striking-women.org<http://www.striking-women.org>).

**Gita Sahgal** is a filmmaker and writer active on issues relating to secularism, feminism and human rights. She was a founding member of Women Against Fundamentalism, and of Awaaz: South Asia

Watch, which worked on religious right networks such as the Hindutva movement, originating in South Asia. She made numerous documentaries for *Bandung File*, a Black current affairs programme on Channel 4, and for *Dispatches*, including: 'Hullaballoo over the Satanic Verses', the only film that examined the Rushdie Affair as a debate among secular and fundamentalist Muslims, and 'Struggle or Submission', on women and the Rushdie Affair, in which the demonstration of WAF in support of Rushdie was shown. These films are on Secular Zone on Youtube. She made 'The War Crimes File' for *Dispatches*, a documentary investigating the role of three prominent British Muslims who were members of the Jamaat e Islami in crimes committed in Bangladesh in 1971. This film was important in mobilising a mass movement in Bangladesh for war crimes trials, alerting a new generation to genocide committed in 1971. She was co-editor with Nira Yuval Davis of *Refusing Holy Orders; women and fundamentalism in Britain* (1992). Other publications include: on the rise of Hindu fundamentalism in Britain: 'Diaspora Politics in Britain: Hindu Identity in the Making', in *In Quest of a Secular Symbol, Ayodhya and After*, edited by Rajeshwari Ghose (Curtin University); 'Legislating Utopia: Violence against Women, Identities and Interventions', in *The Situated Politics of Belonging* (Sage 2006); 'Purity or Danger? Human Rights and their Engagement with Fundamentalisms' (ASIL, 2006) (on the twin origins of Hindutva and the Jamaat e Islami); and 'The Power of Memory', in *Criminal Jurisdiction 100 Years after the 1907 Peace Conference* (2009); on Christian and Muslim fundamentalism in Britain: 'The Question Asked by Satan: Doubt, Dissent and Discrimination in 21st century Britain, in the Struggle for Secularism in Europe and North America', WLUML 30-31; and 'The Return of the Grand Narrative: Relating Secularism to Racism and Belonging' in *Secularism, Racism and the Politics of Belonging* (Runnymede Trust).

Following her departure from Amnesty International in 2010, after her complaint regarding Amnesty International's relationship with Cageprisoners, a salafi-jihadi influenced campaigning group, she established a think tank called the Centre for Secular Space (www.centreforsecularspace.org). The first publication of the Centre, by co-founder Meredith Tax, was 'Double Bind; the Muslim Right, the Anglo-American Left and Universal Human Rights'. She has written for openDemocracy, WLUML, and the *Guardian*.

**Hannana Siddiqui**

Hannana has worked for Southall Black Sisters for twenty-seven years, and has been working in the field of race, gender and human rights for thirty years. She has carried out extensive work on violence against BME women and girls, including domestic violence, forced marriage and honour based violence, and the inter-related issues of suicide, self-harm, immigration and lack of recourse to public funds. She been involved in a number of high profile campaigns, including those to free Kiranjit Ahluwalia, and battered women who kill, which led to a reform in the law on provocation in 1992. She also helped to introduce the Domestic Violence Immigration concession (1999), and the Destitution Domestic Violence concession (2012), and was an original member of the Home Office Working Group on Forced Marriage (1999-2000). She worked with Lord Lester to introduce the Forced Marriage (Civil Protection) Act 2007. She also helped to found the End Violence against Women Coalition (2005), and Women Against Fundamentalism (1989). She has won a number of awards (she declined an MBE in 2004) and published widely – most recently as a co-editor of *Moving in the Shadows: Violence in the Lives of Minority Women and Children* (2013).

**Eva Turner**

Eva moved to London from former Czechoslovakia in 1978. From 1986 she worked as a university lecturer, retiring in 2011 from the post of Principal Lecturer at the University of East London. Throughout her academic career she lectured, researched and published in the fields of Gender and Computing and Computer Ethics. She taught a variety of computer science and information technology subjects in schools of Computer Science and Sociology. From 1994 she was an active member of Women into Computing, an organisation which published, organised conferences and campaigned for the role of women in the development, construction and use of digital technologies. She joined Women Against Fundamentalism in 2006 after attending a WAF public meeting on the war on terror and fundamentalism. She is active and interested in the politics of gender and environmental issues, and in the political activities of her local community.

**Rashmi Varma**

Rashmi was born and raised in India. She moved to the US in 1990 and received her PhD in English and Women's Studies from the

University of Illinois at Chicago in 1998. The same year she became Assistant Professor of English and Cultural Studies at the University of North Carolina in Chapel Hill. Since 2004, she has taught English and Comparative Literary Studies at the University of Warwick in the UK. She is the author of *The Postcolonial City and its Subjects* (2011) and of the forthcoming *Modern Tribal: Representing Indigeneity in Postcolonial India*. She has published numerous essays on feminist theory, activism and literature. She lives in London and has been a member of Awaaz-South Asia Watch and Women Against Fundamentalism.

**Georgie Wemyss**

Georgie is Senior Research Fellow at the University of East London. She studied at UCL before becoming a youth and community worker in East London, where she was active in anti-racist initiatives. After completing a PGCE she studied Bengali in Dhaka and taught adults at Tower Hamlets College whilst studying for her MA and PhD part-time at the University of Sussex. She became involved in WAF in 1989 after having worked with women from SBS on forced marriage. In 1993, following the election of a BNP councillor in Tower Hamlets, she was active in the campaign group Women Unite Against Racism. She is the author of *The Invisible Empire: White Discourse, Tolerance and Belonging* (2009); and 'Littoral Struggles, Liminal Lives: Indian Merchant Seafarers' Resistances', in R. Ahmed and S. Mukherjee (eds), *South Asian Resistances in Britain 1858-1947* (2012).

**Nira Yuval-Davis**

Nira is the Director of the Research Centre on Migration, Refugees and Belonging (CMRB) at the University of East London. She has been President of Research Committee 05 (on Racism, Nationalism and Ethnic Relations) of the International Sociological Association, and is a founder member of both Women Against Fundamentalism and the international research network Women In Militarized Conflict Zones. She has written extensively on the theoretical and empirical aspects of intersected nationalisms, racisms, fundamentalisms, citizenships, identities, belonging/s and gender relations in Britain & Europe, Israel and other Settler Societies. Among her written and edited books are: *Racialized Boundaries*, 1992; *Refusing Holy Orders: women and funda-*

*mentalism in Britain* (1992); *Gender and Nation* (1997); *Warning Signs of Fundamentalisms* (2004); *The Politics of Belonging: Intersectional Contestations* (2011).

# Index